Scotland the Bold

Scotland the Bold

Gerry Hassan

FREIGHT BOOKS

First published 2016

Freight Books
49–53 Virginia Street
Glasgow, G1 1TS
www.freightbooks.co.uk

A CIP catalogue reference for this book is available from the British
Library.

ISBN 978-1-911332-04-6
eISBN 978-1-911332-05-3

Contents

Acknowledgements

This is a book about hope and change. It is about Scotland, ideas, culture, politics and the future. Even though it addresses the terrain of our nation post-indyref and post-Brexit, it attempts to use examples of our near past to understand where we are, where we might be going and indeed, where we might actually want to go.

In a Scotland that has been recently characterised by increased democratic and political engagement, but also in places by an over-exerted partisanship, tribalism and sometimes intolerance, this book is written and offered in exactly the opposite to this latter spirit.

The Scotland this book is offered to isn't primarily divided into Yes and No, or pro-independence and pro-union. Instead, it is written for people who both see themselves as living in one Scotland and the multiple, infinite country that already exists and many of us would like to see more championed and encouraged.

Many people assisted and offered encouragement and advice in the writing of this book. They include Simon Barrow, David Bell, Lucy Hunter Blackburn, Madeleine Bunting, Jean Cameron, Roanne Dods, Douglas Fraser, Ken Gibb, Russell Gunson, Gordon Guthrie, Scott Hames, Walter Humes, Ian Jack, Joe Lafferty, Jim Livesey, Jim McCormick, John McDermott, Alastair McIntosh, Gehan Macleod, Joyce McMillan, James Mitchell, Ken Neil, Verene Nicolas, Fintan O'Toole, Stephen Reicher, Douglas Robertson, Alan Sinclair, Nigel Smith, Willie Sullivan, Lesley Thomson, Katherine Trebeck, Graham Watt, Christopher Whatley and Eleanor Yule. Many other people over the years have inspired, challenged and encouraged me – and sincere apologies if I have missed you out of this immediate list.

Thanks also go to the great team at Freight who have been a joy to work with and in particular to Adrian Searle who has seen this through as a project from beginning to its publication and always been passionate as well as committed to it. I can think of no finer champion to work with from the world of publishing.

My biggest debt of gratitude and humbleness goes to my partner Rosie Ilett who, with a packed schedule and many commitments, read the manuscript of the book more than once – and offered advice throughout the process from the intellectual to proofing. I am as ever deeply indebted and aware that this book might never have seen the light of day without such support and encouragement. I can only hope Rosie knows how much I appreciate this and thank her profusely for her backing and insights.

Finally, a quick word on style and terminology. I have intended to avoid jargonistic terms or obscure words and to use an open, accessible style while providing background references and sources for those who wish to delve deeper. I have also for brevity and style used the term indyref as it is common usage and much shorter than the words independence referendum.

I hope people find the book as enjoyable and stimulating as I did researching and writing it, and I welcome thoughts and observations from readers in due course.

Gerry Hassan
September 2016
gerry@gerryhassan.com

Chapter One:

Scotland's Place in Today's World: Where are We Now?

Ah dinna ken whit like your Scotland is. Here's mines.
National flower: the thistle.
National pastime: nostalgia.
National weather: smirr, haar, drizzle, snow.

Liz Lochhead, Mary Queen of Scots Got Her Head Chopped Off,
1987

For Scotland, the UK, Europe and much of the world, these are challenging, tumultuous and perplexing times. Has there ever been a year as dramatic as this one?

Well, yes, there have been other dramatic years of uncertainty and rupture such as 1968 (the year of protest and rebellion), 1979 (the year of counter-revolution), and 1989 (the fall of the Berlin Wall) and there will certainly be more to come. Change though does seem to be speeding up – and becoming more unpredictable, disorganised and messy.

Traditional centres and sources of authority have never been more in question across the developed world. The forces of left and right, which gave shape and meaning to much of 19th- and 20th-century politics, no longer appeal or provide explanations for the state of the world which they used to.

This is a book about modern Scotland; what it is, what it could become, and what our future might entail. In order to discuss this, we have to understand the times and world we live in beyond our shores.

Scotland has a population of 5.3 million people in a UK state of 65 million, representing 8.2% of the people. But Scotland is also almost one third of Great Britain's landmass, 57% of its coast, and crucially, occupies a place of major geo-political significance in terms of the West – witness not just the location of Trident, but also its critical role in military, intelligence and security issues.

Therefore, this small country on so many criteria matters much more than population size. So any debate about self-government, independence and our collective future has important ramifications beyond these borders.

Our Scottish debate is taking place in a world changing so rapidly that it is difficult for most of us to keep up, recognise and assimilate events and their implications. Economic assumptions of the last 30-40 years are in ruins. The free market revolution of Thatcher and Reagan that promised freedom, dignity and prosperity for all has delivered nothing of the kind. Instead, our societies have become characterised by the enrichment of an increasingly privileged few, while the vision of a more dynamic, liberal capitalism has morphed into a cannibalistic crony capitalism, and a corporate order and politics of cartels and closed elites.

Nearly a decade has passed since the economic crash of 2008 which was meant to herald a new age of responsibility, and a more socially aware economics. Such hopes were doomed from the start. As we know, in the UK (unlike Iceland) not one senior banker was ever jailed. Instead, the story was of restoration. This embodied a fixation with what can be seen as the British Magic Money Tree – the creation of money from supposedly nowhere to pay pampered elites for, at best, doing nothing, and certainly not creating anything physically real or adding any real value. Welcome to the Britain of the present – a country economically and socially unsustainable. A system which carries huge costs for all but a tiny number.

Then there are the many crises of the European Union, from the fiscal fascism imposed on Greece by Berlin and Brussels, to the huge youth unemployment of the Southern Mediterranean countries of Greece (50.4%), Spain (43.9%) and Italy (36.9%)[1], the straightjacket of the Euro, and now Brexit which will create massive waves for the UK and continent over the next couple of years.

This is an age of huge unprecedented global movement of people. In the past year, 65.3 million people – the equivalent of the entire UK population have been displaced – resulting in one in 113 people across the world being either an asylum seeker, internally displaced, or a refugee.[2] To put that in context, the only other time which saw movement of this scale was at the end of the Second World War when 60 million people were displaced, including 12 million Germans forcibly moved as Germany's eastern territories were given to Poland.[3]

What do today's mainstream politicians have to say about these burning issues? Some play to the very worst instincts – Donald Trump in the USA, Marine Le Pen in France, Nigel Farage in the UK. But even those attempting to come from a place of decency and liberal values – such as Angela Merkel in Germany, François Hollande in France, and Barack Obama in the US – are either swept along by what seem elemental forces, or have to appease sentiments of racism and xenophobia. More than likely none of the aforementioned political leaders will be in office by the middle of 2017: two are not standing in their country's elections (Obama and Merkel), while Hollande faces huge obstacles. Political office, as David Cameron illustrated in 2016, is a less secure calling than once was, and the aura of authority and deference that national leaders once enjoyed is significantly diminished.

Not surprisingly, this has become an age of insurgency and protest against conventional politics, and of racists and populists even more objectionable than the likes of Trump and Farage. Across Europe a swathe of extreme right-wing opinion and even neo-Nazis have emerged as electoral forces such as Golden Dawn in Greece, Jobbik in Hungary, the Law and Justice Party in Poland, the authoritarian turn of the Fidesz-

Hungarian Civic Union, and even in the Nordics, the True Finns in Finland, and the Sweden Democrats. Seemingly everywhere, reactionaries and the hard right are on the march.

In most countries, these authoritarians haven't yet achieved the electoral support needed to form the main party of government, Poland and Hungary, for the moment, being the exception. However, these forces and their anxieties aren't going away anytime soon. Take the US Presidential bid of Donald Trump. This has caused all kinds of turmoil in US politics and the Republican Party. Trump was always likely to fail on sheer demographics alone, but the longer question is what happens to these nativistic, anxious, angry sentiments? They don't just disappear into the ether, and so far what passes for the centre-left in the US and elsewhere has no idea on how to confront and defeat them.

One profound set of changes underpins all of the above and is critical for the future of Scotland. This is that the managed capitalist order of 1945-75 is no longer. The vision of Bretton Woods (where this international order was agreed in 1944), of full employment in the West and fixed currencies now seems a half forgotten dream. It was the security of this international order which made the welfare state of Britain and the West possible.

In its place for the last 30-40 years has been a disorganised capitalism which has seen great shifts in power, wealth and influence – from workers to capital, from the real economy to the financial sector, from West to East, and also within the West, from older, more organised forms of labour to new, more individualised types. All of this has contributed to huge changes in work, employment, gender roles and the expectations people have – from the workplace to family, friends, support networks, and wider society.

Scotland's Place in a World of Uncertainty

This forms the context and backstory to the dramatic changes we have recently experienced, and are currently living through. This is a time in which the world has seemingly turned upside down. Changes have had enormous impact and repercussions for Scotland, and have influenced the debates we have been having, and will continue to do so in the future.

Scotland has, in recent decades, undergone numerous shocks and transformations. There is the familiar story of the upsurges of 2011, 2014 and 2015 – now added to by the insecurities of Brexit. In my previous book, *Caledonian Dreaming*, published in 2014, I argued that the indyref and these other moments did not come from nowhere.[4] Instead, they are part of a longer story – explored in light of the indyref result and Brexit in the following chapters.

The referendum was *a product* of deep-seated, fundamental shifts in Scottish society: namely, the dispersal of the traditional closed social order that ran and administered public life. At the same time, the indyref itself was *a further catalyst* of change way beyond the formal question being asked, as it disrupted normal business and many of the conventions of public engagement. In an age of disruption it is not that surprising, but many sections of society were caught unawares and disliked the unpredictability and fluidity that emerged.

This book is an attempt to understand the times we are living through in relation to Scotland's debates and experiences. Moreover, it aims to place our own changes, hopes and anxieties – what can be called, in the words of Tom Devine, our own 'quiet revolution' (itself a reference to the dramatic changes which Quebec went through in the 1960s as it became more Francophile and self-governing) in this international context.[5] In so doing, the intention is to shed some fresh light on where we are and the real choices we will face in the future. It aspires to challenge our inbuilt tendency at times to insularity – something every nation on planet Earth has – and our propensity to sometimes believe we are special and unique (also shared widely across the world).

In so doing, this book refers to many recent events we are still coming to terms with. It doesn't aim to be about this near-past, or to try to rewrite or rigidly reframe it from one political perspective. Rather, it is about seeing past, present and future as one continuous conversation – and in which the arguments within try to use the first two to make observations and suggestions on the third.

All of this is written with a sense of engagement and hope. Two obstacles face us in this. First, despite all of the change Scotland has undergone, issues remain about our collective confidence as a society, or at least, parts of society. This was evident in some debates in the indyref, and is still present in some of the silences and evasions that characterise public life. There are still huge sensitivities, even taboos and no-go areas of discussion in Scotland. They range from talking honestly about our own shortcomings as a society and the role of Scottish people in that; limitations in some of our public services and how we reform and transform them with the active involvement of those who use and work for them; the nature of the power elites and how they self-reproduce and maintain their dominance; the role of culture and official cultural bodies; and critically, the overshadow of failed British economic policy and practice, and the extent to which Scotland can embark on a different path. Addressing our confidence gap contributes to all of this, and requires scrutinising and holding to account power, while recognising the power that we hold in our hands collectively as a people, society and nation.

Another dimension worthy of exploration is what I would call the empathy deficit. Scottish people have a 'reputation' for being emotional and sentimental, but these are sweeping generalisations of a whole people and thus problematic. Hard evidence is seldom offered and difficult to find. It isn't too controversial to say parts of our society have a serious problem with emotional intelligence. By this I mean an ability to feel the complex emotions in any issue, recognise the feelings of others, and act beyond one's own gut and instinctual feelings.[6]

Much of this can be witnessed in the binary politics of the Yes/No show of the indyref, the way anti-Labour and anti-Tory sentiment are used by some as sticks to metaphorically beat people over the head, with Labour deemed 'red Tories', with 'Tory' being a dismissive four-letter word in Scotland. There is the problem with football, in particular, the 'Old Firm' duopoly of Celtic and Rangers historically and all that flows from it.[7] And there are particularly distressing elements of masculinity, manifest in problems with aggression, violence and drink across Scotland, and particularly in sections of youth culture.

All of these can be seen as having a relationship to an empathy deficit – by which people find it difficult, near impossible, to imagine the world from someone else's vantage point. This hurts us; it hurts us badly. It hurts hundreds of thousands of Scots individually and us as a society. This has to matter and be central to our politics and public deliberations.

In my earlier book *Caledonian Dreaming* a central tenet was the power of dreaming; its limits, as well as its positives. Abstract, utopian idealism has positive aspects but also a host of negatives – if it gets in the way of real action and change. What was perhaps not too surprising was that in all the numerous reviews and citations of the book, not one picked up this point. There was one lone exception – a retired Scottish academic in social policy who thought that this double meaning and limiting notion of dreaming was self-evident.

This isn't an accident. It is indicative of our instinct to stay away from the split between words and action, thinking and doing. Thus, there is a propensity to be drawn, particularly on the left, to grandiose, well-meaning gestures and visions, and to show much less interest in the detail, and in making small-scale, incremental change.

These three areas – the confidence gap, the empathy deficit and the action-words divide – all mitigate against building the belief and capacity that collectively we can employ to bring about lasting change. They each have deep historic origins and roots in Scotland's experience as a brutally unequal society throughout most of its history; where power and authority have traditionally laid in a few hands and often beyond our borders – whether politically or economically.

Scotland stands at a fascinating juncture in its history: one where the old institutions and pillars of a very controlled, hierarchical society – and one in which those bodies were overwhelmingly liberal unionist – have fallen into decline. This is a massive change which has taken decades, and which is unlikely to be reversed in the near future. The implications of this are explored in the next chapter, but suffice to say that authority, power and influence have shifted dramatically in society, and the dispensation of today's Scotland, however impregnable it may look to some on the inside or outside, is likely to be but one chapter in a much bigger story. There is underneath the surface, a state of flux and transience as the old order has withered and lost much of its hold and credibility, but the new forces of authority such as the Scottish Government and the SNP are still learning the ropes. That impermanence is something that should be welcomed and celebrated, not resisted. But what is certain longer-term is that power and authority are more contested, and that the debate about these is centred around what is the best form of self-government.

There will be along our future roads many blocks and obstacles. Some will be of our own making. Take the view, for example, still found on large parts of the left of a pessimism about much of the modern age – which can spill over easily into a rather sour miserablism, asserting that nothing is going right in present times. At an event last year organised by the *Soundings* journal I made this very point, only to have an ex-

Socialist Worker's Party member declare with certainty that 'the last 40 years have seen the destruction of nearly everything we have cherished and built over the post-war period.' When I replied that domestically there were such significant gains as formal equality for lesbian, gay, bisexual and trans people; and internationally, the collapse of the Berlin Wall and apartheid, he didn't reply.

An opposing sentiment can be found in sections of the Scottish left and the pro-independence community that have bought into a panglossian optimism, and think that because they have bought into the phrase 'Another Scotland is Possible', this is literally true. At the Radical Independence Campaign conference in Glasgow in November 2013 I overheard two middle-aged male left-wingers who had clearly been politically active for decades but still carried a sense of optimism. One said – 'Of course it makes sense that Scotland can become the world's first democratic socialist country. We were part of the world's first capitalist country.' That is a sort of first in, first out principle but political change rarely conforms to such tidy, ordered patterns.

A sense of hope and belief in change is healthy. But believing that the global forces of the markets and the power of capital can be single-handedly defeated by the political will of a small-sized country such as Scotland is, to put it mildly, going to lead to disappointment. Some of this naivety is based on the absence of large right-wing conservative forces, and the lack of public face and advocacy for a neo-liberal, market capitalist approach in the domestic life of the country. Yet, this doesn't translate into believing that the international economic order can be ignored in a post-independence Scotland.

There was another strand in our indyref that understandably hankered after Scotland becoming more Nordic, co-operating with our northern friends, and rejecting the blighted model of Anglo-American capitalism.[8] However, such were the hopes raised by the indyref that some people thought that we could become completely Nordic and turn our backs on the influence of Anglo-America. Apart from the fact that an independent Scotland would be situated in a number of international influences, there would be little chance of becoming completely Nordic. There has to be a recognition that the Nordics are not by any measure utopian, ideal societies, and typically at the moment feel under attack from a voracious capitalism and pressures of immigration and mass human population movements.

Scotland beyond the Great Divide

Our politics now and for the foreseeable future are shaped by the great divide of the indyref. For some on either side of the independence question, politics can be likened to the emotions of a football match – cheering on one side and booing on the other, reducing our politics to tribalism, trench warfare and point scoring. It used to be said of Scottish football reporters that they were 'fans with typewriters'; this behaviour reduces politics to this level of fandom.

This book isn't written in that spirit, but instead is aimed at the huge sections of Scotland who are curious, want to be challenged, and to challenge others. There are no final answers or conclusions, but instead this is a search to ask questions, to explore possible answers and to address some of the big issues that we face – to aid a different kind of Scotland.

In between the two statements of certainty post-Brexit vote – that an indyref is inevitable, and that it is not going to happen (both of which I am told by people everyday who are 100% certain about their belief) – is the terrain of this book.

This is the landscape of 'the third Scotland' I identified in the referendum – the self-organising, self-motivating independence of the Scottish mind.[9] Post-indyref this sentiment has even more morphed into being supportive of independence – but not completely unconditionally.

It is not signed up without qualification to the Nationalist Scotland project, and instead sees independence as a means to an end, not an end in itself. It wants to support policies which devolve and decentralise power within Scotland, not just to Edinburgh. This is the difference between independence as focused on the full powers of the Parliament and the vision of self-government leading to self-determination – not just in terms of a nation, but individuals, communities and society.

A word should be made about the state of the United Kingdom – one of the main strands running through the book. It is clearly broken, does not work for the vast majority of people, and looks to be unreformable in the long run – an assessment explored in later chapters. It is not just, in Iain Macwhirter's words, a 'disunited kingdom'[10], but an unequal, unbalanced, lopsided kingdom, where too much of the wealth, resources and power is hoarded in a tiny economic elite over-concentrated in a micro part of London: a capital-ism of capitalism.

How we live and act on a set of islands next to such turbo-charged grotesquely unfair capitalism and its nexus of power in the city of London is one of the biggest questions facing Scotland. The two main answers before us are either 'independence in the UK' – a phrase in inverted commas as it was briefly in the late 1980s Donald Dewar's description of far-reaching home rule and for a period actual Labour Party policy[11] – or independence within the EU.

The first would be a uniquely Scottish-British solution whereby everything domestic came back to Scotland, and only defence and foreign affairs were pooled at Westminster. The second would be more conventional, but see sovereignty pooled at the level of the EU.

There is common ground between these two competing visions: of Scotland inside political unions, sovereignty not seen as an absolute, independence as very unlike the traditional 19th-century version, and external affairs in particular shared at a higher level. Both also have problems: the first, the unreformed nature of the British state and its inability to share sovereignty or enter the 21st-century; the second, how Scotland navigates the UK realities post-Brexit. For the moment, I am leaving the option of independence outside the EU as an outlier – which does have the virtues of addressing the post-Brexit landscape, but carries its own baggage.

The defining question about both main competing visions should be independence – or indeed, inter-independence – for what? How does either aid Scotland become a better, fairer, more content country? How does each advance the search for an alternative economic model, close our social divisions, reach out to the 'left behind' Scotland of the last thirty years, and nurture the wellbeing of our citizens? That, more than formal statehood, should be the criterion upon which we decide our constitutional status.

This is the rationale of this book – of a Scotland that doesn't give blank cheques or blind obedience to any political tradition or authority, and that doesn't see our possible future in easy answers or simple clarion calls. A first step in all of this is understanding the epic, sweeping changes which have already dramatically altered Scotland, are still in process, and are not yet finished. To some who hanker after the old ways, this is a time of feeling unsettled and unsure, but that is always the way of change. Some of these changes are long term, some more immediate, but this often leaderless 'quiet revolution' has to be understood, for in it we can begin to see the maps and contours of a future Scotland.

Chapter Two:

Scotland after the Long and Short Revolutions

Words are important – to fight silence, alienation, and violence. Words are flags planted on the planets of our beings; they say this is mine, I have fought for it and despite your attempt to silence me, I am still here.

Mona Eltahawy, Headscarves and Hymens, 2015

People think they know Scotland. They have assumptions, perceptions, even the occasional prejudice that adds up to how they see us.

This is true for people who live here and people outwith the country – some of whom think they know us better than ourselves. Much of this is unavoidable and just part of the human condition, but much of the latter has become a major issue – both for Scotland, and for how the UK understands and misunderstands us.

Numerous examples illustrate this. Scotland is changing at such a bewildering and far-reaching pace in such a short space of time that it is increasingly proving impossible for Scotland to be represented back to itself in an accurate way – either from inside the country, or from outside.

The Story of the Long and Short Revolutions

Scotland has undergone two very distinct, but intertwined revolutions through which the above accounts (and many more) need to be understood. They share some common characteristics, in that they were and are owned by not one political party or perspective exclusively, and were for the most part, leaderless and not, by origin, facilitated by organisations. That makes them very unusual in the recent history of Scotland.

The first of these has been the Scotland that revealed itself in the indyref. This is a society that is diverse, disputatious, and sometimes difficult. For large parts of Scotland this represented something hugely positive. It was the overthrowing of the established order and even, in the words of some pro-independence opinion, a 'festival of democracy'. But for others, it was the exact opposite – unpleasant, disorientating, and filled with a palpable sense of loss. Both accounts are accurate from their perspectives. The future Scotland has to recognise the validity of both, and that there are many more stories.

The second has been the long revolution – of a much more prolonged timescale. It could even be seen as Scotland's own kind of 'velvet revolution' in the words of Tom Devine – whereas we have become much more secular, less deferential, and more pluralist (related to the 'quiet revolution' outlined in Chapter One).[12] The nature of authority has shifted, become much more contested and temporary, and the characteristics of the economy, society and culture altered for good.

These two revolutions have crisscrossed and cross-fertilised each other. The long revolution contributed to the shorter, more immediate revolution – weakening the old pillars of unionist opinion and their elites. In the immediate period before the 2014 indyref, one question asked many times (and that I was asked dozens of times) was 'How did we get here?'

The superficial answer put forward, even by some commentators, was that the whole thing was an unintended 'accident' – a product of the May 2011 surprise victory.[13] The real answer is much more complex. First, Scotland's long revolution created the conditions for the SNP victories in 2007 and 2011, which then in turn led to the calling of the indyref.

The scale of change is bewildering. Scotland post-2014 looks dramatically different from the Scotland of 1955, or even the nation of 1975. It is important to grasp what has happened and why, for it has critical implications for what Scotland's future will look like.

Trouble at the Top: The Backstory to Scotland 2014

First, let's examine the Scotland that was the backdrop to the indyref experience. A number of the most established institutions in the country experienced difficult times and huge turmoil. These included the Royal Bank of Scotland (RBS) – the fifth biggest bank in the world at its peak, headquartered in Scotland, and led by a management team fronted by Sir Fred Goodwin, Scottish-born (educated in the much lauded Paisley Grammar School) and based in Edinburgh. He was feted nearly unanimously by the political classes – from Labour's Gordon Brown to the SNP's Alex Salmond.[14] Post-crash, Labour and SNP went into rapid reverse – each trying to accuse the other of having fawned more and got closer to Goodwin, by then reviled and renamed 'Fred the Shred'.

There was the painful, public experience of Glasgow Rangers FC, historically Scotland's most dominant club on the footballing field and in origins and traditions representative of the country's predominant religious tradition – Protestantism. In February 2012 it went into administration, then in July of the same year liquidation, going through several stages of questionable businessmen owning it (Craig Whyte and Charles Green having brief periods of tenure before ending up in the current Dave King era).[15] The club had to undergo the shock therapy of starting life again as a new legal entity ('newco') in the lowest league, taking four years to get back to the senior level. No matter how successful Rangers now are in the future, they will never quite be the same again.

From the other main religious tradition, the Catholic Church, emerged a series of sexual and ethical scandals – from the top down and including priests at all levels.[16] A large element of senior church figures and authorities turned a blind eye or deliberately didn't ask the right questions on such serious matters as systemic abusive and problematic behaviour – from child and adult sex abuse to the hypocrisy of priests engaging in long-term gay relationships including the then head of the church, Cardinal Keith O'Brien, who was forced to resign in February 2013.[17]

Two observations spring from the above examples. First, in each of these cases, influential sections of Scotland tried to prevent the unethical and questionable behaviour from coming to light. There were opinion formers and powerful forces in each who actively attempted to prevent scrutiny being shone on RBS, Rangers FC and the Catholic Church: these ranged from 'the succulent lamb journalism' evident with Rangers, to the numerous apologists for RBS and the Catholic Church.

Second, all of this told a story about elements of the mainstream Scottish media. Not only did they show a disinterest in these areas, but revealed a wider set of characteristics about the media and its historic and contemporary relationship to power. It begs the question: where is the space to bring unaccountable elites to task when they go wrong? A major challenge in a Scotland becoming increasingly autonomous and self-governing is how power (in all its manifestations) is properly scrutinised and restrained.

Third, another dimension was the attempt to minimise the scale of these scandals once they became public. One way to do this was to individualise them and blame them on the actions of one rotten, rogue apple in a good barrel. Thus, 'Fred the Shred', the free spending years of David Murray at Rangers FC, and Cardinal O'Brien were all trashed. It was all supposedly down to them as the institutions were sound, and it was all about business as usual. Yet, the emergence of such dysfunctional leadership and their ability to get away with such damage to their organisations and individuals, says much about the nature of authority and lack of oversight in these bodies. It is always easier to blame the lone individual gone wrong rather than address cultural norms and structure.

The Slower Decline of Other Elites: the Labour Party and BBC

These events caused seismic shocks when they occurred. They were comparable to massive, once impressive and intimidating towers toppling; mostly, if not exclusively, as a result of internal explosions. As significant were a series of slower timed crashes and implosions that need to be seen as having longer-term consequences which the indyref brought to the fore.

There was the fate of the Scottish Labour Party. It was once Scotland's leading party, its political establishment, and central to the country's place in the union.[18] Just under twenty years ago in 1997 it won 45.6% of the vote, legislated for and delivered a Scottish Parliament emphatically backed in a popular referendum. It looked to many observers that it would continue to dominate politics well into the foreseeable future.

It did not work out like that as Scottish Labour showed that it had little idea of how to adapt to devolution, or indeed what to do in the institution it had helped to create. It was subsequently challenged and outmanoeuvred by the SNP who once they narrowly won in 2007, saw Labour's fortunes fall off a cliff – in 2011, 2015 and 2016. There was no one single moment which made this happen, but a series of factors – from Blair and Iraq, to Brown's command and control politics and seeing Scotland as his 'fiefdom', and the weight of 'London Labour' producing a Scottish party which wasn't fully accountable and autonomous. That is still the case to this day and costing the party dear.

Another institution which once invited confidence and respect, and which has failed to adjust to the new Scottish landscape, has been the BBC in Scotland. The BBC has increasingly struggled to represent and reflect contemporary

Scotland – not just politics, but the arts, culture, science and any other aspect of society you care to mention. STV does not do any better, and in some respects is actually worse, in areas such as commissioning new content. Like the BBC it has a statutory obligation to public service broadcasting, but the ITV network has been lobbying to have this diluted and eventually dropped – which would have consequences on its scant Scottish-specific content.

Now the BBC, along with STV, did not have a good indyref. But this was more nuanced than some pro-independence critics alleged, claiming that it 'stole' the referendum, meaning that its bias tipped the result in favour of the union.[19] This begged the question of how did the indyref become the BBC's property in the first place, allowing it to 'steal' it? Such overstatement, the result of years of resentment and problems, gets in the way of understanding deep-seated problems.

The BBC has many common characteristics with Scottish Labour. Both are basically branch offices in Scotland that struggle to find a way to have accountability to Scottish audiences. Both are ultimately accountable to London bureaucrats in their respective organisations. 'BBC Scotland was a fiction' said one savvy media player and insider.[20] While this might seem an overstatement, it captures an essential truth of where power has historically lain.

There is a democratic deficit in the BBC – 48% of viewers and listeners trust BBC news and current affairs in Scotland, compared to 61% in England. Then there is the licence fee and the problem of how much is spent in Scotland: in Wales the figure is 95%, in Northern Ireland 72% and in Scotland 55% – from the BBC's own figures.[21] The indyref brought these kind of tensions into the open and to a head.

Then there were the smaller implosions and institutional reverses which belied deeper problems. Thus, the Scottish Council for Voluntary Organisations (SCVO), the national umbrella body of the voluntary sector, attempted to position itself post-2011 to be part of and help shape a campaign for a two-question referendum, in part to aid the SNP after their unexpected election victory. This brought out tensions about SCVO's leadership, legal concerns, and even anxieties about how independent the voluntary sector can be when so much of its funding is from the government. This even led to Lib Dem leader Willie Rennie calling on the long-serving head of SCVO – Martin Sime – to resign.[22] The rich mosaic of voluntary activities across the country goes on uninterrupted, although somewhat reduced by less public donations and tightened government budgets, but SCVO's reputation at a senior level will take a longer time to rehabilitate.

More serious was the car crash that was CBI Scotland. In the midst of the indyref it decided to register as a supporter of the No camp, only to find out this had negative consequences.[23] Many of its public body members such as Scotland's universities resigned or suspended their CBI membership, forcing the organisation into a hasty U-turn that it blamed on an administrative error. The damage was done, and in a not unrelated move, Iain McMillan, its Scottish director for two decades, announced his retirement at the end of 2014.

This episode touched on the fact that CBI Scotland, who claim to speak for 'Scotland's business community', have a tiny membership, are not fully autonomous, and are arguably not very representative (even at a UK level), speaking for big corporates and multinationals. Their miscalling in the indyref came after decades of being on the wrong side of public opinion – having been anti-devolution in 1979 and 1997, as well as anti-independence in 2014. They have had a consistent 'No, No, No' position, and have been at every opportunity against greater democracy in Scotland. Never in nearly four decades have they come up with any counter-proposals for democratisation. That's because elite Scotland has, over that period, worked well for CBI Scotland and its agenda.

Scotland in the age of disruption

In this there is some similarity between Scotland's experience leading up to and including the indyref, and much more dramatically, Ireland after the crash. Of course, Ireland was subject to seismic shocks, but common ground can be found in Fintan O'Toole's influential analysis that the leading institutions and their raison d'être were found wanting in Ireland. There was in Ireland pre-crash a powerful self-delusion of the elites that held sway over the population. O'Toole wrote that such self-delusion is not of itself unusual, but 'the degree of collective misapprehension was rather extreme' and went on:

Many people knew, from their bitter daily experiences of poverty, abandonment and squalor, that everything was not for the best in the best of all possible worlds... The idea that Ireland had found salvation in its embrace of so-called free-market globalisation ceased to be an ideology and acquired the irrefutable authority of common sense.[24]

Scotland's shift has been much more subtle, but the collective grip of the old order and traditional unionist establishment has withered, and the years leading up to the indyref witnessed a public crisis of confidence in unionism and institutions long identified with it. Not only that, this touched on the nature and basis of power, legitimacy and status in society: RBS, Rangers, the Catholic Church dramatically, the BBC and Labour Party in much slower, incremental decline. The old networks and cosy relationships of that previous era have become much less palatable and increasingly contested.

This transformation of Scotland is understandably unsettling for some. Well-known anchor points and references have withered or disappeared, and for sections of society there is a tangible yearning and grieving for a lost Scotland which isn't coming back.

All of these shifts have a longer backstory in which the indyref was only an added catalyst, in some cases merely speeding up or bringing scrutiny to already existing trends. The Church of Scotland's peak membership was in the mid-1950s, just after the Scottish Tories had won over half the popular vote. On existing trends, there will not be any Church of Scotland membership within 20-30 years: which is quite a scale of transformation – from seeming omnipotence to impotence and possible future oblivion.

The decline in social authoritarianism, a sort of personal conservatism and the proscriptive society of limitations on behaviour and opinions, and numerous no-go areas, has been a long time fermenting and brewing. It is only fourteen years between the bitter cultural war over Section 28/Clause 2a on the 'promotion' of homosexuality in schools, and legislation for same-sex marriage.[25] Twenty years ago, there were no 'out' public figures in Scotland, the word 'homosexuality' barely spoken in public, and now three of the five main political parties have gay or bisexual leaders, along with the Scottish Secretary of State David Mundell and UKIP Scottish leader David Coburn. No one makes a big issue of this epic turnaround, but the change across society is off the scale in a relatively short time.

From the vantage point of today some people question whether Scotland was really that different and authoritarian in the not too distant past, and to underline the change later chapters will offer a number of detailed examples which illustrate that the Scotland of the past was in many respects a foreign country compared to today.

This was for long the society of 'the Scottish tut' – where a whole host of restrictions, repressions and resentments were articulated by a class of moral guardians, usually elders, feeling that they had permission to admonish others if they judged they were acting above themselves. That Scotland – personified in the strip cartoons of the *Sunday Post*'s *Oor Wullie* and *Broons* family – pushed at omnipresent authority and against often ridiculous rules, has mostly disappeared. That poses new dilemmas for how we organise and govern ourselves in our daily lives. After the tut – which was a metaphor for a whole social order – what will be the ethics of living together in modern Scotland? We are going to have to agree new rules collectively and more democratically than before.

From Labour to Nationalist Scotland: Change and Continuity

Some see the end of the Labour era and its dominant party rule and the rise of the SNP as the continuation of a familiar Scottish story: serial one-party rule, farewell to the old establishment and welcome to the new establishment, normal service being resumed after only a short interlude.[26]

This is one possible outcome of the multiple changes we are living through. It is true that some in the SNP leadership – and certainly some of their sympathisers in numerous public bodies, public affairs and consulting – would like to see this state of affairs come about.

Yet, a degree of caution and context is required. 'Labour Scotland' – that vision of society which Labour built – lasted nearly fifty years, being dominant from 1959-2007; while its West of Scotland roots go much further back. Labour first broke through in Glasgow at a parliamentary level and won the city in 1922, and first won the council in 1933.

Scottish Labour became incredibly insular, self-serving, self-reverential and nostalgic for its own past (Red Clydeside, the ILP, 1945, council housing). It also, the longer its reign continued, became more imbued with a politics of cronyism, particularly through local patronage, quasi-business practices and shady deals it acquiesced in and facilitated, irrespective of whether this was under an Old or New Labour banner. Sometimes the personnel and their actions were indistinguishable between one and the other in some of the party's traditional strongholds.

The scale of this and its corrupt, sometimes criminal nature, cannot be over-exaggerated. While much of the focus historically has been on the manner in which West of Scotland Labour expressed its monopoly control of local government, this was the pattern across numerous places in the country. For example, one of the biggest British post-war local government scandals came to a head in Dundee in the 1970s when J.L. Stewart, chair of the council housing committee, engaged in dodgy contracts with builders for millions of pounds. He ended up in jail, challenged by such local young turks as a then untainted George Galloway.[27] All of this was brought to the surface in a pattern to become familiar, not by the efforts of the Dundee press or Scottish media, but by an ITV *World in Action* special. Its producer Ray Fitzwalter called the city of the 1960s and 1970s a 'mafia town'[28] with all the connotations, both in crime and violence and police complicity that flow from that, minus the style. Such was the nature of unchecked Labour rule.

It goes without saying that the SNP are far removed from this multi-generational politics of incestuousness and preferment. There are concerns of centralisation, the absence of serious opposition in the Parliament, the lack of serious power in the Parliament in relation to holding the Scottish Government to account, and a lack of alternative centres of power. These can all come together under concerns about how Scotland embraces and encourages pluralism, how it puts in place checks and balances on the concentration of political power, and limits any cultural propensity to conformity and degree of groupthink. It is too early to tell, but there is a world of difference between asking these questions and just labelling the SNP as a 'one-party state', a dictatorship, a cult, and a whole lot worse.

However, the more germane debate is to raise concerns

over how a small country with a small network of an insider class holds power – political, economic, social and cultural – to account. One undercurrent of many of the institutional collapses which have taken place – RBS, Rangers FC, the Catholic Church, the Labour Party – was the absence of a sustained, informed, investigative media culture. This has always been the situation – with all of the mainstream newspapers once upon a time originating in the liberal unionist establishment and thus, not surprisingly, historically failing to question or investigate such groups. This is a thorny issue exasperated by the now significant decline in sales and resources of the print media, leaving unanswered the issue of who holds the elites and power brokers to account in Scotland, and how this impacts on diversity and accountability in the light of greater self-government and, potentially, independence.

The Right-Wing Counter-Story of Scotland

In Scotland there is evidence of what can only be described as cognitive dissonance – of people clinging to antiquated notions that offer consolation or reassurance even though they often know these to be false or outdated. One burning issue is how Scotland's mainstream media have failed to keep abreast of these epic changes, and instead have been behind the curve and, in many cases, in denial.

An influential group worthy of note are the disgruntled right-wing commentators, journalists and opinion formers who see themselves as some kind of underground samizdat opposition to the forward march of the SNP and the widespread collusion and appeasement this has elicited. This position is articulated by a number of right-wing titles and platforms; pivotal in this is the role of a group of London Scottish journalists such as Andrew Neil (previously editor of the *Sunday Times*), Fraser Nelson (editor of the *Spectator*) and Iain Martin (a former *Scotsman* editor). They see it as their role to challenge what they perceive as the collective groupthink of Scotland – oblivious to their very own collective groupthink and ideological dogmas.

This troika often pen florid, and influential, commentary on Scotland via their access to UK media platforms and play into the right-wing consensus so influential in the Westminster bubble. Neil has written and commented at length on Scotland showing his disdain for present arrangements, calling it 'the land of the big state… where the state was more important than in any country in the world, bar Cuba, North Korea or Iraq.'[29] Nelson has spoken of Scotland as a land with 'Soviet levels of state spending.'[30]

This right-wing counter-offensive can reach such heights of passion and fury with modern-day Scotland that it effortlessly falls into disinformation and deliberate misreporting. Two recent examples show the scale of this. First, there was the *Daily Telegraph* spin of the Frenchgate memo in April 2015 involving First Minister Nicola Sturgeon, which had the front page headline: 'Sturgeon's secret backing for Cameron.'[31]

The paper insisted that the memo, written by a senior British civil servant, showed Sturgeon had expressed a preference for a Tory Government led by David Cameron, as opposed to a Labour Government led by Ed Miliband, in a meeting with the French Ambassador to the UK. Within one hour of the story becoming public, Sturgeon took to Twitter and declared this account '100 per cent untrue'.[32] This was in the midst of a UK general election where the SNP's profile and influence at Westminster was a key issue. The press watchdog, the Independent Press Standards Organisation, found the *Telegraph* story 'significantly misleading', while it also emerged that Scottish Secretary of State Alistair Carmichael leaked it.[33]

Another was the London right-wing media, from the *Daily Telegraph* to the *Daily Mail* post-Brexit vote, claiming that the Scottish Government said that it had a 'veto' on the UK Government 'triggering' Article 50. The only problem was that the interviews and comments they were citing from Nicola

Sturgeon said nothing of the kind, with her going out of her way to avoid using the word 'veto'.[34]

This right-wing account has grown more defiant and damning in its critique as Scotland has grown more autonomous. It isn't an accident that after the 2015 SNP landslide – which seemed like some inexplicable 'tartan tsunami' to such opinion – a host of pieces arose pathologising Scotland. They stated at the extreme: 'Scotland has gone mad'[35] or talked about 'mad Celt Disease'[36], while the more mild-mannered Alex Massie asked: 'How do you defeat a faith-based party whose voters are animated by quasi-religious zealotry?'[37] This is an extreme form of denial of reality. Sadly, this take on Scotland will not go away in the near future, and as our country grows steadily more different from the rest of the UK we can expect more of the same. We will return to the right-wing interpretation of our future in the concluding chapter.

After the 'Big Bang' and the Competing Claims of Two Nationalisms

If the indyref can be characterised as a creative, transformative 'Big Bang' of engagement and enthusiasm, we have to understand that the high-octane energies it released cannot be maintained at the same level forever. In any 'Big Bang' after the initial moment of explosion, there is first a throwing out and creation of new forces, and then there is retrenchment, followed by a new equilibrium. However, not to take the analogy too far, energy and movement are always present in the post-'Big Bang' universe. That sounds like an accurate description of Scotland post-2014 – but there is a difference between the tensions of retrenchment and restoration. We are now in a very different place, living in a new political universe.

This new environment cannot be defined just by the claims of Scottish nationalism or the counter-claims of British nationalism – the latter mostly being in denial that it is a nationalism; unionism being by its very character a nationalism – British state nationalism. Such are the dynamics the world over. Minority nationalisms (Scots, Welsh, Catalonian) are stigmatised and demonised by the official and majority nationalism of a state (British, Spanish). The latter sees itself as cosmopolitan, outgoing and as the opposite of nationalism that is presented as primordial and a throwback to past ages. This is a battle of different claims; and there is even a respectable left-wing version of the British version from the historian Eric Hobsbawm where he placed himself in the tradition of 'I am an internationalist not a nationalist'.[38]

For all the positives of Scotland's indyref, there were undoubted negatives. One was that a large part of the campaign was conducted by the competing claims of these two nationalisms, and for all their democratic credentials it was a war of attrition of argument and counter-argument to the end.

A contest centred on two nationalisms fails to do justice to the values most Scots want to see nurtured now and in the future. Instead, this produced an essentialist element to some of the debate. Thus, to some Scotland was inherently progressive; the UK by its very history and being, reactionary. Both sides drew on an element of faith-based arguments. To some on one side, Scotland had to be independent to recover its rightful statehood on the journey to its citizens having dignity. For a section of the other side, the UK was unique and precious: an incredibly intricate political and social union constructed over the centuries by the efforts of its people.

When I wrote a *New Statesman* piece post-referendum about the perils of a politics dominated by two nationalisms it was fascinating to see the wider relevance and readings.[39] The father of a friend of mine was a leading South African National Party minister in the latter days of apartheid, not something my friend often mentions. A few months after this piece was published, my friend mentioned that their father and another former National Party minister had read it – and in very different, much more extreme circumstances, saw themselves reflected in it. This isn't about anything as insensitive as which side in our debate is closer to apartheid South Africa, but about a polarised debate – in this case between Afrikaner minority nationalism and black majority nationalism.

The two situations are totally different. Any comparison made has to be heavily qualified. One truism can be made from the above. It was made by Fintan O'Toole when comparing Ireland's experience post-independence with Scotland's today. O'Toole said that nationalism was similar to a 'rocket fuel that can get you out of an old order', but 'burns up quickly' and is inadequate on its own to make the contours and characteristics of a new state. That is true the world over – from South Africa to other emerging countries, the Nordics when Iceland and Norway became formally independent, and newer nation states that emerged from the old Soviet Union.

Instead, the siren calls of this narrow kind of debate should be self-evident. For some 'freedom' and 'sovereignty' are enough, and the trappings of a new state as important as what it does and looks like. There is a need to resist such romantic, unreflective nationalism. In very different and much more difficult circumstances, many have been here across the world and such predicaments never end well. Nationalism is never enough; nor is a nationalism that claims to be progressive, centre-left and social democratic. Ours undoubtedly carries all of these credentials, but is still a nationalism first and foremost, and everything else secondarily. As, of course, is British nationalism that carries with it its own problems for those making the case for Britain.

Therefore, we have to be careful about what we invoke, the traditions we celebrate, and the stories we tell about ourselves. 'Freedom,' as O'Toole writes, is an 'act of deliberate disillusion,' and goes on:

What has to be broken free of is not just the big bad Them. It is also the warm, fuzzy Us of the nationalist imagination – the Us that is nicer, holier, more caring. What a free country quickly discovers is that the better Us of its imagination is not already there, fully formed, just waiting to blossom in the sun of liberation. It has to be created and in order to create it you have to genuinely decide that you want it.[40]

Sounds familiar. It should do. For that account of 'Us' is a too familiar story in modern Scotland. One we have to be wary of the charms and conceits of, telling us how special, liberal and progressive we are. Instead, we have to imagine and dare to reach a Scotland beyond Them and Us, and for some that is going to be a struggle. But there is no future in a mindset of each side othering the opposition in Scotland's constitutional debate. The release from such a limiting, damaging approach is nothing short of liberation.

Chapter Three:

What's changed and what's not changed?

Cultural integrity, local self-respect, the redistribution of Highland estates, the survival of the Gaelic language, the control of the exploitation of North Sea oil – all those and many more of the dreams close to the heart of Scottish nationalism will depend on the hard facts of world political and economic structures. They will never become realities unless the struggle for them is seen in the context of world struggle against the imperialism of international, largely, American capital.

John McGrath, Scotland: Up Against It, in The Red Paper on Scotland, 1975

Scotland 2016 is a very different place from the country of 1999, 1979 or the 1950s. We have already looked at a number of the landmarks and while many would still be familiar to a visitor from Scotland of the 1950s they would find much new and disorientating.

Our politics, while still involving most of the same parties, has turned topsy-turvy, new institutions have emerged such as the Scottish Parliament and Scottish Government; and besides that culture, the economy and wider society are dramatically different to how they were in the 1970s, let alone the 1950s.

It's not all about Thatcher: The Transformation of the Economy

Firstly, take the economy. Judging from a baseline of 1951, or even nearer to the present of 1971, huge changes have occurred.

Manufacturing is a much smaller part of the economy. There has been the emergence of a service-dominated economy. Employment patterns have changed, as have career and work patterns.

There has been pain, dislocation and anger as a result for some. 'Thatcher destroyed our industries', 'she closed Ravenscraig' (John Major's Tory Government did in 1992) and 'she hated Scotland and all we stood for'. All of these comments have been heard over and over again in the last couple of decades. You would find similar sentiments in South Yorkshire or South Wales: industrial areas with a tradition of mining and worker resistance. But in Scotland this became interwoven with a collective rejection of Thatcher and Toryism.

Scotland's economy, just like its society, should not be split into two separate periods – between 1945-79 and from 1979 to today – one where the former is viewed by the left and nationalists as an upward curve of prosperity shared fairly and evenly, and the latter in which nearly everything goes wrong and only a tiny minority prosper. Instead, Scottish living standards have per head increased dramatically over the post-war period; UK GDP per head is five times bigger now in real terms than in the early 1950s, and it is more than twice the size in real terms compared to the early 1980s.

The Scotland of today would appear a land of abundance and of milk and honey compared to one hundred years ago, or even to the society of 1945 – long interpreted as the left's holy grail. That is not to say that there are not huge problems and limitations. It is just that we need to qualify and contextualise the scale of changes to the economy. The powerful pessimism that says that everything has gone wrong in recent decades, and that all, or nearly all of it, can be traced back to Thatcher isn't based on any historical or factual basis.

Just take the oft-painted picture of the decline of manufacturing and heavy industry. Their decline predates the arrival of Thatcher by decades, and manufacturing in

Scotland was plagued by the same lack of investment, amateur management and poor industrial relations found across the UK. Heavy, extractive industry such as coal, iron and steel, along with shipbuilding, faced decades of problems in Scotland and the UK, along with the rise of cheaper international competition.[41] The decline of the Clyde in shipbuilding, which pre-World War One built one fifth of all the ships in the world, was a long time coming.[42] The decline thesis also dismisses that there are lots of quality, high-end manufacturing companies in Scotland today; just as there is still, over a century after the peak of the Clyde, shipbuilding and shipyards on the river.

The workforce of Scotland has become more feminised than ever before, more skilled and more educated. There are endemic problems associated with 'left behind' Scotland, and the relative poverty of hundreds of thousands of Scots in what is a wealthy nation. There are big economic challenges about the nature of capitalism, corporate power, what to do about finance capital, and the sustainability of the West's economic model since the crash of 2008. Living standards in the UK have barely recovered to pre-2008 levels – indicating a lost decade in terms of prosperity and growth.

There are concerns about Scottish businesses. Once the economy was dominated by Scottish owned and run companies, but that hasn't been the case for decades, and concern about a 'branch line economy' has worried economic analysts since the 1930s and 1940s. Where are decisions about the economy in Scotland made? Being part of the UK, and thus an 'open Scotland' in a UK 'open for business', we are vulnerable to foreign takeovers, inward investment which can come and go, and with no real concept of strategic national goods. Our economy is open to the same global forces as the rest of the UK.

This is primarily a result of Scotland being part of the UK. Scottish capitalism and the economy here are interwoven with British capitalism and the UK economy. Despite the many

Scottish debates in recent years we have yet to begin a specific Scottish one on our economic priorities, shifting from the Anglo-American model of capitalism, and even identifying and protecting strategic national goods. An example of the latter was the revelation that Scotland's main airports, Glasgow, Edinburgh and Aberdeen, all of which used to be in public ownership, are now owned by companies using offshore arrangements in tax havens – Edinburgh in the Cayman Islands, Glasgow and Aberdeen in Jersey.[43]

This raises the thorny subject of whether there is any such thing as a Scottish culture and practice of business different from elsewhere in the UK. Is there any distinct Scottish ethos which marks itself out from the behaviour and practices of the City of London's endemic short-termism and self-interest? The answer, considering the collapse of RBS and HBOS, along with the record of Scotland's financial sector must be for now, a resounding negative. Isn't that something we might want to acknowledge and look at how we begin to rectify?

Scottish based corporates such as RBS and HBOS acted in the cavalier, buccaneer style of the rest of finance capitalism at its worst. Scottish bankers like the former Sir Fred Goodwin, head of RBS, were personifications of the worst 'masters of the universe' class. They felt that anything was possible, they could lever any deal, and would not take no for an answer. That kind of charismatic leadership always ends in disaster, unless it is challenged and stopped.

Somehow as Scotland becomes more self-governing and the Anglo-American model of capitalism implodes, we have to begin to map out a very different path. It has to be based less on the perils of short-termism, deal making, and the tyranny of finance capitalism. Instead, it has to utilise the state and public agencies to encourage and back innovation and investment. It has to back with legal force different models of business and different structures of corporate governance. In Scotland this debate has barely begun. Much of this can draw upon examples and inspiration elsewhere, but it does seem that such an approach of breaking with the failures of the past and an unsustainable, anti-social capitalism, are beyond the British government, politicians and business, such is the strength of the ideological blinkers and dogma which has captured them.

The Decline of Council Housing and Trade Unionism

Secondly, the above changes have contributed towards Scottish society becoming much less collectivist, more individualist and fragmented. To take housing tenure: council housing rose as a percentage of housing throughout the post-war era peaking at 54.4% in 1977. Since it has remorselessly fallen back year on year. In 1988 owner occupation passed council housing, standing at 46.6% to 43.9%; subsequently it has fallen further to 27.8% in 1997 and 15.1% in 2005.[44]

In the 1945-81 period council housing gave nearly two generations of working class people a very different experience compared to those before. It was one which was secure, cleaner and with better amenities. Many of us grew up in this world, knowing that our parents were experiencing a very different and better life compared to their parents. This included – besides the qualitative improvement in housing – stable employment, rising incomes, and the assumption that prosperity would continue and grow, giving new opportunities for the first generation of council house tenants and their children.

This was at its peak in the 1950s and 1960s, a markedly different world from what came before and what was to follow. I was a child who experienced that world directly in Ardler, Dundee from 1968-81 and it was one where there was little unemployment or crime, with a sense of community and connectedness amongst the cross-section of people living there – from the public and private sectors, teachers, nurses, small business owners, bank managers and shopkeepers. There was also a gender dimension: many women who had children worked in the nearby Timex multinational, later to be the site of a bitter industrial dispute in 1993 – which has been called 'the last major strike in the UK'[45] – and saw the US company eventually pack its bags and leave the city.[46]

Today is very different. Not only is council housing an aging and minority stock in long-term decline, the dream of owner occupation has turned sour for many, having peaked in the last decade and become out of reach now for many twenty and thirty-somethings.

Trade union membership – once 55% of the workforce in 1980, fell to 39.2% in 1991 and 32.2% in 2010.[47] At its peak it not only had majority public sector employment, but representation in growth points of the private sector. In Scotland today, just as across the UK, trade union membership is heavily clustered in the public sector which still has majority trade union membership; the difference is the collapse in the private sector. There is also a skewing of membership towards older workers with job protection and rights, and very little membership amongst younger workers or growth parts of the economy such as the tech economy or self-employed workers.

This has consequences for the world of work. How do workers collectively counter the power of management, owners and ultimately, capital? Work without the constraining influence of unions facilitates exploitation and makes treating workers not as human beings but as commodities much easier. The decline of the influence of trade unions with government, public bodies and business, means that the Scottish Trades Union Congress (STUC) is less listened to as a result. It forces national union leaders such as Len McCluskey, head of Unite, to become more sectional and appeal only to their activist base, rather than to a wider labour interest. Trade unions for the last thirty years have been in a downward spiral – which has contributed to the diminution in skills and representativeness of union officials and leaders. The STUC, once one of the key organisers of the managed settlement of the post-war Scottish semi-state, has been quietly pushed into a more marginal position, one where it is still listened to with respect, but less crucial than it was in its halcyon period.

Where is the Local in Local Government?

Finally, local government's place has shifted dramatically. This used to be one of the main ways a large range of services were delivered, and it had an important part in how people saw themselves and lived their lives. In Scotland pre-NHS it was possible to be born into a Glasgow Corporation hospital, educated in a council school, and finally, when you died, buried in a municipal graveyard: truly, municipal officialdom 'from cradle to grave'.

Moreover, this omnipotent version of the council offered more. Glasgow Corporation produced a 'Glasgow: Our City'[48] guide to the city for schools and adults, held civic lessons, and produced the biggest number of public information films anywhere in the UK outside London.[49] The latter covered all sorts of challenges: public health, slum clearance, improved living conditions in new council flats, and while they were clearly patrician and from an 'expert knows best' outlook, they did tap into a shared vision of the city, progress and the future.

Local government, of course, developed an intricate network and culture of patronage, preferment and clientism. This expanded hand-in-hand with the growth of the post-war welfare state and electoral rise of Labour in Scotland, proving in the long run to be a mixed blessing for the party, aiding it in becoming the party of the local state and establishment.

Local government provided one of the three pillars of 'Labour Scotland', along with council housing and trade union support.[50] Now all three supports have gone, and the electoral map of local government looks completely different from Labour at its peak. In the 2012 local elections the party only won outright two out of 32 councils – Glasgow and North

Lanarkshire[51]; there is widespread expectation that they could even lose these in the 2017 local elections.

In more recent decades, the powers and autonomy of local government have been slowly eroded, first, driven by the need of UK governments to cut public spending, and secondly, to more formally force them to not block, and then deliver central government policies.[52] The first predates the Thatcher government, with the Labour Government, its predecessor, announcing 'the party's over' in local spending in 1976 due to the IMF crisis. The second became pronounced post-1979 over such contentious matters as forcing Labour councils to process council house sales which met with ferocious Scottish Labour opposition.

There has been no return to an era of local discretion. New Labour and the subsequent establishment of the Scottish Parliament have seen further erosion. The election of the SNP as a minority administration in 2007 saw a landmark Scottish Government-COSLA agreement to reduce ring-fencing restrictions on how councils spent monies. However, the implementation of a council tax freeze which lasted nine years further reduced the financial autonomy of councils. This has produced an environment in which there is little 'local' left in local government, with the size of councils per head, the largest in a Western democracy, aggravating this.[53]

The Importance of the Missing Scotland

Human nature tends to focus on what has survived and succeeded; not on what is missing. This is known as the 'survivor ship bias'[54] with one example being the work of Abraham Ward of the Statistical Research Group during World War Two. He examined warplanes that had been shot at and the amount of bullet holes in their fuselage and not around their engine. A superficial response might have been to strengthen protection around the fuselage, but instead, he recommended the authorities strengthened around the engine. His reasoning was simple. The warplanes with bullet holes in their fuselage had made it back. The ones shot in the engine had not.[55]

Survivor ship bias means that the data at the end of a process omits the casualties and those who have not made it through to the end point. Politics is defined and distorted by the prevalence of looking at successes and victories, while neglecting the failures and missing elements.

This is as true of Scotland as elsewhere. To give one example from the indyref. Early in the long campaign I coined the term 'the missing Scotland' – and the related concept of 'the missing million'.[56] This referred to the part of the electorate who had become permanently disenfranchised from participating in elections over the course of the last 20-25 years.

My point was that politics in the form of Scottish Parliament contests (and to a lesser extent, Westminster elections) had acclimatised itself to dramatically reduced turnouts – running at the 50% level for the former. Political activism and commentary had become accustomed to this, and stopped noticing or trying to do anything to counteract it. Instead Scotland had morphed into having a truncated electorate – more middle class, affluent, older – distorting politics in ways often never realised. Of course, 'the missing Scotland' were not just missing in relation to votes, they were missing in lots of other ways, forgotten and neglected.

A significant part of Scottish politics is, despite the warm inclusive rhetoric, really about insiders – the included and networked – and less about outsider groups and those socially excluded. The indyref, by offering an existential choice, mitigated and kicked against this, and reached out to the many parts of our nation that politics (or at least party politics) had stopped trying to.

Yet, that doesn't mean that several decades of damage by the effects of 'the missing Scotland' have been suddenly overcome. For one, insider Scotland is still better organised and entrenched in the system, but, as a caveat to the hype of some independence supporters, for all the optimism about turnout it is an incontestable fact that voters turned out more in middle class, affluent areas than in poorer communities, and in No more than Yes areas. Never ever fall for your own myths: the indyref turnouts speak for themselves. The highest council areas were East Dunbartonshire at 91.0% and East Renfrewshire at 90.4% and Stirling at 90.1%, and the lowest, two of the four Yes areas, Dundee at 78.8% and Glasgow at 75.0%.[57]

By naming this phenomenon 'the missing Scotland', defining it and quantifying it, the contours of the restricted political debate that had grown up were to a small extent challenged. With the assistance of the Electoral Commission, 'the missing Scotland' was literally counted – 989,540 voters who would have voted if turnout had been at the 1992 Westminster level in Scotland.[58] Further more, the Electoral Reform Society Scotland were commissioned to undertake focus groups in Dundee and Glasgow of non-voters, which found that this group were just as political as voters – but the difference being that they saw little point in voting.[59] All of this contributed to understanding the nature of the systematic exclusion of a whole swathe of the country over a generation, at a time when their vote counted and could make a difference: in the indyref.

The Limits of #the45 and how to stop preaching to the converted

Similarly, there is an inherent problem in how progressives, the centre-left and even the most radical left-wingers see themselves. There is a built-in tendency to see themselves as good guys, and the right-wing as bad guys. This has been manifest throughout history, and was on display in the indyref, and more recently, in Jeremy Corbyn's election and first year as Labour leader from September 2015. Gaby Hinsliff wrote on this mindset:

...the belief found close to many left-wing hearts that they, and they alone, are the good guys – and therefore incapable of prejudice. They don't need to question their assumptions, or take a long hard look in the mirror, because the racists are the other guys.[60]

In the messy world of identity politics today – gender, sexism, religion, Islamophobia and anti-Semitism – too many on the left think they are above intolerance. One doesn't need to rise to the full denunciation of seemingly all things on the left in Britain today by the likes of Nick Cohen to recognise there is a problem.[61] Elements of the left would not hesitate to call out misogyny, but significant sections of progressive opinion have a problem with understanding and challenging racist, anti-Semitic or Islamophobic attitudes. One terrible example in April 2016 was Ken Livingstone on what was and wasn't anti-Semitic, which culminated in him discussing ad nauseam Hitler's policies and intentions, and what he was like 'before he went mad'.[62]

Scotland might see itself as immune from such mental mindfields, but these are evident and potent trip wires across the West. It is also worth reflecting that the politics of the indyref for some were not this upbeat 'festival of democracy', but contained a number of problems in language, name calling, insults and a degree of intolerance. It is never very good politics to call your opponents a 'quisling' or 'traitor' as then Scottish Labour leader Jim Murphy did, or to compare the SNP with the Nazis as regularly happened over the course of the campaign.

However, there is a big difference between Yes as a motivation and invitation to hold on to something precious and use it to creatively aid political and social change, and to continually hanker back to the 2014 indyref as a 'summer of independence'.

In some articulations of Yes there was a distinct strand of the moral superiority of independence supporters, which of course wasn't invented by Yes, but draws on a long historical lineage in Scottish culture. Some of this came from Yes supporters only talking to and understanding people like themselves – which is one definition of bad politics and confirmation bias. There is a connection between this and the most incestuous self-referential aspects of the left: both of which have a religious, evangelical flavour to them. The left has had a long, checkered practice of talking to itself and feeling it has the self-evident correct answers, from the attitude of framing Labour voters as 'our people' to the semi-messianic behaviour of some of Jeremy Corbyn's most fervent supporters.

Political zealotry is a problem the world over in any campaign or movement. It is never a virtue. Any successful political campaign – of left, right, or for the independence of a nation – has to understand the need to keep its zealots under control. Zealots scare away swing and uncommitted voters.

There was in the mobilisation and boundaries of Yes and No a palpable sense of closed tribes, othering and stigmatisation of the opposing side – from elements in both Yes and No. The invention of the hashtag #the45 was very understandable in the immediate aftermath of the indyref. People were grieving, working through the implications and taking stock. Independence supporters felt they needed something to hang on to and make themselves feel they were part of something bigger which wasn't over.

Unfortunately, beyond this immediate period, #the45 didn't offer any future project or hope of success. It didn't claim or try to understand and reach out to the winning 55% majority. In its most hyper-tribal versions it wanted to browbeat the majority into submission: recant, admit you are wrong, look what you have done, and now you are going to have to live with the consequences of life in the land of perpetual Tory rule.

Similarly, the continuation of Yes as an idea was not difficult to understand. Yes voters had become part of an active, energised political community. There was a desire never to return to the old ways, to status quo, steady as she goes, don't rock the boat Scotland. Instead, Yes as an ongoing vision was about a commitment to a very different Scotland and future.

Any future indyref will not be won by such sentiments and the mindset of #the45, however well-intentioned some of it may be. A war of attrition, wearing down and questioning the motives of the majority is always unlikely to produce the desired outcome. In fact it is taken straight out of 'The Big Book of Bad Left Politics' that has a very long track record. It goes along the lines of: when you lose, get bitter, blame the stupidity of voters, the perfidy, treachery and lies of the other side, search out various propaganda vessels (usually Murdoch, but in the indyref with the BBC centre stage), and question the motives of the other side ('the Vow' and others who stole it).

This can then be taken even further. To underline bad politics never once seriously reflect on the motivations, hopes and fears of voters who disagree with you (citing false consciousness or a reference to Herman and Chomsky's 'manufacturing consent'[63]). Finally, do not spend one minute considering the outlandish notion that the voters might have called it right, and that there could be flaws and pitfalls in the offer you put to them: a classic example being when Labour suffered in 1983 its worst electoral defeat since 1918 because it stood on a left-wing manifesto. Tony Benn declared the result a victory as: 'A party with an openly socialist policy recorded the support of over eight million people.'[64]

Instead, a future campaign will be won by a careful appeal to the hearts and heads of those who resisted the charms of independence in 2014. A large part of the No vote was contingent and pragmatic. It was resistant to the flaws of the Yes offer, while seeing in principle the appeal of independence. Post-indyref surveys show that a mere 27% of the No vote was mobilised by the idea of the union per se (47% saying the risks of independence were too great and 25% a No vote meant more powers); thus the vast majority of No was a cool-headed and pragmatic consideration of the appeals of both sides.[65]

Instead, people choose the three S's: strength, security and stability – all of which have been fundamentally undermined by the Brexit vote of 2016.[66] A fourth contentious principle was also claimed: solidarity (the 'pooling and sharing' argument). The first three S's had power and resonance: of addressing how voters balanced and assessed risk and uncertainty on both sides' offers – and that part of No's appeal was as much 'better the devil you know' as the more upbeat 'the best of both worlds', aided by a dash of 'Project Fear'.[67]

So much of this is about how voters in very different individual ways navigate uncertainty in a world of instability and constant change. It does not really get you very far to pose the answer as certainty and to deal with doubt and anxiety by the retort of faith-based messages and politics that invite people to believe it will all be all right on the night post-independence. All of this will be even truer in any second Scottish referendum.

From the Age of High Unionism to making it up as you go along

This brings us to the changing place of Scotland in the union. The élan, confidence and once seemingly impregnable nature of high unionism (meaning in the sense of 'high and low politics'[68]) has all but gone forever.

If we go back in time to one of the foundation moments of Scotland's constitutional journey: the Kilbrandon Royal Commission on the Constitution, set up by Harold Wilson in 1969 with the express aim of stemming the SNP and Plaid Cymru's electoral advances, and parking the thorny issue of constitutional change in the long grass. The submissions of Scottish Labour to the Commission, given just weeks before the 1970 UK general election, make for fascinating reading. No more so than the oral evidence from the then Scottish Council of the Labour Party (as it was so called until 1994) on 4 May 1970. It is worth quoting a lengthy extract from the Commission's exchanges with the Labour delegation:

W.G. Marshall (Labour): There is, however, no such thing as a separate political will for Scotland...

Maitland Mackie (Commission): Surely you must accept that there is a political will for Scotland?

Dr. Hunt (Commission): Where a Conservative Government was in power at Westminster, would you really feel under those circumstances that the Scottish Grand Committee or the Select Committee on Scottish Affairs would have adequate power of control over Scottish Office administration?

Jim Pollock (Labour): If we accept the United Kingdom structure, as we do, such a situation may be the inevitable outcome of it. We must add that as Scottish members of the Labour Party, we see our interest as being the same as members of the Labour Party in England and Wales on a vast range of issues...

Chair (Commission): You cannot be in exactly the same position as English members of the Labour Party... In the extreme, but perhaps not entirely hypothetical case that Labour held all 71 Scottish seats in Parliament, but there was a Conservative Government, how in those circumstances would Scotland exert any control over the Secretary of State?

Jim Pollock (Labour): I think that situation is hypothetical and almost impossibly extreme.

Dr. Hunt (Commission): The odds are that with a Conservative

Government for the UK, there would still be a majority of Labour MPs for Scotland.

Jim Pollock (Labour): The only effective way of solving the Scottish problem is to have a Labour Government at Westminster, but we are prepared to put up with the short period in which a Conservative Government might be the administration because we can more than make good in our next administration.[69]

The stark language of the above exchanges looks even more so with the passage of time: 'we are prepared to put up with the short period' and 'we can more than make good'. For these comments are firmly located in the politics of the period 1945-79 when there was an expectation and reality of regularly alternating UK governments. The years after the above exchanges and, in particular, from 1979 onwards have not seen such regular alteration. Then there is the issue of Scotland and that from 1959 it began to turn against the Conservatives. By the 1970 election (held on 18 June, just over a month after the above exchange) when Ted Heath was elected with an overall majority of 30 seats, he was in a minority in Scotland. Scotland voted Labour 44.5%, Conservatives 38.0% and returned 44 Labour to 23 Tories: a picture we were to get used to, but was only going to get worse for the Tories north of the border.[70]

If we look at the picture post-Kilbrandon, and the fifty-year period from 1970-2020 and assume that the 2015 Tory victory under David Cameron and subsequent Theresa May premiership runs to 2020 at the minimum – then this fifty years divides into 32 years of Tory or Tory-dominated government and 18 years of Labour: a 64:36 split. Over that same period, Scotland voted Labour for what covered 45 years of Parliaments, to the SNP's five and Tories zero: a split of 90:10:0, but still ended up with 32 years of Tory complete or dominated government it didn't vote for.

This problem has grown over the years. The Tories under

Heath had 38.0% of the vote. Thatcher was first elected in 1979 with 31.4% of the vote and 22 MPs; by the end of eighteen years of Tory administration they were down to 17.5% and zero MPs. The Conservatives under Cameron came back in 2010 and entered government in coalition with 16.7% of the vote and one MP[71], and won an overall UK majority in 2015 with 14.9%, their lowest vote in Scotland since 1865, and again a solitary MP: David Mundell.[72] Leaving aside the Tory recovery in the Scottish Parliament in 2016, a political union cannot in perpetuity survive such blatant political misjustices and lack of political accountability. Over fifty years, Scots have cumulatively been excluded from a choice of government at Westminster as Scotland and rUK have diverged politically.

But the assumptions in the second remark are even more damning: 'we can more than make good' – meaning in relation to Tory Governments and the damage they do. This captures the post-war era of centre-left optimism – that Labour Governments were presiding over an expanding state, public services improving and rising public spending, living standards, and greater equality. The future, of course, did not exactly work out like that.

However, that Labour attitude of high unionism – of even preferring Tory Governments to a self-governing Scotland has remained, albeit diluted and weakened and shorn of its previous arrogance. The indyref experience gave it one huge shock to its system, and the second tremor of Brexit has provided even more convulsions, which have yet to fully work themselves through Scottish Labour. And that's without mentioning the ripples of the Corbyn leadership and Scottish impact.

Unionism's Long Retreat: From Indyref to Brexit

Finally, coming to events closer to the present: the period from the 2014 indyref to the 2016 Brexit vote displays the deep-seated problems and decline of unionism in Scotland and across the UK. In the 2014 campaign, Scotland was frequently love-bombed from pro-union opinion telling us how respected and regarded we were in this partnership of four equal nations that is the United Kingdom.

David Cameron, with days to go to the indyref vote, eventually brought out the gut, emotional case for the union – a few days after his 'don't give the effing Tories a kick' speech – saying:

For the people of Scotland to walk away now would be like painstakingly building a home and then walking out the door and throwing away the keys.

He declared that our nations had 'only become Great Britain because of the greatness of Scotland.' And then pleaded:

Please don't lose faith in what this country is and what we can be. Don't forget what a great United Kingdom you are part of. Don't turn your backs on what is the best family of nations in the world and the best hope for your family in this world.[73]

This was the time of the 'We Love You Scotland'[74] letter of historian Tom Holland and other initiatives such as 'Please, Stay With Us' from the right-wing *Spectator*.[75] While these annoyed many on the pro-independence side, they were respectful and heartfelt, and completely understandable from a pro-union position.

Fast-forward to the 2015 UK general election and the spectre of SNP influence over a Westminster Government was used by the Tories to powerful effect. There were the famous posters showing Alex Salmond, then Nicola Sturgeon, with Labour leader Ed Miliband in their coat pocket: the implication being that the SNP were pulling the strings, and Miliband was nothing but their puppet.

Cameron attempted to legitimise SNP influence at

Westminster; the strategy being to use this to undermine Labour. The SNP, he said in one speech 'want to achieve the breakup of our country, so therefore if you have a Labour Government backed by the SNP, you have got a government backed by people who don't want the country to succeed.'[76]

John Major spoke of a Labour-SNP post-election deal as a 'recipe for mayhem'[77], but the biggest hyperbole award went to future Prime Minister Theresa May who claimed it would produce the 'biggest constitutional crisis since the abdication' of Edward VIII in 1936.[78]

Speed-forward again to 2016 and we find the threat of Scottish independence being used by those politicians who sang Scotland's praises in 2014, and then used the threat of the SNP in 2015 to aid the election of a Tory Government. Cameron with his back to the wall in the EU referendum raised the threat of Scottish independence as a result of Brexit. He implored people:

If you love your country you don't want to act in a way which could lead to its break-up.[79]

John Major claimed that Brexit would 'tear apart the UK' and that 'the plain uncomfortable truth is that the unity of the UK itself is on the ballot paper in two weeks [sic] time.'[80]

Post-Brexit vote, the tone and content changed yet again. Both the Scottish and UK Governments engaged in an initial war of manoeuvre akin to a multi-dimensional game of chess. Apart from the two Governments, there were as players, pre-Article 50 'triggering', the EU Commission and the German Government. Theresa May, who had talked of 'the biggest constitutional crisis since the abdication', in her first week as Prime Minister met with Nicola Sturgeon, commenting:

As far as I'm concerned, the Scottish people have had their vote, they voted in 2014 and a very clear message came through. Both the UK and Scottish Government said they would abide by that.[81]

This zig-zagging might confuse some of you. You might have taken the emotional pleas and platitudes of the indyref at face value, however you actually voted in the end. Now it is completely clear beyond any doubt, if it wasn't before, that Cameron and company were just playing desperate tactical and short-term games – attempting to win individual contests and ignoring the longer-term position, and anything as trivial as consistency.

Cameron's attitude to Scotland became public when David Laws, ex-Lib Dem minister, revealed that in the weekend after the indyref, Cameron and Nick Clegg, Lib Dem leader and then Deputy Prime Minister, had a conversation about its aftermath. Already, Cameron had the morning after the vote declared his intention to legislate for 'English votes for English laws' or 'EVEL' as it has become widely known, to widespread dismay from Labour and Lib Dems.[82] Clegg said to Cameron that 'the Prime Minister was in danger of guaranteeing the break-up of the UK, with the only beneficiaries being the SNP.' Cameron responded angrily:

Look Nick, I just don't care. We've only got one Conservative MP north of the border. Let Labour sort it out.[83]

The columnist Hugo Rifkind (himself the son of Tory Malcolm Rifkind) gave words to the misuse and abuse of a principled unionist politics in this. They had been used and blatantly so. The above amounts, he recognised, to nothing less than a seismic moment and utter disaster for both Labour and Tory unionism. English Labour unionism has a very pragmatic and qualified perspective about the union: one of its main motivations being the fear of being left alone with England, unrestrained by Scotland. It is not a good place to base your politics: namely, a unionism centred on a pathologising of

England and using Scotland at least until the watershed of 2015 to keep the project afloat. But, as for Tory unionism, Rifkind was even more contemptuous:

Remember all those decades when there was a Tory PM and almost no Scottish Tory MPs? Remember the way they'd shrug and explain that this was just how a Union works, and that the reverse could as easily be true? Call me a mug, but I actually thought they meant it. They don't want a partner, these people, but a pet.[84]

This has led, he wrote, to 'Tories abandoning unionism for their own self-interest (while pretending they haven't) and Labour cleaving to it for theirs (while pretending they aren't).' This led Rifkind to realise something big was up and plainly wrong:

It is not the SNP who are the real threat to Britain, for all their swift and startling resurgence. It's their secret English allies, who are many and various and hiding in plain sight. And they pretend to oppose the Scottish separatists, and the Scottish separatists pretend to oppose them, but both are giggling behind the backs of their hands.

Scottish, English and British unionism – as popular, confident and forward-looking political philosophies – have never been weaker, more disorientated, and more inconsistent. They have been reduced over the last few years to the most obvious and desperate tactical considerations to try to win each individual battle – through the 2014 indyref, 2015 UK election and 2016 Brexit vote. But it has come at huge cost and long-term damage.

The once proud and powerful forces of unionism, that once carried all before them across the nations of the United Kingdom, have been humiliated by numerous figures and forces. Central roles have to go to Cameron and George Osborne, Tory Chancellor of the Exchequer in Cameron's administration, who played fast and loose over this critical period. It cost them dear, losing them their jobs, but much higher stakes were at play.

They also cannot be landed with the main responsibility, for this is a story about a long, painful decline in which they played walk-on roles in the near-to-closing scenes. This isn't even just about Thatcher, as it is about more than any one individual's contribution, or Thatcherism, or the decline of a more genteel Toryism. Instead, it is about how politics and society have transformed over decades. It is about Labour's failure to challenge Conservative Britain and the bastions of privilege and inequality, the end of Empire, the decline of religion, the loss of a clear external enemy which aided cohesion: Napoleonic France, Nazi Germany and the Soviet Union, all made Britain feel it was united against something; however, 'the war on terror' and challenge of ISIS/ISIL in Syria and Iraq, don't quite carry the same threat.

Moreover, all of this happened in the context of Scotland changing. The ordered, controlling society, once synonymous with high unionism and which also contributed to a genuine, popular, low unionism, has withered and fallen into historic decline. That social change has aided the huge political shift which has taken us to where we are: to a Scotland which is in a very different place from the country the Labour delegation spoke to during the Kilbrandon Commission in 1970. Two generations later it is still part of a United Kingdom, but one which is united in name only, and far removed from the days when the union was seen as an unquestioned good across the land. Those days are gone forever. They will not return.

Chapter Four:

21st-Century Nation: Scotland's Changing State

Scotland will need to be led,
But never by one man only,
of whatever wrongs a righter:
Not that for any excuse!
These days are dead,
Dead with Wallace and Bruce.

Naomi Mitchison, The Cleansing of the Knife, in The Cleansing of the Knife and Other Poems, 1978

Scotland has had a very different experience in the UK compared to Wales and Northern Ireland. For one, Scotland was never, as many Scots like to remind the world, conquered. Its experience of union has been very different from the brutal way that Ireland became part of the United Kingdom in 1801. But nor did it disappear legally as Wales did post-1536, when it was assimilated into the legal concept of 'England', only to eventually reappear again in the 20th century.[85]

Scotland's continuous legal existence post-1707 in areas such as education, local government and the Church of Scotland, and the elite autonomy that was negotiated in the Acts of Unions (note the plural), are central to how the self-government debate has evolved, not just in recent times, but since the late 19th century.

The critical compromises of 1706-7 which are described as an incorporating union, fell short of the maximum positions on both the English and Scottish sides. The former wished for the biggest degree of assimilation and common British institutions, the latter, a looser, even proto-federalist solution. The hybridity and ingenuity of it, leaving aside its lack of a democratic mandate in both countries (which was conventional practice in that period) was, as well as being a compromise, innovative for the time. This was after all the age of absolutism and monarchical rule, and decades before the twin peaks of democratic revolutionaryism of 1776 and 1789. Its subtlety, as well as its emergent flaws, would be a significant part of Scotland's journey towards democratic self-government.

The current Scottish Government should be understood in this context – namely, the backstory of elite and institutional autonomy. Scotland post-1707, in particular since the establishment of the Scottish Office in 1885 has been marked by the evolution of an increasingly distinctive, semi-autonomous set of spaces aided by the expansion of the state over most of the 20th century.

Scotland's Government today is seen as the focal point of much of public and political life. However, in previous times the incursion of the state into the lives of citizens was much smaller. The scale to which Scots used to live in a land of minimal state intervention, and how this completely altered over the course of the 20th century, is made clear by this extract from the Kilbrandon Royal Commission final report in 1973:

The individual a hundred years ago hardly needed to know that the central government existed. His birth, marriage and death would be registered, and he might be conscious of the safeguards for his security provided by the forces of law and order and of imperial defence; but, except for the very limited provisions of the poor law and factory legislation, his welfare and progress were matters for which he alone bore the responsibility. By the turn of the century the position was not much changed. Today, however, the individual citizen submits himself to the guidance of the state at all times. His schooling is enforced; his physical well-being can be looked after in a comprehensive health service; he may be helped by government

agencies to find and train for a job; he is obliged while in employment
to insure against sickness, accident and unemployment; his house
may be let to him by a public authority, or he may be assisted in its
purchase or improvement; he can avail himself of a wide range of
government welfare allowances and services; and he draws a state
pension on his retirement. In these and many other ways unknown
to his counterpart of a century ago, he is brought into close and
regular contact with government and its agencies.[86]

What do the Scottish Public Think?

Today this has changed in so many dimensions of domestic
public policy. Scottish post-devolution attitudes have been
measured by the Scottish Social Attitudes Survey which has
consistently since the beginning of the Scottish Parliament
been asking: 'Which institution do you think has the most
influence over the way Scotland is run?'[87] Over the period the
perceived influence of the Scottish Government (prior to 2007
Scottish Executive) has increased from 2000 to today whilst
that of the UK has declined. One recent analysis stated that
there is 'a clear and fairly steady increase in the proportion
choosing the Scottish Government...'[88] Yet, the picture is
much more complex than that sometimes painted in the rosy
account whereby all that supposedly matters is the Scottish
Parliament, as the influence and legitimacy of Westminster
slowly withers on the vine.

The initial establishment of the Scottish Parliament saw a
brief honeymoon in attitudes – where people perceived it as
being the most influential political body. But disappointment
soon crept in at Labour incompetence and lack of vision. In one
year there was a dramatic reversal as a 2% lead by the Scottish
Executive over UK Government became a 53% UK lead (see
Table One). The story of devolution is the slow pullback from
this sudden abyss to approximate parity between the two.

Other indicators paint an equally dramatic picture. Asked

who they trust to look after Scotland's best long-term interests, voters said the Scottish Government by 81% in 1999 and by 73% in 2015; with the UK Government receiving 32% in 1999 and 23% in 2015 – these figures on occasion adding up to more than 100% because they could choose to trust both.

Such is the constancy of public opinion over a period of just under two decades. They amount to a democratic gap between the perception of the Scottish and UK Governments in relation to Scotland. Such a chasm raises long-term questions about the role and legitimacy of how Westminster is perceived north of the border.

The above describes mostly how voters see domestic policy, but the picture is different in relation to defence and foreign affairs. For all the popular invoking of Tony Blair, the Iraq war and Trident and its potential replacement, a much more nuanced picture emerges than the one assumed by much of the rhetoric.

Whereas in 2013 there was majority support for welfare (57%) and taxation (59%) being the responsibility of the Scottish Parliament, the opposite was the case with defence and foreign affairs: 39% selecting the Scottish Parliament and 53% Westminster. This has been the consistent pattern for over a decade.

Table 4.1.:

Who has the most influence over the way Scotland is run?[89]

	1999	2000	2001	2003	2004	2005	2006	2007
Scottish								
Govt.	41	13	15	17	19	23	24	26
UK Govt.	39	66	66	64	48	47	38	47
Gap	+2	-53	-51	-47	-29	-24	-14	-21

	2009	2010	2011	2012	2013	2015
Scottish						
Govt.	33	37	38	34	30	41
UK Govt.	39	45	38	41	47	42
Gap	-6	-8	=	-7	-17	-7

The Accidental then Planned Re-emergence of Scotland International

None of this should be seen in isolation. One of the big stories of recent times has been the re-emergence of Scotland on the international stage – more importantly, the first appearance of a modern Scotland. Over a decade ago British Council research into how the four nations of the UK were seen across the world[90] showed that England was viewed as being about Premiership football and London, whereas Scotland was tartan, kilts and castles. There was no football, golf or Edinburgh Festivals. It was a timeless 'Brigadoon' Scotland: a land of myth and make-believe, and all the more dispiriting for it. Yet, in the last few years this sense of invisibility has been shaken and challenged and not just by the indyref.

First, the Abdelbaset al-Megrahi case introduced the world to the fact that there was a legally defined and semi-autonomous entity called Scotland. In August 2009 then Justice Minister Kenny MacAskill released Megrahi who had been convicted of the Lockerbie terrorist attack on 'compassionate grounds'. This was a hugely controversial decision: in Scotland, the UK, and internationally.[91] It got US congressmen, UK politicians and experts, and even some voices here into quite a mess. Some politicians thought the UK Government could just over-ride Scots law – thus indicating their complete ignorance of the UK and law. Even John Curtice, doyen of election studies managed to get himself in a bit of a fankle:

...because Holyrood was not sovereign but accountable to Westminster, the British Government could have rushed through legislation to prevent Megrahi's release.[92]

Worse a Gordon Brown aide revealed that they had even less of an idea what the UK was:

A Conservative backbencher said Lockerbie should be looked into but he realised that the UK Parliament didn't have any sway over the Scottish Government and I thought he must be out of his box if he thinks that. Britain is a unitary state. There was an emergency cord that could have been pulled.[93]

One wonders what that 'emergency cord' might be and look like.

But alongside such revelations was the reality that a modern-day nation – not just a set of historical relics and images of castles, clans and bagpipes – was seen before the world's eyes, and critically, some of its political elites. It was a transformative moment, irrespective of your opinion on the Megrahi release.

Second was the indyref which, since the advent of the Scottish Parliament, was a likely occurrence and the most likely event to re-introduce Scotland to an international stage. This produced three years of global coverage of Scotland as a different country from the rest of the UK, as a country having a profound, existential debate, and being invigorated by the resultant democratic engagement.[94] Much commentary reflected upon the unprecedented and completely peaceful nature of this debate. Most nations do not become independent in such benign circumstances, although Scotland's neighbours, Norway and Iceland, did.

A number of strands were evident in this international coverage. One represented a romantic yearning for the potential loss of the UK. This was not surprising: a similar strand was self-evident in the Quebec referendum of 1995 with a strain of international coverage asking: 'Wither Canada?' The lament for the possible demise of the UK was always going to be part of global coverage, considering the legacy of Empire, the existence of the Commonwealth, and the allure of the English language. Some of this coverage coalesced around English-speaking coverage in the Anglosphere, and the US and Canada in particular.

A further perspective questioned how this could be happening. It was particularly evident in some American commentary, and often displayed complete ignorance of Scotland and sometimes of the UK. There was the infamous *Time* magazine article which contained so many basic errors about Scotland, the list of corrections was hugely embarrassing. These included the following:

The original story said that England suspended the Scottish Parliament in 1707. The Parliaments of both England and Scotland voted to create a single united British Parliament based in the Palace of Westminster in London in 1707.

The original version of this story said Salmond formed a coalition government with Labour in 2007. He and the SNP formed a minority government.[95]

However, a large part of international coverage was accurate and informed – and a lot better than a significant percentage of the London-based media. They came and covered the story as a huge international news story in the context of the relative decline of Britain, the end of Empire, the European dimension and Britain's then semi-detached status from the rest of the continent, and the explosion of new independent nations with the collapse of the Soviet bloc.

Some came with open-minded curiosity about how this potential divorce settlement had arisen, and where the love and affection in the union had gone. Others referenced it around the experience of decolonisation – not that Scotland was being decolonised, having never been colonised. But it gave an entry point for some global coverage given how far the British Empire had stretched, the role of Scots in it, and the number of countries which had become independent from Britain: the sum total of which is 58 (since the USA and then Ireland left).

This brings us to the current debacle the UK has got itself and thus Scotland into: Brexit. The Scottish Government and First Minister have so far played a very cautious and astute hand in the immediate months following the Brexit vote of June 2016. Nicola Sturgeon has been trying to create a political space whereby she can maximise Scottish options, build political consensus at home, and reach out to create European alliances.

In this Scotland's First Minister has rightly earned a wide range of admiring notices. But she has also been constrained by one factor: the Scottish Government's lack of diplomatic skills to draw upon. Foreign affairs require insight, expertise, contacts and strategic intelligence – none of which the Scottish Government has in terms of international affairs, not having been in a position to build up capital and resources in these areas.

While there is a Minister for External Affairs, Fiona Hyslop, (sharing the responsibilities with being Culture Secretary) and a newly appointed Minister for Brexit, Mike Russell, at this important crossroads, the Scottish Government has to think urgently about how to rectify this situation in the immediate and medium term. Could it resource a network of thinkers and practitioners, draw together an ad hoc international cluster of former diplomats from the diaspora and other well-wishers, and even look nearer to home drawing from international affairs experts at Scottish and UK universities and institutes? All of this would be good investment for what might be the emergence of a Scottish Foreign and Commonwealth Office (SFCO) a few years down the line.

Bureaucratic Enlightenment: The Legacy of the Scottish Office

The above considerations relate to the strategic capacities of the Scottish Government on matters close to home. There is an absence of tangible, practical statecraft – the art of doing government – in the Scottish administration. This is mainly because of the Scottish Government's evolution and the capabilities it was bequeathed with from its predecessors. The Scottish Government was previously the Scottish Executive and before that until 1999, the Scottish Office. Its remit and responsibilities were to oversee administrative devolution as a Whitehall government department operating within the mandate of a Westminster framework.

This meant that the Scottish Office often dealt with Scotland in a minimalist, reactive and defensive manner. It fed Scottish concerns into the UK Government, and delivered a Scottish mediated agenda – one with which the UK Government was comfortable and with which it could live.

Increasingly, as government and public spending grew, along with the complexity of public policy, the Scottish Office did not possess the resources or skills to adequately adapt and lead. In the period post-1945 this became increasingly apparent, even long before the old system of administrative devolution became discredited, and support for a Scottish Parliament reached a tipping point.

Thus, in the post-1945/pre-devolution era, the Scottish Office only rarely showed the capacity to be imaginative and far-reaching in policy or legislation. One example was the creation of the Highlands and Islands Development Board in 1965 – a kind of progression from Tom Johnson's Highland Hydro-electric ambition and grand vision. The other was the creation and legacy of the first Kilbrandon Commission on the subject of children in trouble – what were then called 'juvenile delinquents'. This process began under a Conservative Government in 1961, the report was published in 1964, legislated for in the Social Work (Scotland) Act in 1968, leading to the introduction of children's panels, which came into operation in 1971 and are still with us today.

This latter example provided a distinctively Scottish example of legislation, avoided English draconian measures of stigmatising young people, and was one of the first and few examples in this country of openly drawing upon Nordic practices. This entailed being more informal in settings and practices, taking the child's whole social circumstances into consideration, and involving lay opinions in their deliberations.

The Official Story of the Scottish Parliament

The above two examples are the exception pre-Scottish Government. This historic lack of capacity has been carried from the Scottish Office to the Scottish Executive and now the Scottish Government. Indeed, over the near two decades of a Scottish Parliament, it is worth asking what have been the transformative laws which the Parliament has passed which have fundamentally altered lives for the better? The answer would be sadly too few.

Most of Scotland's political commentary, arch-devolution sceptics apart, has taken the Scottish Parliament's word that it is participative, consensual and makes decisions in an inclusive, reflective manner. That, after all, was the dream pre-devolution and the work of the Consultative Steering Group.[96] This hasn't been the reality. Seldom are the laws the Parliament makes given close scrutiny and subjected to these fundamental questions: What kind of democratic process is this? What kind of country does all this lawmaking produce?

The official account of Scotland's nascent democracy and new Parliament is one which believes 'the new politics' have been realised – and offer a different and better model of practice compared to Westminster. The Scottish Government's prospectus on independence, *Scotland's Future,* expressed this satisfaction with the way things are working, and promised more of the same under independence:

Scotland already has a modern, accessible parliament, elected on a proportional representation system. It will remain the parliament of an independent Scotland. The Scottish Parliament has set an example within the UK on how a modern legislature should operate. In line with its founding principles of power sharing, accountability, access and participation, and equal opportunity, the Parliament has successfully put into practice the principles on which it was founded: the petitions system makes the Parliament accessible and improves accountability; the legislative process gives civil society and individuals significant opportunities to participate before and during the formal Parliamentary processes...[97]

Recent debates around the Offensive Behaviour at Football Act (Scotland) 2012 and the Children and Young Person Act (Scotland) 2014 – the latter of which legislated for the named person's scheme – has brought into sharper focus the specifics of what makes good and bad laws. Not surprisingly this has caused many to defend the Scottish Government's record. The academic Aileen McHarg commented that there is:

A kneejerk tendency to criticise the quality of Holyrood's lawmaking, when actually its record... is very good. Three limited strikedowns in 17 years, given the extent and vagueness of the limits of its competence, is really not a lot.[98]

Blogger and academic Andrew Tickell dismissed concerns saying, 'Don't listen to the chicken littles.'[99] McHarg and Tickell are both law academics, but it is noteworthy how high McHarg set the bar of legitimate concern: ECHR non-compliant. That's a very blunt instrument of measurement.

What Scotland has been transformed by devolution?

A more penetrating way to look at this after seventeen years of legislation is to ask which Scottish Parliament laws have positively liberated and enriched individual lives? What good has been added to Scotland by the activities of our legislators? And even more fundamentally, what laws have directly empowered people?

We can find a number of examples. First, there are the land reform laws passed in 1999-2003 by the first Labour-Lib Dem Executive led by Donald Dewar, Henry McLeish and then Jack McConnell. These administrations passed four specific land reform pieces of legislation dealing with a historic backlog built by the absence of a Parliament and blocking power of the House of Lords with its powerful vested interests in land ownership.[100]

These included the Abolition of Feudal Tenure etc. (Scotland) Act 2000 which abolished feudal land ownership, feudal tenure, and feudal superiors, along with their right to collect feudal dues. The Title Conditions (Scotland) Act 2003 clarified and reformed the law relating to the burdens and obligations of land use.

The Agricultural Holdings (Scotland) Act 2003 brought in two new forms of tenure: one of limited duration of a minimum fifteen years and one of short duration which cannot last beyond five years. This act offers the tenant security of tenure and a right to buy for secure tenants. The most high-profile and for some controversial measure was the Land Reform (Scotland) Act 2003. This established a right of responsible access to land, established the community right to buy, and allowed crofting communities to buy land at any time.

This latter act allowed the community buyouts of the islands of Eigg and Gigha. This has undoubtedly had a direct impact changing lives and turning around once declining communities – led by the people living there. In short, this is a model of enabling government: setting the framework, providing financial assistance, but letting people decide for themselves what is best for them. It is in this an exception in Scottish legislation of the devolution period.

A controversial measure to consider would be the experience of housing stock transfers of municipal housing – as set out in the Housing (Scotland) Act 2001 – and that had to be facilitated by a ballot of local tenants. Glasgow and Inverclyde voted for stock transfers, whereas Edinburgh and Renfrewshire voted against; the former contained some of the most dilapidated council housing in the country. The Glasgow stock transfer was always the most contentious, involving the city's entire council housing stock, the largest municipal housing in all Western Europe, being transferred to a new body, the Glasgow Housing Association.[101] This was attacked by critics as privatisation and selling off publically owned assets breaking any accountability.

Yet, what it also did was break the search for a single 'Big Bang' solution to management of housing in the city. Glasgow's council housing had from the very beginning been plagued by bad design, poor upkeep and years of huge debt payments. A major reason for this was not that municipal housing is necessarily inferior, but the scale of a problem the city faced and the legacy of decades of slum housing, landlords and overcrowding. The original Glasgow Labour vision for the city formed in the idealism of the Independent Labour Party (ILP) was to build garden suburbs and villages in the city, but by the 1930s it was obvious that there was not the space (Glasgow's population was to peak at 1.1 million in 1951, nearly twice what it is today[102]), nor the resources or expertise.[103]

There have been numerous concerns about the financial model of the housing stock transfer in the city and Glasgow Housing Association, yet what it has allowed is the writing off of debt – which could have been done while retaining the housing in public ownership. But by a mixture of demolishing old stock, building new and transferring some stock into smaller community housing association ownership – the pattern of social housing has been reshaped. The result, whether you agree with the methods, has been a dramatic change in the life of Glasgow. The skyline of the city has been altered with dozens of huge tower blocks demolished – some of them famous or infamous landmarks on the city skyline: the Red Road flats, the Hutchesontown C flats of the Gorbals. Even more importantly, the quality of life for thousands of citizens of the city has been improved as they have moved to better housing under more responsive management.

Another measure which has transformed and saved lives has been the smoking ban. The Smoking, Health and Social

Care (Scotland) Act 2006 was a pro-active public measure and began life as a private member's initiative led by SNP MSP Stewart Maxwell, before being adopted by First Minister Jack McConnell and coming into force on 26 March 2006. Unlike the English ban that followed, led by English Health Minister (and Scottish Labour MP) John Reid that had all kinds of exemptions, this ban was relatively straightforward – banning smoking in all wholly- or partly-enclosed public places.

The legislation took on publicans, and was met with suspicion and scorn from critics and devolution cynics who claimed it was another example of 'the nanny state' and interference in individual choice. Very quickly, despite various shades of reservation, the ban became popular, made a visible difference to pubs and public spaces, was proven to be instrumental in achieving improved health outcomes, and seen as a success. One reason was that it went with the grain of people wanting to give up smoking or have a drink and evening out in a smoke-free zone. The measure can be seen in a long line of successful public health measures which date back to the mid-19th century: clean water supplies and the creation of Loch Katrine, sanitation and health drives against a host of contagious diseases.

What lessons can we draw from the above very different examples? The first has already been stated with regard to smoking – all three went with the grain of social change. They went with the drive towards greater individual respect. This leads to the element of empowerment in each and in particular, recognition of choice. Third, none of the above changes were clearly identified with one person or politician, but involved advocacy by collective effort. Fourth, each of the examples wasn't about proscriptive legislative change but how individuals live their life and how the state, public agencies and the law aid this. Thus, the most important aspect of each of the above bills was how individuals choose to change their behaviour as a result of these laws. That seems an important benchmark for progressive legislation: setting a framework and direction which people can choose to act on or not.

Another noticeable feature about the above list is that the examples end in 2006 and there are no clear cases from the last near-decade of the SNP in office. That is not to say that the SNP have not passed lots of decent legislation, as they have, or the previous Labour-Lib Dem administration didn't pass other well-meaning legislation. It is just that an awful lot of Scottish legislation is tidying up and rationalising, while another strand is virtue signalling: indicating that something is a good or desirable thing. Being seen to do something is one of the realities of how governments across the West act, and the Scottish Government is no exception. A final strand sees more overt centralisation and standardisation – as in the creation of Police Scotland and Scottish Fire and Rescue.

Putting Devolution into our Historical Story

One uber-critical view of the above blames this on the whole devolution project, or in more partisan versions, puts the blame specifically on the SNP Government. In the real world, a more complex pattern is at work whereby the historical background of the main institutions, where they came from, and their capabilities and limitations, is of major importance. Therefore, the fact that the Scottish Government has its origins in the Scottish Office, and its lack of capacities, strategy, policy-making and policy development, matters. It's no surprise that the pattern of legislation under devolution saw an explosion of activities in the early years and the first Parliament, and then a slow downward curve. In the first couple of years, there was a long tailback of bills to draw from which could not get Westminster time, would be blocked by Tory Governments (which have been 64% of our most recent period) or the House of Lords, or just couldn't be justified as the one or two Scottish pieces of legislation per year cherry-picked and championed to go through the UK Parliament. This is one major contribution to the slow drying up of high-profile legislation.

After this experience post-1999 we should ask ourselves what we want from the Scottish Parliament – as an institution, in legislation, and in how it does things and conducts its business. We can take some comfort in Aileen McHarg's point that there are very few bad laws, either in terms of ECHR or even using a wider criteria, such as the problems with the Offensive Behaviour at Football (Scotland) Act. But the bigger challenge is to ask ourselves whether we can do better, and create more examples of laws, policy and practice which enrich peoples' lives, give them more say and influence over decisions which affect them?

Such a question is integral to a future Scotland where the Scottish Parliament gets more powers. This is about a politics of self-government becoming one of self-determination: the former about politics, politicians and formal institutions, the latter, more focused on individuals, communities and cultures. This would entail an independence of the mind which is not focused on the Parliament having full powers, but instead sharing them and facilitating their dissemination throughout Scotland. Shouldn't we be talking about, instead of a concentration of powers in the hands of the Scottish Government and Parliament, a power-sharing Scotland, where authority and voice are diffused and spread throughout the nation? We should at least begin to discuss this, and stop talking only about the 'idea' of the Scottish Parliament. We should reflect on its record, its failure to hold the executive to account, and how, in many respects, in 21st-century Scotland as elsewhere in the world, power lies not within it, but elsewhere, in government elites and the power of business.

Power and Patronage and the continuation of Court Politics

All of the above can be placed in a longer timeframe of how Scotland has done politics and patronage that goes further back than the Scottish Office and administrative devolution. How Scotland has traditionally – whether as an independent nation or not – practised political power at the centre.

A politics of power and patronage has a long, seamless lineage – and is one of the continuities between Scotland pre- and post-union. Pre-union, the politics of the Scottish Parliament were divided between a group of distinct factions: the Court Party, the Country Party, the Cavaliers and the New Party, or as they came to be known, 'Squadrone Volante'.[104]

The Country Party represented forces who opposed the union and were associated with the Duke of Hamilton. The Cavaliers were Jacobites who wished to see the return of the Catholic Stuart Pretender. The New Party was an offshoot from the Country Party and were supportive of union.

By far the most important grouping in the Scottish Parliament pre-1707 was the Court Party led by the Duke of Queensberry and who were pro-union. In Tom Devine's words: 'It helped to carry out the policies of London and controlled patronage, essential to the management of Parliament.'[105] Critically, in an age when party did not mean what it does today, the Court Party were given a sense of coherence and purpose by the trading and exchange of power, patronage, access to the courts of the elites and king – hence their name.

The Court Party was one of the pivotal bodies in the passing of the Acts of Union during 1706-7 – safeguarding the autonomy of special status of the Kirk in the Act of Security of the Church of Scotland 1706 – and thus taking out any potential for the Kirk to lead the political opposition to union. However, what is inherent in this is the expression of the Court Party as a form of elite, preferment and insider politics. For all the rhetoric and dramatic changes in society and public life, it has preserved itself over the years.

A few choice examples of Scotland in the union make this case. Archibald Campbell, the 3rd Duke of Argyll, the 1st Earl of Ilay, became known as the 'King of Scotland' by the official monarch, King George II, such was his reach and influence. Major achievements included assisting in the foundation of the Royal Bank of Scotland and becoming its first governor in 1727. Similarly, Henry Dundas gained the nickname 'Henry the Ninth' and the 'Grand Manager of Scotland', itself a play on the Masonic Grand Master of Scotland; he was Solicitor-General for Scotland from 1766-75, before serving as War Minister and later surviving impeachment. Fast-forward into the 20th century and the Secretary of State for Scotland in Churchill's wartime coalition government, Labour's Tom Johnson, also earned the name, 'King of Scotland'. In more recent times, Labour's Willie Ross who held the same post from 1964-70 and 1974-76 became known as 'Hammer of the Nats'.

The above have a number of characteristics in common. They presented a collective, corporate Scottish interest, but did so often by presenting Scotland as a special case, even a basket case. Another angle was to suggest that Scotland was a nation which had been badly wronged, and if this wasn't rectified as soon as possible would soon be in a state of near-permanent rebellion. This was leadership of a far-flung province winning favours from the centre, and in so doing, creating a problematic relationship with it, one constantly simmering and filled with numerous mutual resentments. It is testament to something about the Scottish and English that in many respects it worked so well and lasted so long. But cumulatively it contributed to a slow souring of the atmosphere, aiding a Scottish mindset of co-dependency and at its worst, grievance. It contributed to English elites seeing the Scots as parsimonious and in patronising terms. We are still living in the shadows of such attitudes.

This set of relationships overlaps with how the modern era of party politics has evolved. Scotland's sequential dominant parties – first, the Liberal Party in the 19th century, the Labour Party in the mid-to-late 20th century, and the SNP today, can all be understood in relation to court politics. The latter two in particular, can be seen as modern-day equivalents of the Court Party. It could in fact be argued that the Court Party never really went away in unionist Scotland, but just took on different names and guises while retaining the same modus operandi.

Scottish Labour was explicitly and in many respects unashamedly a Court Party – both in how they operated vis-à-vis London and within Scotland. In either its Old Labour variants from Tom Johnson to Willie Ross, or New Labour with Gordon Brown seeing Scotland as his 'fiefdom', their political practice was never about greater democracy or self-government. Instead, as Labour's hold over Scotland solidified in the 1960s and 1970s, it became solely about the management and maintenance of power, supposedly to do progressive things, but ultimately to perpetuate its own rule and keep the whole show on the road.

The modern-day SNP have a long and proud tradition seeing themselves as 'outsiders' and underdogs. It is written into the anti-establishment ethos of the party, created by the long cold wilderness years of electoral oblivion which, Hamilton 1967 apart, existed for most of the party's first fifty years of 1934-74. In most respects, this attitude will endure as part of the core DNA of the party until the day after Scotland becomes independent. This is for the obvious reason that until then the SNP can always see itself as standing up to Westminster and its political class: the British establishment.

Yet, the contemporary SNP, its ascendancy and unchallenged dominance, as it approached ten years in office, is slowly seeing its outsider credentials eroded. It is becoming at senior levels a party of insiders and a new class of politicians, advisers and interest groups, who see it as their business to maintain the existing state of affairs with the SNP on top and their preferred access to its inner sanctums.[106] In the otherwise very different leadership styles of Alex Salmond and Nicola Sturgeon as SNP leaders and First Ministers of Scotland, there is a common thread of court politics. Indeed, in the Salmond era, such was his risk-taking that the barriers and boundaries of his court were more fuzzy, moveable and accessible than today, whereas around Nicola Sturgeon, a much smaller and more fixed group of people make the key decisions. Whereas there was an identifiable 'Team Salmond', this is much less true of Sturgeon.

This is not a peculiarly Scottish way of doing things. Politics all over the West have become reduced to court and courtier politics. This is to a sizeable degree due to the global rise of free market liberalism and its articulation of a crony capitalism where corporates and pseudo-businesses make deals and win favourable terms of trade and commerce, often with the connivance of government.

There are numerous examples of this: Blair's New Labour, Berlusconi's Forza Italia, the Clintons' (Bill and Hillary) not-so-new Democrats in the USA, and Putin's dominance of Russian politics. This was originally presented to us, at least in the Blair and Bill Clinton versions, as being progressive and enlightened, making an accommodation with globalisation to get the right things done, and that opposition to it was the equivalent of being a flat earther: i.e. unable to understand the way the world now worked. Blair once said in a brilliantly revealing speech to the 2005 Labour conference: 'I hear people say we have to stop and debate globalisation. You might as well debate whether autumn should follow summer.'[107]

Yet even the most progressive version of this politics ended up in a reactionary, corrosive, and, frankly, amoral politics. It led to Blair's debasement of nearly everything Labour stood for in his post-Prime Ministerial afterlife; or in the perception that no one really trusts or knows what Bill and Hillary Clinton stand for and whose interests they represent apart from their own. Even more dramatically, this has produced a form of elite politics which the academic Colin Crouch has called post-democracy[108] – based on the coalescing of political, business and media elites and their horizontal commonalities usurping the old vertical interest groups.[109] It encourages decisions being taken in favour of and for the maintenance of elite views and interests. In so doing, it damages and diminishes the wider body politic and public realm. That revealing phrase, 'Britain open for business' is always about corporate and multinational power getting what it wants. A classic example of this was the way in which now former Chancellor of the Exchequer George Osborne went out of his way to secure Chinese Government investment in the Hinkley Point C nuclear power station by running roughshod over any national security or intelligence concerns (let alone health and safety).[110] By sheer accident the arrival of Theresa May as UK Prime Minister in July 2016 and Osborne's sacking saw her administration pause in the finalisation of the deal, before doing so after a short re-assessment.

Scotland has never reached this point of moral abasement, but caution and vigilance is required. The SNP's court politics are miniscule compared to the above. It has not, as we have previously examined, gone down the route that Labour did in its local government heartlands of engaging in all sorts of shadowy, unsavoury business deals.

However, there is no room for complacency north of the border. First, Scotland has major limitations on its democracy in practice, experience and culture, as well as shortcomings in the Scottish Parliament and Government. Second, one reason for Scotland not being as advanced or regressive as the British state is that the Scottish state is not an independent state and thus lots of powers and responsibilities are not yet run here. In short, Scotland today is just a less interesting and rewarding place for corporate scavengers and the big consultancy firms than the rest of the UK. But they are here, doing nicely, and embedded in the system should independence and the prospect of more contracts from government occur.

Scotland has not had a very rich tradition of practising political democracy. This has been concealed by a sentimental rhetoric from the left and now from Scottish Nationalists. Scotland obviously joined the union as a pre-democracy, but the politics of preferment, patronage and elites which preserved the negotiated partial autonomy of Scotland in the union, maintained many of the elements of pre-democratic life and norms. Now as we enter the age of post-democracy, Scotland rather than hurrying to catch up with the past, has to dare to take a different course. That would entail exploration and experimentation in finding new forms of democracy and participation, looking honestly at the contours and dynamics of public life and the public sphere, and addressing how legislation, policy and practice is done by the Scottish Parliament and Government, along with what kind of expertise they have and can draw upon, and how they are held to account and scrutinised. We will return to how this can practically happen in later chapters.

Chapter Five:

What has gone wrong with Britain?

What would Mussolini have done after such a triumph? He would have crushed the mutineers into smithereens, he would have shot hundreds of sailors... And what did the Conservatives do? They kept their heads; they were not intoxicated by success. They won a tremendous victory and said to the mutineers: let's forget the past! Yes, these people know how to rule. They need to be taken seriously.

Sergie Kirov to Ivan Maisky, Soviet Ambassador to Britain 1934- 43, 12 December 1934, reflecting on 1931 British general election

The United Kingdom is in crisis. That much is widely agreed and understood. But beyond that any consensus stops, with little widespread agreement on what has gone wrong. This economic, social, cultural, democratic, geo-political and psychological crisis has brought the very 'idea' of Britain to its present impasse. It even carries within it an existential threat to end long-standing notions of the UK.

The End of the Great British Economic Miracle

The words and hyperbole of 'the Great British Economic Miracle' were first trumpeted by Thatcher and her first Chancellor, Nigel Lawson, in the 1980s. They became, under Cameron and his Chancellor, George Osborne, along with right-wing cheerleaders, nothing short of a mantra.

The second version of this mirage has run along the lines of a record number of jobs created, the highest employment rate ever, a rebalancing of the economy with less public sector jobs and significant private sector growth. *The Spectator* even went to the trouble of regularly producing lots of graphs to show us how wonderful everything was, and that we had no need to worry about widening inequality (as the main shift, they argued, happened under Thatcher[111]). The downsides in this would be regularly ignored, and the profound structural and long-term weaknesses of the British economy seldom, if ever, cited.

a) The Crisis of Living Standards

British living standards were hit by the 2008 crash and have yet to fully recover. In 2016, living standards finally reached pre-2009 levels, after what the Resolution Foundation described as 'the longest squeeze on households in living memory.'[112]

That is the overall national picture. However the pain, just like the gain, has not been equally shared. In the period 2002-15 over half of all households across the working-age population have experienced falling or flat living standards.[113] There is a generational breakdown. UK disposable pensioner income has grown three times as much as that of young people over the period 1979-2010; in the US the under-thirties are now poorer than retired people for the first time.[114]

b) Poor Investment and Productivity

UK Research and Development represented 1.7% of GDP in 2013 below the OECD average of 2.4% in the same year, with the USA on 2.8% and Germany on 2.9%.[115] *The Economist* summarised this dire state of affairs in the following way:

If Britain cannot get more from its legion of cheap workers… the French could take Friday off and still produce more than Britons do in a week… Britain's workers are a bargain all the same, because their pay is so pitiful.[116] *UK productivity is 19% lower in output per worker than the rest of the G7. It has been hit hardest by the crash with productivity 14% lower than it would have been if pre-crash trends had continued – twice the G7 average.*[117]

c) The Rising Tide of Total UK Debt

Public and political discussions of UK debt usually focus on one component – government debt. This was the sole focus of the George Osborne deficit reduction plan – which is the part the government is responsible for, but that ignores the wider economic terrain of debt. Government debt is only one of four components of debt, the others being corporations, financial and household.

Taking all four of these together the UK has become in the last couple of decades one of the most indebted countries in the developed world – with the only relevant comparators being Ireland and Japan. The UK has seen the biggest rise in this overall debt in the last twenty years, with the exception of Japan. The UK percentage of debt was under 200% in 1987 (according to consultants McKinsey), rose to 300% in 2003, to 487% in 2008, and then continued rising, despite the crash, to 507% in 2011.[118]

d) The Balance of Payments

The UK Balance of Payments – the balance between what the UK exports to the world and what it imports – is at a record historic deficit in 2016, an imbalance unseen for nearly seventy years; although post-Brexit it has, at least for the short term, come down due to the fall in the pound. It is the largest it has ever been since 1948 – another period of severe economic crisis and what was then the post-war austerity of the Attlee Labour Government.

The Balance of Payments deficit is now much bigger than in 1967 and 1974 – when in times of economic turbulence it caused apoplexy in government and policy makers. Labour's Harold Wilson thought he lost the 1970 general election on one month's bad figures such was their importance (along with England as reigning World champions being put out the World Cup in Mexico by West Germany).

Why, if the Balance of Payments caused such anxiety in 1948, 1967 and 1974, does it not seem to matter today? Brexiteers even attempt to portray Britain's deficit with the EU as a sign of strength and an advantage in negotiations. This goes alongside the argument that as the Germans sell one million cars to the UK, they will not want to stop selling those cars. Brexiteers dare to suggest that this gives the UK the upper hand. This is flipping economic realities. The UK Balance of Payments deficit is a measurement of the economic weakness of the UK economy; the German economic surplus indicates that they are one of the strongest economies and exporters in the world. It is also a sign of the widespread prevalence of economic illiteracy in Brexit Britain.

Britain's Corporate Capture Capitalism

There is a deep-rooted malaise in corporate capitalism in Britain – of its governance structures and norms, the role of the firm, and how ownership and corporate decision-making actually occurs. Endemic short-termism, the cult of shareholders and takeovers, and deal making, has always been intrinsic to British capitalism, but in the last thirty years it has gone into turbo-charged overdrive. It is a well-worn cliché to say that modern life is speeding up, but British short-termism gets more short-term by the day, increasingly frenetic and impatient.

Certain moments capture the spirit of an age. Peter Rachman and irresponsible landlordism in the 1960s (producing the descriptive word 'Rachmanism'), Tiny Rowland and 'the unacceptable face of capitalism' in the 1970s, and Gerald Ratner calling his products 'total crap' in the 1980s. Similarly, this year saw Philip Green selling BHS and the fate of 11,000 staff, on the back of a roughly written promissory note to Dominic Chappell, as both of them freeloaded and squirreled millions out of the business.

Worryingly, that isn't as dark as it gets. The UK is a global centre for dirty money and for laundering large amounts of criminal cash. London in particular is a favourite for Russian or Saudi plutocrats investing their money in (literally) safe houses, buying up large swathes of the high-end property market, that often stand empty as they continue to increase in value. Roberto Saviano, author of a best-selling book on Naples and the mafia, reflected that the UK is now 'the most corrupt place on earth.'[119]

What has happened to long-term innovative companies which invest in research and development, high-tech jobs and products, staff and skills? The structures, norms and financial models of British capitalism can allow them to succeed as start-ups, but then the problems begin in terms of finance or banking or a hostile takeover. In 2016, one of the UK's leading tech companies, Cambridge-based ARM, which makes many of the microchips for smart phones, was bought by Japanese company Softbank.[120] All the usual guarantees were given on investment, jobs and headquarters, but it is a familiar story. British politicians have been programmed to believe that ownership and control doesn't matter, whereas every bit of evidence here and across the world says the opposite.

The UK has a complete absence of clearly defined strategic public or national assets or areas not for sale or not for potential sale. There are no restrictions on foreign ownership – whether infrastructure, airports, and until Theresa May's recent pause, nuclear power stations. Britain is 'open for business' basically meant that everything was for sale and often at knockdown prices.

It is not a coincidence that alongside this fire sale of all things public – including the running of the British nuclear deterrent, its maintenance and research by outsourcers Serco and US companies Lockheed Martin and Jacobs Engineering, as well as the Atomic Weapons Establishment at Aldermaston, Coulport and two other sites[121] – people feel a lack of ownership, increasingly powerless in the face of such corporate self-interest and the power of money over shared interests.

Blaming Britain's Problems on the Poor and Welfare

It also isn't surprising that the UK along with the US has seen a systematic squeeze on living standards and the status of middle class incomes and lifestyles. In the US in 1973 5.4% of wages and salaries went to the top 1% of earners; in 2007 it was 12.2%. Britain's top 1% were 6.1% of earnings in 2010: a rise of 77% since 1977.[122] The nature and basis of the social contract – that unwritten compact between government and citizens based on security, safety and wellbeing – is slowly breaking down. This is not an accident or caused by forces beyond our control. It is deliberately being undermined and represents the dominant political zeitgeist of our age.

The UK has one of the most parsimonious, punitive and punishing welfare states in the West, not quite at the grotesque standards of the US, but one that is lacking in any real sense of its original mission to be a positive tool, or genuine empathy and compassion. Lost long ago was the ethos behind Beveridge's original intent and the crusade against the 'five giant evils' – disease, want, ignorance, squalor, and idleness[123] – or T.H. Marshall's idea of welfare as part of social citizenship.[124] Both of these came from the Whig view of British history as an inexorable upward progress, and in relation to welfare and social security such an enlightened approach has now disappeared.

Much time and passion has been spent on the bedroom tax, but much more iniquitous has been the pervasive regime of sanctions inflicted on benefit claimants. This, in what we were told everyday during the EU referendum campaign is 'the fifth richest economy in the world', is a return to the Dickensian logic of the Victorian workhouse. People are sanctioned in Britain for the most petty irrelevances, humiliated and made to feel like they count for nothing, left with no money, and reliant on friends, families, the kindness of strangers, and of course, foodbanks. People have committed suicide and many lives and families have been destroyed due to the sanctions regime, yet its reign of terror continues and shows no sign of abating.

This brutal regime dehumanises those who are poor, struggling or on welfare, into what became known in the 1980s in the US as 'the underclass'. This was invented by a right-wing academic and writer Charles Murray and then popularised by Andrew Neil in his first life as editor of the *Sunday Times* in the 1980s. Neil pushed it hard as a convenient term which not only stigmatised those on welfare, but those deemed to be losers. He would even, post-*Sunday Times* in his role as a BBC anchor, regularly peddle the line that the underclass 'are not like the rest of us' – a pithy summary of othering.[125]

Today such a proselytising view of Britain's poor has become standard. Phrases such as 'welfare dependency' which began as part of the underclass thesis are now part of day-to-day debate: many politicians and professionals use it without any idea of its origins or ideological baggage. This is what happens when an ideology becomes 'commonsense' and presents itself as not an ideology. Thus we have had *Benefits Street* on Channel Four – which itself became a trailblazer for a whole wave of poverty porn programmes, with some of the 'stars' going on to achieve tabloid-style celebrity status and social media scrutiny. The BBC even have a series on benefit cheats called *Saints and Scroungers* and least you think Scotland immune, a few years back we had *The Scheme,* based in Onthank, just outside Kilmarnock, depicting life in forgotten, welfare-dominated Scotland.

The Rise of the Serco State

Public services are increasingly commercialised, outsourced and fragmented under corporate capture in England, if not directly given over to the private sector. Scotland is no different. In the immediate run-up to the indyref, the respected writer Neal Ascherson lamented the state of present-day Britain, turning to the diminishing of the public sector. He reflected that England was embarking on 'the transition to a "Serco state" that would soon cripple public services in Scotland.'[126]

This is an accurate description of England, but the inference from Ascherson's analysis was that Scotland was different and had resisted the charms of such an approach: the familiar argument that England has lost its moral compass, but that this is still maintained and treasured in Scotland along with a sense of public duty and proper public services. The trouble is that 'the Serco state' (Serco: 'the biggest company you've never heard of'[127]) is alive and kicking here as well. It maybe is not as big or as all-encompassing as in England, but it is entrenched and has secured many lucrative contracts including ferry services from the mainland to the Northern Isles, Glasgow City Council's IT services, tagging in prisons, management in PFI hospitals, and to top it off, ran the Dungavel Detention Centre for two years. There are literally no limits to their talents if the price is right.[128]

Living in the Past: The Cultural Nostalgia Industry of Britain

Today much of what passes for mainstream culture is reducible to its financial worth. This can be seen in the blatant selling of work from the Frieze London art fair to plutocrats, despots and anyone with a pile of cash, or on a small, more humble level, the monetising of everything, so that Edinburgh Festivals and the Scottish Government make great play of it drawing £313 million into the city.[129] What pass for cultural programmes address how much financially the once exciting, on the edge 'Young British Artists' of twenty years ago – such as Damian Hirst and Tracey Emin – are now worth, and that being used as a measure of cultural impact.

In policymaking there has been the rise of the term 'creative class' which was championed by the UK Government Department of Culture Media and Sport. This was embraced in Scotland by the creation of Creative Scotland – which in a previous life was two bodies: the Scottish Arts Council and Scottish Screen.

This is about arts and culture as being instrumental, with creativity as an economic tool and gain, and about winners in society. All of this draws sometimes directly, sometimes indirectly, from Richard Florida's *The Rise of the Creative Class* [130] which was about encouraging those who gain from global connectivity and clusters, such as urban mobiles, young lesbians and gays, and multi-cultural neighbourhoods. This was the age of 'fuzzy capitalism', where some observers gave credence to the California Silicon Valley post-hippie dream of Apple, Google and Facebook as genuinely proposing a different kind of ethics of business and work.

Then there is the growing power and packaging of retro-culture that has several strands. One is centred on pop culture and has been widely written about by the likes of Simon Reynolds as well as many others.[131] This is the Britain which is forever young, or at least, forever stuck in the 1960s and the world of swingin' London, The Beatles, The Rolling Stones, The Kinks, and The Who. It has become endlessly referenced, repackaged and presented in documentaries, films and books as if it were some kind of 'Enlightenment' period of great breakthroughs in understanding what it means to be human. This has resulted in the entire period losing its dangerous and radical edge, and instead being reduced to one long party and celebration.

Other strands go much further back into Britain's past. There is the appeal of toffs in the past, English country houses and the English countryside (nearly always the English). There is the continual invoking of the Second World War: the last great, almost foundational story of Britain which has become 'a kind of creation myth, the noble story of modern Britain's birth'.[132]

As we have grown ever more distant from the war, and the stories of Britain in recent times have become less appealing, so the war has moved centre stage again – but not as history, but as an idealised past. This is a place where Britain stood united, alone and on the side of democracy; it was of course more complicated.

Many think, however, that this is a commercially exportable image of the UK and good for box office takings; think ITV's *Downton Abbey* for example. But it is increasingly how Britain culturally represents how we see ourselves, and tries to shape how we are seen globally. That story of the past is problematic in the here and now, and for the future. It presents a Britain where any consciously alternative future that breaks with this past is closed down, and instead, a costume drama interpretation of the past defines who we are. History and politics are affected in this as Jonathan Freedland wrote, reflecting on the massive success of *Downton Abbey*: 'It's a little like studying history before E.P. Thompson and Raymond Williams taught us that the past was not the exclusive preserve of the aristocracy.'[133]

More critically, and mirroring economic and social interpretations, there has been a narrowing of what is and what isn't part of mainstream cultural Britain. This can be seen in the popular historian Dominic Sandbrook's take on British culture, *The Great British Dream Factory* and the related TV series, *Let us Entertain You* (itself a nod to great British entertainer Robbie Williams) and its first episode called 'The New British Empire'.[134]

Sandbrook has a superficially inclusive version of popular

culture – which seems to come down to the base line of what sells and shifts units, and nothing else. Beyond this his reach is hideously narrow and deliberately selective. Thus, key icons in Sandbrook's cultural Britain are Catherine Cookson, J.K. Rowling, Elton John, and those titans of the 1960s, the Beatles and the Stones. However, it is much more partial and exclusionary than that, for Sandbrook's cultural Britain is really London with a few add-ons. Not only does it omit Scotland and exclude any mention of Scottish independence, it ignores Northern Ireland, or any mention of the thirty-year troubles – both of which had and are still having huge cultural ramifications. And of course, you can just forget Wales – as Sandbrook obviously has.

Not only is this a cultural Britain with no Edinburgh Festivals (so much for the 'Athens of the North' and 'biggest arts festival in the world'), or mention of a single Scottish author – J.K. Rowling apart. There is no England beyond the M25. No Manchester, no North of England, and no understanding of the cultural imagination and activities of such real places. And with the exclusion of outliers and outsiders, there is no room for provocateurs; so there is no punk (beyond the Sex Pistols), no post-punk and no 1980s indie music scene.

Sandbrook calls British culture an 'empire of the mind', in that the UK has supposedly conquered the world with its cultural products. In reality, it is a double-edged comment. His take illustrates an increasingly unsophisticated dominant culture's psychological colonisation of public culture, space and art. This is a Britain where the mainstream reflects uncritical acquiescence to money and commerce, and its ultimate triumph in incorporating or stifling any alternative accounts. Culture becomes what money and power approve of, buy or give patronage to; for what is meant to be the story of a cultural powerhouse this is a pretty grim prospectus.

Sandbrook's cultural Britain isn't even generous enough to be a history of just England, but is a tiny slither socially of society.

It is also a mean-spirited place. So in the usual tour of the 1960s which adds nothing new, the individual personas of the Beatles and Stones are examined, and special condescension given to the obvious rebels in each, John Lennon and Keith Richards, because they wanted the good life and the big houses while also criticising it.[135] In many respects all of this is a bit Richard Florida, with culture reduced to being about the winners and the rise of a new creative class and how success allowed them to join the elites. It is a very old British story.

The Democratic Deficit of British Politics

The British state has the pretence and appearance of being of a democracy. It self-mythologises its Parliament as 'the mother of all Parliaments'. This disguises the reality that the United Kingdom never fully democratised. Its limited, qualified embrace of democracy, and that the conditions under which the people were slowly allowed to enter the inner sanctums of power were not those of the people or the radicals (Chartists, suffragettes, the labour movement) but those of the elites (Whigs, Liberals, Tories).

The first two great Reform Acts of the 19th century, 1832 and 1867, passed by Liberal Earl Grey and Tory Benjamin Disraeli, were to maintain the existing order of things, to cut off pressure for radical change and sweeping democratization. They intended to bring firstly, parts of the middle class, then, select sections of the working class into the electorate and politics, with the latter representing what Disraeli called 'angels in marble'.

The fact that the United Kingdom never fully democratised can be seen in remnants of feudalism scattered across public life. This isn't just the obvious cases of the monarchy and House of Lords. After all quite a few countries have monarchies – including three of the five Nordic nation states (Norway, Sweden, and Denmark). But in the UK the monarch is not only formal head of state but sits at the apex of a set of powers and institutions called 'the Crown' (and which include such property empires as the Crown Estate). There is the issue of the Crown powers or Royal Prerogative as it is also known, used by the executive to govern; in short, used by the executive to cloak the reality of its role, aid patronage, and to limit the expression of democracy.

Until 2003 British governments refused to confirm or deny what the Royal Prerogative did or did not cover, and then issued a list. In domestic matters it then covered:

- the issuing and withdrawal of passports;
- the appointment and dismissal of ministers;
- the appointment of Queen's Counsel;
- the granting of honours;
- the appointment and regulation of the civil service;
- the commissioning of officers in the armed forces;
- the dissolution of Parliament;
- the calling of elections.

And in foreign affairs it covered:

- the declaration of war;
- the making of treaties;
- the recognition of foreign states;
- the accreditation of diplomats.[136]

The powers also cover strange quirks such as the royal ownership of swans in open waters. Post-Iraq war, calls arose to change the Royal Prerogative right to make war, and in 2011 then Prime Minister David Cameron announced that future military interventions would involve a parliamentary vote. However this is merely a convention, no legislation has been brought forward and it has been confirmed the Royal Prerogative right to make war remains.[137] The 2003 contentious

Iraq war vote had, as it was made clear at the time, only been 'advisory.'

There is huge irony in the recent Brexit vote for the United Kingdom to come out of the EU. The Leave campaign railed against 'unelected bureaucrats' in Brussels – whereas the House of Lords, the second chamber, is unashamedly and unapologetically 100% unelected. Worse than Brussels it comprises unelected legislators. While the House of Commons retains much more power, and is where governments have to have a parliamentary majority or mandate, the numbers and balance between the two show the allure of patronage and preferment. The Commons, if the Tories get their way, will be cut from 650 to 600 elected members, while the Lords just grows and grows with no end point on its final membership: currently sitting at 797 members in August 2016.[138]

Being a member of the House of Lords means having no accountability to anyone or any standards; with no requirement to regularly turn up, contribute, or operate for the greater public good. It is literally membership of a select private member's club for life (or beyond, with the remaining hereditary peers) and a club nearly impossible to get ejected from. Convicted criminals such as Jeffrey Archer, Conrad Black and Mike Watson retain their membership of the Lords, despite spending time behind bars after becoming Lordships; Watson even managed in 2015 to make a mini comeback as a Shadow Labour spokesperson in education, despite his criminal record.[139]

Every now and then the need for reform is articulated, such as 'Peers guilty of serious criminal offences to be expelled from House of Lords',[140] but nothing happens. House of Lords reform occurs at a snail's pace in Britain: with legislative calls for its abolition lasting over a century since the Parliament Act 1911 of the radical Liberal Government of 1906-15 first circumscribed the powers of the upper house.

The upper house has also diminished in its claims of expertise, although there still remain some stellar examples of world-class authority in their respective fields. The 7th Baron Sudeley can try to claim that 'The virtue of aristocracy is wisdom',[141] but today's debates can be a little bit less edifying than that. The maiden speech of bra millionaire, and Government Tsar for small business, Michelle Mone, involved her citing the late singer Whitney Houston as inspiration, quoting 'I believe the children are our future: "teach them well and let them lead the way."'[142]

The wider absence of democracy can be seen in the absence of any fundamental or entrenched laws in the UK, a position soon to become rather germane with the departure of the UK from the European Union. UK Parliaments are not restrained in the same way as those with written, codified constitutions. Once upon a time this wasn't meant to matter, as a system with time-honoured and tested checks and balances subtly worked, but no longer is that the case.

The limits of British democracy allowed the Thatcher Government to upend all sorts of economic and social rights and norms, and never on more than 44% of the popular vote at their peak. This is not a partisan party point. The philosophy of Thatcherism and its related market liberalism never won majority support for its tenets with the public in all its time in office. But it was still able to ram through its proposals and defeat parliamentary and popular opposition, hugely aided at times by Labour divisions, splits and incompetence. Some things never change in Britain.

The British political system can be characterised as a pre-democratic form of government and politics that clings to archaic concepts and myths such as parliamentary sovereignty – and makes quite a fuss about rejecting popular sovereignty. This produces all sorts of contradictory attitudes. For example, the EU referendum – an expression of popular sovereignty – has been for supporters of Brexit to defend parliamentary sovereignty.

Yet conventional democracy is in crisis and retreat all

across the West, aided by the march of post-democracy – the collusion of powerful elites, whether in politics, business and professional life, or senior media executives. The UK finds itself in the unique position of being a pre-democracy in much of its political norms and limitations, but has found that these have been captured for the purpose of post-democracy – the narrowing and constraining of any democratic impulse. This lethal combination of two elite forms of rule – pre- and post-democracy – is one of the main reasons for the success of the right-wing counter-revolution in recent years. It poses huge challenges for any attempt to row back the Thatcherite changes, and any centre-left project to reform and democratise the UK.

The Gathering Storms of where the UK situates itself in the world

The UK has for all of its existence had significant international reach and influence in both hard and soft power. This has operated in a number of dimensions – Europe, the Commonwealth, the so-called 'special relationship' with the US and the more than 40-year membership of the EU. Winston Churchill understood this as being the basis of British influence and talked of the country at the centre of a series of alliances such as Europe, the Commonwealth and the English-speaking world.

In recent times the phrase that 'Britain can punch above its weight' has become a threadbare cliché, stretched to breaking point by Blair and his desire for military intervention which came to a juddering halt in the Iraq war. Andrew Gamble, in the aftermath of this, wrote that the idea of England as a 'world island' sat within four intersecting circles: the union that is the United Kingdom, the Commonwealth, Europe and Anglo-America.[143] More and more right-wing commentators prior to, and after, the UK vote for Brexit have started to refer to 'the Anglosphere' meaning the English-speaking developed democracies in the world.[144]

All of this has come at a cost. The UK has endured a post-imperial hangover, never fully became a believer in the European project or saw itself as a European country in the way others do, and developed a hugely unbalanced relationship with the USA which came over at times as desperate and created a British dependency mixed with an element of entitlement. Macmillan talked of the US as 'the new Roman empire' and the UK as 'like the Greeks of old [who] must teach them how to make it go'[145]; while Christopher Meyer, UK Ambassador to the US in the run-up to the Iraq war, was given the instructions with relation to the US to 'hug them close'.[146]

The UK still has global clout in some areas. It is the fourth largest arms exporter in the world. It has long-term commercial relationships with brutal authoritarian regimes such as Saudi Arabia, putting human rights concerns second to British business – irrespective of the use to which the Saudis put the hardware, such as in the Yemeni civil war. The UK has the fifth biggest defence spending in the world in real figures – only surpassed by the USA, China, Saudi Arabia and Russia.[147] The UK's armed forces in terms of effectiveness are ranked sixth with India added to the list.[148]

On the plus side, UK international aid under Cameron's Conservatives reached the UN target of 0.7% GDP – one of only a handful of countries which met this figure. The UK is seventh – only out-aided by Sweden (1.41%), UAE (1.09%), Norway (1.05%), Luxembourg (0.93%), Denmark (0.85%), the Netherlands (0.76%) followed by the UK (0.71%).[149] Whether this will survive the fall of Cameron and Brexit Britain is for the moment unclear.

One study has examined all the parts of the world the UK has been in military conflict with. According to the author there are only 22 from 193 nation states with which the UK hasn't fought over in some form (although some of the judgements are a little suspect). Such has been the UK's military prowess that a large number of the 22 are microstates such as Andorra, Liechtenstein, Monaco and Vatican City.[150]

The serious point is that the UK has historically been a warrior state. Alarmingly, in the more than one hundred years since the onset of the First World War in 1914 there is according to one study not a single year in which UK armed forces have not been in active combat. Ian Cobain surveying this commented:

The British are unique in this respect: the same could not be said of the Americans, the Russians, the French or any other nation. Only the British are perpetually at war.[151]

The hangover of Sandbrook's 'empire of the mind' has many damaging consequences. Blair's liberal imperialism (which is often the worst kind; it is how the US got involved in Vietnam in the first place) did not appear from nowhere. It was located in 'Great Powerism', 'the special relationship' and Britain's continual mistrust of Europe (and Europe's mistrust of the UK). This led to the disaster of Iraq which played such a part in the corrosion of any kind of trust in politicians. None of this has yet been resolved – despite the publication of the Chilcot inquiry into the Iraq war a mere thirteen years after the UK engaged in military action.

Britain's political classes even post-Iraq still see themselves as being some of the self-appointed policemen of the world. Cameron took the UK with the French militarily into Libya in 2011 to overthrow Gaddafi, then tried to win a parliamentary vote for intervention in Syria in 2013 and lost to his fury. Subsequently, he won a Syria vote for limited bombing in 2015 – where Jeremy Corbyn and Hillary Benn spoke from opposing views from Labour's front bench. This turned out to be very limited, and subsequently no parliamentary mandate was requested for UK special forces operating in Syria assisting anti-Assad rebels.[152]

Trident and After and the British Nuclear Fixation

Then there is Trident and the British nuclear obsession – a nationalist shibboleth if ever there was one. This directly links to Britain's political, military and security elites' desire to still see themselves as significant global players with an automatic seat at the international top table. In reality, the status of Britain's so-called 'independent' nuclear deterrent fails to meet two of these three criteria: it is, at least, nuclear.

The history of the UK deterrent is bound up in the UK-US relationship. The wartime Manhattan Project – the secret project to build an atomic bomb which ultimately led to the devastating dropping of 'Little Boy' and 'Fat Man' on the Japanese cities of Hiroshima and Nagasaki – involved UK co-operation and input, albeit at the level of a junior partner.

Wartime co-operation meant that this was formalised in the Quebec Agreement in August 1943 and the Hyde Park Agreement in September 1944 that committed the UK and US to continued nuclear co-operation after the war. This was the expectation in the UK. Post-war attitudes changed in the US and in 1946, to the horror of the UK, they passed the McMahon Act that forbade the passing of classified atomic energy information to any foreign country (including the UK) on pain of life imprisonment or death.

This was a body blow to British prestige. Attlee, within one month of coming to power, set up a secret Atomic Bomb Committee in August 1945 known as GEN 75. The British nuclear programme began in 1946 under the banner of the Atomic Energy Research Establishment with the initial aim of civil nuclear power. The Labour Government nearly simultaneously took a decision to develop its own nuclear weapons, with Ernest Bevin declaring in October 1946: 'We've got to have this… We've got to have a bloody Union Jack flying on top of it.'[153]

A decision was taken to develop nuclear weapons in January 1947, and in October 1952 Britain undertook its first nuclear weapons test, leading to the deployment of Blue Danube in November 1953: a free-fall bomb.[154] Meanwhile, UK diplomacy tried to get a UK exemption to the McMahon Act. An opportunity arose out of disagreement with the US and the achievements of Soviet science: the Suez debacle in 1956 and Sputnik, the world's first satellite in 1957. Thus began the 1958 Mutual Defence Agreement between the UK and US leading to the Polaris Sales Agreement of 1962-63. In short, the US provided the Polaris missiles for UK-built submarines – this being broadly the picture since with the UK 'deterrent' being 'independent' in name only.

Soft Power and Prime Ministerial Foreign Policy Disasters

One area the UK has long prided itself on is soft power, in which the country has traditionally 'punched above its weight', aided by the reach of the English language, through American connections and the legacy of the Commonwealth. This is slowly mattering less and less. These days the decline in the Foreign and Commonwealth Office (FCO), even before it was further diminished by the pilfering of staff post-EU referendum to establish the Departments for Brexit and for International Trade, has affected the quality of advice UK Governments get about the world. This is further aided by cuts to the BBC World Service and the British Council.

The UK has spent nearly two or more decades marginalising the FCO. Thatcher had an innate suspicion of the Department and its mandarins, thinking that many had gone native and accepted the British decline at home and abroad. Systematic ignoring of the FCO began seriously under Blair and was then continued by Cameron. Expertise was deliberately ignored and in its place was put Prime Ministerial diplomacy and foreign policy.

The results of this accruing of power to a more centralist authority have not exactly been positive. Meanwhile, FCO expertise, whether in the Middle East and the Arab world, or on Russia and Ukraine, has been neglected, cut back and not listened to. One former UK Ambassador said of the diminishing of the FCO: 'You can see how its Russian expertise has been hollowed out.'[155]

This shift in the craft of political diplomacy has had lasting damage to the UK's international influence and standing. The previous examples of freelancing Prime Ministerial diplomacy and foreign affairs, and bypassing of formal channels of FCO, intelligence and security, have been some of the biggest, if not the biggest, geo-political setbacks the UK has suffered in the previous century.

They included Neville Chamberlain not trusting the FCO and developing back-door diplomacy with Hitler and Mussolini. This was the basis for his appeasement of the dictator, and the ultimate humiliation of the Munich agreement in 1938 where the UK and France encouraged and supported the carving up of Czechoslovakia.[156]

Anthony Eden, himself, a principled opponent of Munich, read the wrong lessons from history and believed that the Egyptian leader Nasser who nationalised the Suez Canal (previously British-controlled) was a 'new Hitler' and this was the 1930s all over again. This led to the British and French attacking Egypt with Israeli support, Eden being caught lying to the Commons, and the Americans pulling the plug on the whole episode. American President Eisenhower threatened to withdraw financial support for the pound on world markets and blocked IMF support for the ailing currency. Eden resigned in January 1957 under the fig leaf of ill health. After that the British and the French never saw each other in the same light.[157] The French judged they should never fully trust the Americans, and the British felt that they should get as close to the US as possible – all of which shored up problems for the UK in relation to Europe, with the French twice vetoing UK applications to what was then the EEC.[158]

There is a pattern from Chamberlain and Eden's disasters, arrogance and moral certainty, along with simplistic reading of history, and Tony Blair and the perfidy and disinformation of going to war in Iraq in 2003. Yet, again the lessons of appeasement were dragged out and misused to say why the UK and US should stand up to the dictatorship of Saddam Hussein. If Blair wasn't caught directly lying to the Commons as Eden had been, he had just as seriously become sold to the whole prospectus for war put forward by neo-conservatives in the Bush administration during 2001-3 because he wanted to stand 'shoulder to shoulder' with the US.

The result, along with Munich and Suez, produced in the aftermath of Iraq a Britain diminished in how the world saw us, with the Middle East in turmoil, an increase in terrorism – all the product of Prime Ministerial hubris that will impact on the UK and world for decades. A contributory factor in this debacle has been the desire of British Prime Ministers to freelance and deliberately contract out diplomacy and foreign affairs from formal channels to resultant calamity.[159] Increasingly Prime Ministerial leadership and ownership of such areas is connected to the atrophying and decay at the heart of British government, including the abandonment under Thatcher, Blair and Cameron of any pretence of cabinet government alongside the creation of a semi-Presidential operation in No. 10 Downing Street.

The Problem of Empire State Britain

The UK political and military elites have never given up on the Great Power illusion. The recent contours of the EU referendum and its result can be seen in this context, with public opinion clearly influenced by such a backdrop. The mantra of the UK as 'the fifth richest economy in the world' was recited to breaking point in the campaign.

The UK has in effect what can be called an Empire State – a state devised for global pretensions, projection and military expeditions. It is not designed for the care or wellbeing of its own people. This Empire State Britain has been characterised by the fossilised, anti-democratic nature of the central state which has allowed an outdated version of Britain to remain at its core: one which has united the main Westminster classes, irrespective of who forms a government.

The 'special relationship' has been one of the pillars of how the UK has interpreted the world – contributing to us more often than not seeing the world through Atlanticist eyes. This was born in World War Two in the period 1940-41 when Britain, with the backup of Empire, saw itself as standing alone against Nazi Germany. It became even more pronounced after Suez which saw the end of any substantive independent British foreign policy and action, the Falklands War exempted.

There is a connection and trajectory from the overreach of Suez in 1956 to Iraq in 2003 and the exit of the UK from the European Union. On one take of the UK's forty-year-plus membership of the EEC then EU, we never really properly joined or arrived at the club, and always had one foot outside. Brexit has been a product of a rich concoction of psychological convulsions that put into question how UK elites in the future see where the UK sits and with whom it tries to make allies and friends. At the moment none of this is very clear, and the UK's turn away from Europe cannot find satisfactory solution in the 'special relationship', Anglosphere or Commonwealth as they are all pathways of the past.

Xenia Wickett, head of US affairs at Chatham House, a think tank on international affairs, observed that for the US its relationship with the UK rests on a three-legged stool. The first is Britain's military and intelligence capability; the second,

EU membership; and the third, UK soft power in Washington. She observed pre-Brexit vote: 'Cuts in defence would crumble the first leg, leaving the EU would destroy the second. The third might survive, but stools don't balance on one leg.'[160]

A large section of the UK political class still believes that it can cut an advantageous deal with the EU. There is a discernable mood that is almost one of insouciance in elements of the political elite, bordering on sleepwalking into a prospective disaster. This toxic mix has even led the mostly mild-mannered *Economist* to comment pre-triggering of Article 50: 'Breaking up a relationship is never easy, but when one side thinks it is god's gift to political unions it becomes tougher still.'[161]

We have of course been here before. In the three years of indyref campaigning, the UK was presented as unique and special – all the time by pro-union opinion. Thus, the UK was 'the greatest political union ever' (Boris Johnson[162]) and 'the most successful multinational state in the world' (Ed Balls[163]). The nature of the union as 'a partnership of equals' which respected all four component parts including Scotland, was continually trundled out. Scotland was protected in the union, and even, underlying this, Scotland was actually Scotland in all its glories because of the union: a not implausible pro-union argument.

Today in post-Brexit Britain the nature of this partnership looks shakier and even impermanent. The UK voted 51.9% to 48.1% to leave, while Scotland split 62:38 to remain. Despite this the language of Westminster pro-union politicians (explored in detail in Chapter Three) is very different from the summer of 2014 to the autumn of 2016. David Mundell, Scotland's solitary Tory MP and Secretary of State for Scotland commented: 'We have to respect the result on Thursday, even if we don't like it – it was a UK-wide vote – and it was a vote by people across the UK.'[164]

This is the standard line of Westminster politicians and

it is a literal interpretation of the untrammelled expression of parliamentary sovereignty: a world which no longer exists except in the minds of politicians who cite them. There is a certain desperation in the constant incantation of such phrases – as if trying to perpetuate a discredited, contradictory religious faith now fallen on hard times.

This has been a situation foretold by perceptive observers of the strange entity that is the United Kingdom: the most penetrating analysis of which has usually, not surprisingly, come from Scots, or people based in Scotland, but not exclusively: Tom Nairn, Bernard Crick, and Anthony Barnett, being three of the most consistent critics. Crick made his latter-day home in Edinburgh and from this vantage point dissected the strange goings-on which make the UK what it is. Talking about the myth of parliamentary sovereignty and the Whig history of Britain, he wrote in 1988: 'Our rulers have ended up believing their own rhetoric', and therein often lies ruin and disaster.[165]

Britain post-Brexit is showing multiple cracks and faultlines. The EU referendum was in a mostly unsaid way really about England and its place in the union of the UK, Europe and the modern world. Immigration and anger about the state of society were foils for a large section of England's population thinking, rightly, that no one in power listens to them or has their interests at heart. It isn't also very surprising that this unnamed English dimension became more explicit and was even on occasion literally described as English, post-vote. The problem is that in most mainstream avenues England's debate is still being portrayed as Britain's.

One example suffices as a representative example after the Brexit vote. The BBC special programme looking behind the scenes of both campaigns – *Brexit: The Battle for Britain* presented by Laura Kuenssberg – had lots going for it.[166] Enough time had transpired from the vote for some detachment and reflection, but we were still dealing with real live issues. However, in a one-hour programme what was stark was what was missing. Thus, not only were Scotland, Wales and Northern Ireland missing, but this was a UK reduced to London and a vague place called 'the North' made up of three men in a pub and one Leave-supporting woman.

This is the Britain of an insider class making decisions, framing what is debated and what isn't, and marking out the boundaries of what is deemed politically permissible to talk about and what isn't. This doesn't spring from BBC's Broadcasting House as some conspiracy theories suggest, but is about a collective elite view of Britain and its intolerance of others. This Britain has become so narrow and so fixated on the interests of a tiny slither of people and institutions based in London that the BBC's post-Brexit analysis thinks it is not an issue in a one-hour programme to not even have one (tokenistic) reference to prospects post-Brexit for Scottish independence, or implications for the Northern Irish peace process.

This version of Britain has been a long time brewing. It did not arise from the Brexit ashes, but is about a disunited, divided, unequal kingdom where power, status and legitimacy are increasingly focused in a narrow swathe of London and surrounding commuter areas. This version of 'Great Britain plc' is to the direct detriment of the vast majority of the people of the UK, including London and the South East.

There is insularity, self-reverence and confirmation bias in this. Britain's elites are telling themselves and ourselves how special and important they are. Britain's story has become their story. It never used to be so. There is also in the talk of the likes of Dominic Sandbrook a sense of denial and of deliberate forgetfulness – of consciously not understanding and remembering the union that is the UK. This union that supposedly inspires Sandbrook and others is being presented as a unique mosaic and mixture of human talent and insights that contributes something wonderful to the world. The sheer lack of curiosity and insight in the power elite account of Britain reveals that something has gone way wrong with Britain.

The story of Britain has been taken from its people. One can overstate how much they ever were completely in control or influential, but in the past there were hopeful stories of Britain, and accounts of collective change and different Britains of the future. Once upon a time Labour were a party of the future: a place and country that was a better place. Labour's 1945 manifesto was called *Let Us Face the Future* and again in 1964 there was a national mood that Labour were the party of change and progress. The right then knew this about Labour and the left, they grasped that modernity and hope sat on the left and that they were fighting a series of defensive battles.

Now the roles are reversed. The British right sees the future as theirs and understandably sees Brexit as part of that: an opportunity to create a Britain of their dreams – of low tax and light regulation that has escaped the evil European leviathan. The British progressive tradition has been left with its memories, hankering after the past and going on about things like the 'spirit of 1945'. For all the energy around Jeremy Corbyn's influx of hundreds of thousands into Labour, they have become a party of conservative values: preserving past gains and at best reversing Tory onslaughts.

There are huge implications in this but this switch isn't going to remain forever, but nor is it going to change anytime soon. The non-Conservative majority in the United Kingdom is going to have to live in a politics which is tectonically tilted towards one version of London and the South East. This distorts and damages much of British public life, but for the foreseeable future, the centre-left of England are going to be fighting a set of rearguard actions. That carries consequences for the Celtic nations: Scotland, Wales and Northern Ireland, and also throws down a gauntlet to us in not only how we progress our self-government, but also reach out and assist the majority of people in England.

Chapter Six:

The Limits of Scotland's Revolution

I: *Yesterday at Leveson, they were talking about public officials being in receipt of cash. How commonplace was that, that far back?*

Jack: *Every day. I had a black book of cash payoffs and I remember the accountant came down and said he needed to see who the money was going to and I said to him, 'No'. He said, 'I demand to see it'. I said, 'Fuck off out of editorial or I'll have you thrown out'. He then rushed to the gaffer who had been a journalist in his youth...*

I: *And who knew how it worked?*

Jack: *And he came in and said, 'Jack, no worries. The black book is fine.' And when I left The Sun, I destroyed the black book. But there were cash payments in that to policemen, ambulance men, soldiers, social workers...*

Jack Irvine, former editor of the Scottish Sun, *quoted in* Enquirer, *National Theatre of Scotland, 2012*

Scotland is in a state of flux and change. Much is positive, as well as understandably unsettling. It wasn't always like this. Throughout much of our history Scotland has been defined by institutions, for the search for an overarching consensus in public life, and the advocacy of a collective 'Scottish interest', sometimes characterised by a high degree of agreement, even groupthink.

This isn't of course how the situation is usually represented by the agencies and bodies that view themselves as key components of the 'Scottish interest', like professional, business and civic organisations. Instead the reach and status of the Holy Trinity of the Kirk, law and education, which historically characterised autonomy in the union, presented themselves as guardians of the nation and of the popular will. The same could be said in more recent times of 'civic Scotland': that 1980s rebellion against Thatcher by respectable middle class society: the more modern and secular variant of that 'Holy Trinity'.

Today's Scotland may seem far away from that nation of claustrophobia and pervasive authority, but it wasn't too long ago that large parts of public life were characterised by taboos, silences and no-go areas. These covered many issues from religion and sectarianism to sex and sexuality, and all matters relating to the body.

Many in contemporary Scotland may doubt that our country was once the kind of society portrayed in such accounts, a place where public discourse – and what was permissible to say and do – was heavily controlled and also self-policed. Such attitudes sometimes come from the radical Scotland perspective that proposes that we have always been a 'restless nation', warring with and challenging authority. One over-optimistic account of the indyref can seem a modern variant of this older story. Yet, the scale of change we have gone through can only be understood by recognising where we have come from, by studying the power of forces of social control in that past country and mapping how they have declined, so that we can recognise the contours of contemporary Scotland.

One recent detailed study of Scotland over the period 1950-80 by academics Roger Davidson and Gayle Davis found an illiberal, censorious society with a punitive voice of moral authority centred on the Kirk and Catholic Church, but also in wider society including the Labour Party.[167] Trying to push against some of the boundaries in areas such as abortion, contraception or homosexuality was represented by moral campaigners as somehow 'unScottish'. There is a warning in the past for Scotland today and in the future of over-investing in moral certainty and the current manifestation of a monocultural national identity.

How Scotland changed on Sex and Sexuality

Much debate and discourse in this area was conducted at the margins of society until the establishment of the Scottish Parliament in 1999. For example, Scotland didn't have a major public conversation about lesbian and gay rights until the Wendy Alexander-led abolition of Section 28/Clause 2a – a Thatcher inspired measure which supposedly outlawed the 'promotion' of homosexuality in schools.

This brought forth a highly contested cultural war, the like of which has never been seen before or since.[168] The forces of moral conservatism were fronted by Stagecoach millionaire (and SNP supporter) Brian Souter, along with PR adviser Jack Irvine. Both Labour and SNP leaderships reacted nervously and wobbled in the face of such fury and bigotry. The forces of enlightenment and equality won out, but not as a result of politicians, party or Parliament. Instead a wider, very loose mobilisation of trade unions, churches, NGOs and individual campaigners, came together on equality. The Tories were for the old order; the Lib Dems, Scottish Greens and Scottish Socialists were pro-equality.

It was a painful experience at the time: for many pro-equality campaigners it seemed like a warning from the dark, dank Scotland of the past that many thought dead. But the victory has wider pointers about political and social change. Suffice to say it showed the therapeutic nature of taking on reactionaries and the limits of advancing equality by stealth and ministerial diktat. The flushing out of homophobic opinion and those who didn't want any kind of discussion of lesbian and gay lifestyles in schools showed how repressive and intolerant they were.

The forces of equality just won the short-term argument, but longer-term trends shifted dramatically, aided by the Section 28/Clause 2a battle. In the decade from 2000-2010 public opinion saw enormous change. In 2000 56% of the population thought that homosexuality was always or mostly wrong; in 2010 this fell to 27%. Whereas in 2000, 38% thought homosexuality was rarely or not at all wrong, rising to 58% in 2010.[169]

Future change illustrated how the landscape had altered. There was little controversy over the passing of the same-sex civil partnerships in 2004 and same-sex marriage in 2014. Scotland had dramatically liberalised over the course of a decade; and in many respects on this, as well as other moral and ethical issues, come closer to English public opinion.

The Sounds of Silence and Radical Scotland's Impatience

Despite such dramatic change, the legacy of a culture of powerful taboos and prescriptive authority has left a mark. In a previous study, I analysed the cultures of unspace and undemocracy and how tradition defined much of public life.[170] These cultures sat in a Scotland post-union where what mattered was a mix of insider, expert and elder opinion. This gave sustenance to the practices of unspace, whereby certain voices were seen as more permittable and privileged, and others discouraged or silenced. At the same time, a cautious, incrementally conservative mindset put an onus on tradition and continuity above anything seen as too radical, questioning or independent-minded.

It is this old order that, while already weakening and in retreat, was further challenged by the indyref. Visible shifts around what was permissible in terms of authority and voice occurred, and the boundaries of public life became significantly more porous. However, any idea that the indyref itself has brought about a permanent revolution in public debate has to be dismissed, and indeed, overstating its impact aids those who would wish for a return to normal service. There was a rhetoric in sections of the Yes movement which bought into the notion that saying 'No' to the British establishment meant it would somehow be simple to not only defy global markets, but to reject the ideological assumptions of Anglo-American capitalism and neo-liberalism. This suggested that the power of political will would be enough. The experience of Syriza in Greece, as well as the countless wreckages of democratic socialist governments the world over suggest otherwise.

An articulation of a sort of Pot Noodle radicalism – just add water and you have instantly your successful left-wing project – is short-sighted. Some elements of the independence camp assumed that the disorientation and defeat of the British establishment would be enough, when combined with will and the 'correct' programme, for Scotland to radically depart from the economic and social orthodoxies of recent decades.

Prime examples of this kind of left boosterism and naivety were to be found everywhere in the indyref. Then there was the excuse that such overblown claims were just being said to mobilise people, but that's not healthy or honest, and such claims have continued from some of the same sources post-indyref, admittedly less frequently. Robin McAlpine of Common Weal stated with seeming certainty post-indyref that: 'Political change is easy. Social justice is easy. We know what it is and how to get it.'[171] This isn't helpful – or grounded in evidence from Scotland or anywhere else in the world. Just affirming and saying positive and defiant things doesn't make them happen; politics is never ever just about political will, and thinking it is only produces disappointment.

What happens to power when it has to account for itself?

One gauge of how power manifests itself is how it reflects on setbacks and defeats. In a number of recent high-impact case studies we can see that institutions have gone out of their way to talk about their shortcomings and weaknesses. However there are many important examples and events in Scotland in recent times in which this has not been the case.

First and rather telling, there has been no proper indyref post-mortem in the two years since the vote – either by the SNP or Yes campaign. One justification for the SNP post-2014 has been that for the next two years Scotland has been in permanent political campaigning, with the 2015 and 2016 elections and then the Brexit vote.

Yet that is not a sufficient answer, as politicians should be able to multitask. A deeper reason is that the official independence movement in the SNP and Yes have not wanted to look too closely at the reasons they lost in 2014. That's an unhelpful attitude, for defeat offers the potential for renewal. Lord Ashcroft, Tory peer and opinion pollster, commented after the 2014 vote: 'A political movement never flourishes by blaming its defeats on the media, or by deploring the motives or gullibility of the electorate.'[172]

Instead, there has been a degree of self-congratulation and worse on the fringes, believing a rightful Yes victory was snatched away by a lying mainstream media, the BBC 'stealing' the referendum, and the power of the 'Vow', along with threats from Westminster and big business. Now all of these hurt Yes. But rather than just repeat this as a mantra it would be better politics to look at why a majority of people did not want to embrace independence. A whole host of factors need unpacking – from economic wellbeing to future financial prospects, the psychology of voting to leave one union and the setting up of an independent nation state, along with managing risk and uncertainty generally. It just doesn't do the independent camp any favours to not explore these and more.

Some myths of the indyref cannot be dismissed entirely from pro-independence opinion such as the notion that 'the Vow' won it; we know from opinion polling that this isn't the case. If this had been the case, popular opinion would have to believe that Westminster would deliver the pledge of greater devolution, something many Yes campaigners questioned. However, public opinion was very sceptical on whether Westminster would deliver; only 27% of voters believed Westminster would deliver greater devolution if there were a No vote in week one of the formal campaign and 26% in week four.[173] Such figures and trend data show that No was back in the lead before the Vow was unveiled, and in all probability the indyref wasn't lost in the last weeks of the campaign, but in the much longer contest.

Second, it is true that the BBC had a very poor indyref but this is a complex story and not one reducible to conspiracy theories. BBC Scotland did not set out a clear direction on the indyref – from then head Ken MacQuarrie to its Head of News and Current Affairs, John Boothman, who went on gardening leave in the last months of the indyref and subsequently left the organisation.

The BBC, like STV to a lesser extent, approached the indyref in a cautious frame of mind, portraying it as if it were a general election between two competing sides. This produced lots of yah-boo heated exchanges of politicians and representatives of both sides issuing claim and counter-claim, while taking through each other in some of the worst stairheid rammies of recent times on our screens.

Missing from all of this was sceptical, unsure, don't know Scotland. This was, as both Yes and No knew, a huge part of the electorate and the swing voters who would decide the contest. The self-organising, DIY Scotland on the Yes side – such as National Collective and Women for Independence – were not given much coverage as they did not confirm to the party model and, also due to balance restrictions, there was no commensurate forces for No. Similarly, the overwhelming balance of businesses were for No, meaning that BBC and STV felt they had no choice but to put Business for Scotland people up, despite its unrepresentative nature and concerns that is was just an official Yes Scotland front. Constraints of balance can erode quality concerns.

BBC Scotland's problems were exasperated by the absence of leadership – which contributed to avoiding taking risks and playing it safe. Another issue was where power and authority sat in the BBC across the UK, with BBC Headquarters in London and senior management under Director General Tony Hall. BBC London management and journalists came to Scotland's indyref anew, needing to catch up speedily and in places showed incomprehension and even, condescension. London types have a default position which believes they are the Big Boys and that everyone else out in 'the sticks' are 'little people' who have been minding the provincial shop when nothing much is going on, and when an important story breaks need to hand it over to the professionals.

In the last months of the indyref BBC London staff were parachuted into Scotland and committed all kinds of errors. In the final weeks of the campaign a group of BBC London staff discussed the pros and cons of independence in BBC Scotland. One person loudly proclaimed: 'Why do any Scots want independence?' bringing another to retort, 'Who would want to be like Denmark?', while a third added: 'This has just been a divisive, horrid referendum. I will be so glad when it is over.' The BBC *Today* programme was broadcast from Scotland in the run-in to the vote. Such was their lack of knowledge, even of their own employer, that one person from the team could not believe there was such an entity as BBC Scotland commenting, 'You mean you make your own programmes here?' This brought numerous tensions into the open inside the BBC between Scottish and London staff. One senior BBC Scotland journalist said to London colleagues in a meeting on indyref coverage: 'You come up here and make a mistake, and at the end of the day, you go home. We have to live it, deal with it and clean up the damage.'

Despite all of the above and more, there has been no BBC internal reflection on their indyref coverage of any kind either at BBC Scotland or London. This was the biggest story in Scotland for decades, a huge UK and international news item. Reflecting on it matters for future coverage, for any second indyref that may happen and in the case of London, the fact that after the Tory 2015 election victory an EU referendum was going to happen – in which Scotland's experience offered huge pointers.

This reveals how BBC Scotland sees politics – as a minority interest, to be fed to specialist and often directly engaged audiences, rather than the general public. In my academic study of the Scottish media in the context of the public sphere, one observer commented on *Newsnight Scotland* that 'there is an assumption of some kind of secret insider knowledge which many of us have no idea of what it is' while Gillian Bowditch of the *Sunday Times* reflected that when she first listened to BBC Radio Scotland it seemed 'a satire and joke... some kind of ridiculous, but brilliant send-up.'[174]

It isn't an accident that programmes such as *Newsnight Scotland*, and *Scotland 2014* and its successors have been as poor as they are. It is a conscious attempt to make politics something that isn't part of the national conversation, unlike football. When the Scottish Parliament was set up in 1999, BBC Scotland along with STV both axed their news and current affairs programmes which had significant public participation – mediated access programmes they are called – such as *Scottish 500*, *Scottish Women* and *Scottish Voices*. They replaced them with programmes such as *Newsnight Scotland* on BBC which was initially a compromise because of *Scottish Six* and *Crossfire* on STV/Grampian about politics for the select few and professional political class.

Scottish broadcasting has changed dramatically in the last 20-25 years. In the late 1980s and early 1990s both BBC and STV's early evening news and current affairs programmes were widely seen across both networks as being of quality.[175] I undertook research into the main BBC and STV programmes – *Reporting Scotland* and *STV at Six* – measuring outputs in 2012 and drawing on internal BBC research from 1992 to track changes over twenty years; in each case two weeks of programmes were recorded and studied.[176]

BBC *Reporting Scotland* over the twenty years saw politics fall from joint first item with 23.8% of coverage to 10.8%, crime fall from 23.8% to 11.8%, while sport became the most prominent subject, rising from 5.7% to 29.0%. With *STV at Six* (in 1992 *Scotland Tonight*) politics fell from top item with 25.5% to 12.4%, crime rose from 8.5% to 14.9%, and sport became the first item – up from 18.1% to 39.1%. Therefore, both programmes saw a dramatic decline in the amount of time spent covering politics, despite the establishment of the Scottish Parliament in 1999. Without this, one can only surmise this fall would have been even more pronounced.

This backstory played into how both BBC and STV approached the indyref. How could it not? Both had spent years being unambitious and unimaginative on how they covered politics and current affairs. Then along came the biggest story in their lives and they were caught unprepared. Subsequently, the BBC – and I suspect STV too – haven't examined and dug up what they got right and wrong, and the wider lessons.

This leaves us with the problem for the BBC of BBC London. They barely show any interest or understanding not only of Scotland, but of the UK that they are meant to reflect. Rather than change, they have been regressing and reflecting the UK back uncritically for years, presumably with the belief that we will all just keep shtum and accept their selectivity. This set of circumstances cannot last indefinitely and something in the future has to give.

Finally, beyond the political lexicon, but with huge social after-effects was the Rangers FC implosion. This sent major shockwaves through parts of Scotland and before the indyref took off, in its later stages was the biggest news story in the country for years. Now Rangers are back in the top league after administration, liquidation and their time in the lowest league, spending four years climbing their way back to the senior level.

A similar picture can be found to the previous two examples. Despite numerous court cases involving Rangers FC and its winding up, the appearance and removal of various owners, and several official inquiries instigated by the football authorities – such as the Lord Nimmo Smith-led inquiry into the use of Employment Benefit Trusts (EBTs) and tax avoidance and evasion – there has been an unwillingness on the part of Rangers FC, as well as the football authorities, to confront the issues which led to the club's collapse.

Scottish football had four years to observe and comment as Rangers FC slowly and painfully made their way through the lower leagues. This was a huge shock not just to them but to the natural order of the game, from the 'Old Firm' dominance and derbies, to the way the media covered the game. In this, it was a challenge and big opening, giving football an opportunity to learn lessons and bring about change. Sadly but not surprisingly, the authorities decided not to do this.

There has been no enquiry into Rangers FC corporate misgovernance, or how to bring about fundamental change to the game. Such activity would open up the stale predictable diet of the 'Old Firm' and their century-plus dominance and stranglehold of the game, which began when Scottish football turned professional in 1893, and when the era of Queen's Park (the great amateurs) passed.[177] Even more damningly, in the last three decades the Scottish senior league has gone from being in 1986 the most competitive in Europe to the joint equal most uncompetitive with Ukraine: a regression that the football authorities show no interest in challenging.

Instead what Scottish football authorities are praying for is a return as quickly as possible to business as usual and to the old discredited, lucrative, populist model based on the circus of the Celtic versus Rangers 'Old Firm' derby. Throughout this, there has been no overt attempt by anyone – Rangers FC, the Scottish Football Association (SFA) and Scottish Professional Football League (SPFL) or another body – to heal the wounds of the past four years. Rangers FC had felt aggrieved and picked upon. In other clubs there is a near-universal loathing of Rangers FC that, however understandable in its origins, isn't healthy or appropriate in the long term. This was on show in the 2016 Hibs versus Rangers Scottish Cup Final where Hibs broke their 114-year drought to finally win the Cup, their fans invaded the pitch after the game to celebrate, and things briefly turned ugly; but after this the mutual incomprehension between large swathes of Rangers fans and everybody else became evident – to our collective loss.[178]

All of this has just been left to fester away and become, football authorities hope at best, just another element of the unsaid, unacknowledged pains and wrongs about football and its place in society. The whole saga has been one where neither Rangers FC nor the football authorities have shown any leadership, boldness, or even honesty in any part – meaning that the whole experience and its disruption hasn't been used creatively or reflectively. Ultimately it isn't beyond the realms of possibilities that something similar could happen again, given unsustainable business models. At the minimum, we are stuck with Scottish domestic football as a 'Groundhog Day' and no visible escape.

These are three very different examples on first examination – covering politics, media and football – each with its own unique qualities. The SNP's current dominance has come about recently – in the last decade with its breakthrough in

2007 and last couple of years, in winning a parliamentary majority and Westminster landslide. BBC and Rangers have existed in a prominent position for many decades – and both have rarely until now had to face any serious challenge to this position: the rise of, say, STV in the 1950s and 1960s, or Celtic FC in the 1960s, not threatening their long-term dominance.

Reflecting on Power and Leadership

SNP MSP and Government Minister for Brexit Mike Russell has written about the Nationalists: 'The SNP has spent very little time thinking and writing about itself and still less analysing its leaders and their background, influence and motivation...'[179] Clearly, the BBC and Rangers FC are very different cases but touch upon a leadership style which is more often than not sadly timid, unchallenging or stagnant. Indeed, historically, Scotland has embraced a form of public leadership which could be described as invisible: either based on precedent and tradition, or in the case of the pre-devolution era, a political class who were most of the time in Westminster.

Sidney Hook in his landmark study of leadership *The Hero in History* differentiated between 'eventful' and 'event-making' leadership – the former where things happen due to other factors, whereas the latter change the context and make things happen.[180] The former has been too often the way of public leadership in Scotland and there have been few examples which challenge this in recent times. One would be Alex Salmond, winning the 2007 and 2011 elections for the Nationalists and undertaking the 2014 indyref, whereas Nicola Sturgeon, inheriting office and the newfound dominance of the SNP, looks to be more the former. It also needs recognition that in different times, on the way up and challenging, and then maintaining your dominant position, that different leadership styles are needed.

All three examples involve powerful forces having to adapt and check their position and place in society. They touch on the weakness of accountability in public life, and of the fragility and tensions in taking responsibility and self-reflection. Maybe, in some ways, there is an element of comfortableness with the existing order of affairs in each. Opening yourself up to understanding your limitations and weaknesses has obvious risks, including the possibilities that you might not retain the position you have earned.

There is also an element of hope that change will just happen, or the issues and barriers blocking you just go away, particularly if you play a patient, waiting game. Finally, there is the backdrop in all of the examples of living in a world some choose to see in binary colours. This contributes to people being less inclined to open up and appeal to waverers, and instead, remain focused on core business or true believers.

In wider society, power rarely talks about itself as power because that draws attention to itself and its position of privilege. Powerful people and institutions think it the natural order of the world that they are where they are. Seldom do they ever use words like 'chance' or 'a lucky break' to explore or describe their journey to success. They tend to just inhabit the power spaces they are in, see the world from their vantage point and have little curiosity about how things appear outside their circles. Numerous studies undertaken of CEOs of top companies in the UK and US, or of bankers, paint a picture of a dysfunctional, narcissistic class getting high on making deals and moving money and fates to the extent it becomes 'something narcotic' and addictive.[181]

Many manifestations can be seen across modern Scotland. For example, the RBS collapse, along with HBOS, and the now much-forgotten Dunfermline Building Society that went out of business in the crash. Scotland had its fair share of 'masters of the universe' and their bloviator apologists who thought everything revolved around them and their world. We have not yet even begun to come to terms with the economic, social and personal damage this perspective has done to Scotland, let alone the world. We could make a small contribution as an increasingly self-governing nation in pro-actively addressing public ethics, behaviour, and even, the role of morality, in banking, finance and business. A much smaller country than Scotland has chosen such a path. Iceland's Parliament set up a special investigative commission into the crash, pursuing criminal bankers and even, up to January 2016, jailing 29 of them.[182]

One area of society in which Scotland has changed fundamentally and irreversibly has been in relation to sectarianism and religious discrimination. Up until the late 1960s, even early 1970s, there were numerous examples of no-go areas for Catholics in employment. Particular areas were notoriously bad, such as the West of Scotland legal profession, while the *Glasgow Herald* (as it was then called) was until not that long ago a vehicle for the Protestant middle classes, both in its editorial outlook and in its employment.

This has utterly changed in today's Scotland. This is not to say that sectarianism doesn't exist in places; it undoubtedly does, particularly, but not exclusively in relation to football. However, one dimension missing in any explanation from any leading public body has been how they have changed, how they did it, and in what ways they are now non-discriminatory. Scotland has gone from being a society of silence and systematic exclusion to one which thinks of itself as liberal and inclusive. That does not seem a very open or enlightening attitude and not one which augers well for the future if it persists.

How Trust in Institutions has Changed

Trust and legitimacy is shifting across the developed world – Scotland included. No longer is there automatic deference and blind trust in institutional power in the West that there once was. Trust has declined across the UK, but very differently for various areas of life. Some groups have even managed to buck the trend of severe decline and held their position but in a way which means respect and status has become more earned and contingent.

Not surprisingly, bankers have taken the biggest hit. In 1983, 90% of the public thought banks were well run, rising to a peak 92% in 1986, falling to 19% in 2012. Newspapers fell from 53% in 1983 to 27% in 2012; the BBC from 72% in 1983 to 49% in 2009 – at the start of the Jimmy Savile scandal – rising to 63% in 2012. Some declines have been gradual: the police falling from a 77% rating in 1983 to 65% in 2012; the NHS going up from 52% in 1983 to 54% in 2012.[183]

Digging into such surveys there is no completely uniform public mood, but instead a differentiated fall in trust – one which became hugely evident in the indyref and Brexit vote. For some this became captured and seen as problematic in Tory MP and Brexiteer Michael Gove's populist comment that 'people in this country have had enough of experts.'[184] Take trust in government: in 2016 this stood at 37% of the UK public, but sits at 54% with households earning over £100k and 26% for those earning under £15k. Similarly, trust in media is 32% of the general public, but 46% for those households earning over £100k, and 34% for those under £15k.[185]

There has also been a rise in trust amongst certain groups towards established news brands. Trust in traditional media rose to 52% in 2016 among 'informed publics', up 14% on the previous survey; 78% of all respondents agreed that 'there is a lot of bad news in the world and I want to be sure I am getting reliable information about it'; while 59% see social media as less reliable than traditional media.[186]

There is unfortunately scant Scottish data on trust in public life – beyond the questions about the Scottish and British Governments. A 2003 Ipsos MORI survey found 96% of Scots thought doctors would tell the truth, 93% teachers, 78% clergy, 77% professors, 76% judges, but only 21% of politicians and 17% of journalists.[187]

If we examine Scottish Government trust levels – as

previously cited in Chapter Four – there is a dramatic trust gap between the Scottish Government and Westminster: the 2016 Scottish Social Attitudes Survey putting the former at 73% versus the latter on 23%. This has been presented in the following manner: 'Scottish Government: most trusted government in Europe' – with the Scottish figure of 73% more than twice the EU average of 31% and way ahead of our nearest neighbours geographically and on trust: Finland on 60% and Denmark on 55%.[188]

The above figures can be seen as Scotland situating itself in a more Nordic setting in relation to government's role in society and public expectations. Another interpretation is also possible. The question here is: 'How much do you trust Scottish Government/British Government to work in Scotland's best long-term interests?' Because of the positioning of 'Scottish Government' in relation to 'British Government', the wording of the question works in favour of the former.

Thus, the Scottish Government does undoubtedly enjoy high levels of trust, but this is a more qualified trust than the Finnish or Danish figures – which are obviously measures of independent countries and not comparing their authority to such a degree with others. A more nuanced set of figures in the same survey showed that 49% of Scots have trust in the Scottish Government to make fair decisions; broken down by gender – 52.4% men and 46.5% women.[189]

A segment of Scotland still yearns for political change which harks back to the past, is simplistic and conservative, and views the last forty years as not just a mistake but as something which should be, and can be, reversed. Sometimes this takes expression at a commentariat level – as in recent sympathy for Jeremy Corbyn's Labour's leadership – which hasn't been polling well either in England, Wales or Scotland.

That's not the impression from some of the country's centre-left commentators. A selection of recent titles give a flavour: 'Love him or loathe him, Jeremy Corbyn has altered the political landscape'[190] (Iain Macwhirter), 'New Labour, not Corbyn to blame'[191] (Joyce MacMillan), 'Why the powers that be fear Jeremy Corbyn'[192] (Kevin McKenna). Such sentiment deliberately overlooks Corbyn's many flaws and weaknesses, and his poor poll ratings and lack of popularity. Instead, they see his leadership through a one-dimensional lens shaped by New Labour perfidy and continued Blairite manoeuvres. It is too simple and too black and white, ignoring that it is possible to see Corbyn's leadership as weak, New Labour as part of the problem, and the entire crisis as shaped by forces much longer and deeper.

The Great Male Leader Syndrome and its Limits

A large part of history has been shaped by men and then written by men. Thomas Carlyle summarised this attitude perfectly when he wrote: 'the history of what man has accomplished in this world... [is]... at bottom the history of the great men who have worked here.'[193]

There is in places in Scotland (as well as other parts of the UK) a radical nostalgia for the world pre-Thatcher, pre-New Labour, but also a politics of turning away from the complexities of the modern world, and looking backward for a lost Eden that never was. This can be seen in the appeal of the Great Leader theory of political change in Scotland – which of course is also one of Great Men.

Take the examples of two of the leading figures of the left over the last fifty years: Gordon Brown and Jimmy Reid. Both were in their more youthful, idealistic years, unapologetically on the radical left, challenging the tired ways of their elders on the left, spellbinding orators at their peak, with devoted followers, and an almost quasi-religious, evangelical, even mystical way of speaking and pulling people into their argument and worldview.

Brown and Reid shared the experience, despite Reid being

nineteen years older, of becoming Rectors of Glasgow and Edinburgh Universities at approximately the same time: the early 1970s. Reid in his Rectoral address at Glasgow on alienation gave the world the stirring phrase: 'A rat race is for rats. We are not rats. We are human beings'[194] which was printed and applauded in the *New York Times* and is still to this day cited and provides inspiration: *The Independent* for example saying when Reid died in 2010 that it was, 'A working class hero's finest speech.'[195]

Gordon Brown at the same time as Rector of Edinburgh University terrified the university establishment. Prior to becoming Rector he led a campaign forcing the institution to disinvest from apartheid South Africa and ran rings round the university authorities. He did so to such an extent that the university gave in, disinvested from South Africa, and when he became Rector they attempted to change the basis of the Rector's role to prevent it ever happening again.[196]

While Reid achieved little else in his tenure as Glasgow Rector, his powerful words still resonate today, of their time and yet timeless. Whereas Brown's Rectoral address is lost in the mists of time; even his 'Red Brown' period of taking on and defeating the Edinburgh establishment has been mostly forgotten.

Both men had much in common. They had a romantic and emotional as well as intellectually informed view of political change, they possessed charisma and even alpha maleness, combined with an attitude of entitlement often found in left-wing male leaders. As with Reid people felt a connection and projection: some of it tribal, familial, and proprietorial. One problem with the Great Male Leader thesis is that it becomes axiomatic as to why such people are Great Men – they just are, it is given, it is almost an article of religious faith, and don't ask why. This continued until Brown became Prime Minister and disappointed many who choose to believe that he was the opposite of Blair – the keeper of the flame and the party conscience.

Jimmy Reid travelled through the Communists, the Upper Clyde Shipbuilders and Labour; standing for the party in Dundee East and losing to the SNP in 1979; was briefly with New Labour and the Scottish Socialists before endorsing the SNP after Alex Salmond became leader in 2004. Indeed, minus Reid's fame, that is a familiar one of a certain generation of Scotland's left. He even had a walk-on part posthumously in the indyref but because he was no longer alive, he was reduced to a one-dimensional figure who could not answer back and didn't confuse or disappoint. He became another in a long lineage of romantic dead Scottish heroes with all his complexities and ambiguities washed away: recent examples include John Smith, Donald Dewar and Robin Cook.

Some portray Alex Salmond as the latest in the pantheon of Great Leaders. Salmond changed Scottish politics and the SNP, but he didn't do it by himself. It was part of a collective effort and leadership that amounted to a 'Team Salmond' who shared common goals and objectives. Thus, Salmond listened to advice, changed his style in 2006-7 after seeing how he won points in debates, but could lose the bigger argument, and dared to reach out and take calculated risks. Salmond took Scotland to the summit of an indyref that another kind of leader might never have reached.

Yet, post-indyref he has gone the way of many other Great Leaders. The indyref was lost because it was snatched away by 'the Vow' and other such skullduggery, there was the perfidy of the BBC and role of then Political Editor Nick Robinson, who Salmond chose to continue a vendetta with for over a year after the vote. The roar of the crowd continues for him, and of course, 'the dream shall never die'. But shorn of 'Team Salmond' he has become Salmond uncensored – and it is less attractive and sometimes not helpful to his successor or to the greater cause.

Brown, Reid, Salmond – from the traditions of Labour, Communists and Nationalists – can be seen as men much bigger than themselves, who attracted true faith defenders, followers and a community who have an interest in the maintenance of the myth. That at times crosses over into adulation and follow-ism, which when combined with power, as in Brown and Salmond, can lead to the slow dulling of political antennae, hubris, and ultimately, their nemesis.

The idea of Great Leaders as a magnet of social change is an obstacle and hindrance. They only really work in the context of those behind them: a movement, team, and shared vision. Without that there is only rhetoric and empty platitudes. The age of the modern leader does not require blind faith or obedience in one figure, or buying into a messianic vision. Instead, it necessitates such negotiation skills, alliance building, flexibility while understanding core values, and the ability to listen. Brown, Reid and Salmond aren't quite as emphatically of the past as, say, Jeremy Corbyn, but they point to an earlier age of certainty and authority.

The Great Leader Show still has allure, not very surprisingly, to budding leaders and their inner circles the world over. Charles Powell, Thatcher's Private Secretary commented after her reign that there was 'something Leninist about Mrs. Thatcher.'[197] His brother Jonathan Powell, Blair's chief of staff, in an off-the-cuff remark said, 'We wanted to move from a feudal to a Napoleonic system [of government].'[198] Neither are models for today's world or democracies, but they do tap into delusions of grandeur, the legacy of imperial arrogance, and an attempt to overcome complexity with centralisation which offers leaders the reassurance that not only do they matter and can affect change, but that they are the crucial missing ingredient. Such a position is clearly a deceit.

One strand of politics that perpetuates the role of the leader and to reduce everything to the pluses and minuses of personalities, is the mainstream broadcast media. The last two UK general elections have hung on the leaders' debates, sucking the oxygen of publicity from the rest of the campaign.

An obvious example of how ridiculous this can be, when UK politics are not presidential, came after the 2015 election and the surprise election of a majority Tory government led by David Cameron: for thirteen months after this, he was gone, a victim of his own desire to hold the EU referendum.

Similarly, the Scottish independence debate in the last stages went viral with the Alistair Darling v Alex Salmond TV debates. The second saw Salmond bruise his way to victory, getting the Yes vote on a late roll that took it briefly into the lead. It wasn't – from either side – the kind of quality argument and debate that you could hang the future of a nation on but was effective as drama, theatre and stagecraft, and these have always been integral parts of politics.

We now know incontrovertibly from the experience of the indyref and Brexit debates and the huge rises in SNP and Corbyn/Labour memberships that political interest and engagement still exist and have captured something in the ether in recent times. One huge factor has been the dearth and blandness of the mainstream, which the indyref and Brexit experiences shook to the core. This necessitates that we create a politics which isn't just about leaders, and in particular, the cul-de-sac world of great men.

The irony for radicals who validate Great Male Leader politics is that it comes from an old-fashioned, discredited version of how to do things. It was rooted in the late 19th and early 20th centuries, and mirrored the industrial discipline, structures and norms of hyper-industrial capitalism. That external world is firmly in the past, but some on the left still cannot, as they say in Denmark 'put away old flags.'[199]

It is not an accident that the mass party of the 20th century was one borne out of this era – hierarchical; disciplined; top-down; with clear roles, rules and boundaries around who could and couldn't be a member. These parties and in particular the social democratic tradition, have struggled to adapt to the age of disruption and a disputatious culture. Indeed, it could be seen as the last and fatal body blow in a series. This proud tradition has been floundering for the last forty years, since the first explosion against the international order with the 1973 OPEC oil price shock. Many still cling to a leadership style which owes more to what is now called 'the golden age' of social democracy (supposedly 1945-70), but says how far we have fallen and politics has shifted.

There is a need for a very different kind of leadership and party – one which will be explored further in later chapters. Suffice to say that in an age of revolt, questioning, anger and dismay at elites we cannot just believe that the answer lies in the Great Male Leader myth. That is as true for Scotland as everywhere. Our society has undergone far-reaching change in recent decades with the fall of old industries and the rise of new ones; new styles of employment and work; changing housing patterns and consumption; more diverse lifestyles and notions of family and relationships, and how we see and relate to authority. The answers to these are not to be found in replicating older, discredited models.

It is also true that what we have been living through and experiencing is a series of inter-connected revolutions. Scotland has not fully embraced this new world and still in places, including elements of the SNP and self-government movement, clings to a wish to return to the world of safety and security which many knew in their more youthful days, or have heard about from their parents or grandparents. This is chasing and yearning for an unreachable chimera. There cannot be a 'Back to the Future' Scotland. We should not want to and nor should we try. Our only possible future, of which there are many different variants, entails embracing doubt, uncertainty, ambiguity and risk. These are some of the carriers of any future Scotland and we should choose actively to embrace them, and see them as our allies of change, not threats. The future is going to be very different from the past, and that is a major positive and opportunity, as well as a challenge.

Chapter Seven:

Home Truths about Home Rule Scotland

The first step is to crack the magic mirror.

Question: Mirror, mirror on the wall, who is the fairest one of all?

Answer: You are.

A country with the widest health inequalities in Western Europe cannot be satisfied with this answer, comforting though it is.

Prof. Graham Watt, General Practice and Primary Care, Institute of Health and Wellbeing, University of Glasgow.

Scotland is often described as having a 'social democratic consensus'. This is sometimes seen as a virtue and sometimes a vice. This opinion can be found on the left when it is portrayed as a barrier or resistance to Thatcherism and New Labour, and on the right, characterising Scotland as a land of inertia, complacency and worse. It is often used as a summary – of difference, intent and values – and as a surrogate term for centre-left politics.

What is Scottish Social Democracy?

These sort of sweeping generalisations seldom dig down deeper. First, they consistently show little interest in what social democracy truly is – its philosophy with inherent strengths and weaknesses, and the relationship between these values and the social democracy of parties that raise its banner. Second, such comment more often than not shows little curiosity about the relationship between words and actions, for example in questioning how effective Scotland's social democracy is at changing lives and outcomes.

Any definition of social democracy has to start from noting its connection to the socialist tradition. In Bernard Crick's words: 'Equality is the value basic to any imaginable or feasible kind of socialism.'[200] Social democracy carries forth this commitment to equality in a manner more adaptive, pragmatic and less systematic in transformational social change. Robin Cook, months before he died, gave expression to these values and their importance:

Top of anyone's list must come solidarity – the principle that the strength of a society is measured by the extent that its rich members support their vulnerable fellow citizens. Next comes our commitment to humanitarian rather than commercial priorities, and the corollary that the market should be managed to meet people's needs rather than the people harnessed to serve the market.[201]

Considering that Scotland in so many ways defines itself as social democratic, it is curious that little thinking or exploration has gone into what this amounts to: its values, ideas, priorities. It turns out in fact that Scottish social democracy is threadbare at a philosophical level, and instead, has chosen to present itself as pragmatic and rather ad hoc.

British social democracy has produced a range of writers and thinkers such as Harold Laski, Richard Tawney, Tony Crosland and Bernard Crick – many of whom have also been elected Labour politicians. This tradition hasn't existed in Scotland in the Labour Party – apart from in its very early days and the Independent Labour Party (ILP) which disaffiliated from the party in 1932. Nor does it in the modern SNP. Some critics have seen this 'social democratic consensus' as a camouflage against any radical politics. Stephen Maxwell wrote in 1976:

The idea that Scottish society is egalitarian is central to the myth of Scottish democracy. In its strong nationalist version, class division is held to be an alien importation from England. In the weaker version, it describes the wider opportunity for social mobility in Scotland as illustrated in 'the lad o'pairts' tradition.[202]

In recent times the SNP have adopted the language of social democracy. The party's website says: 'The SNP are a left of centre, social democratic and progressive party.'[203] Yet, the SNP's adoption of social democracy does not make the SNP first and foremost, a social democratic party. Instead, the SNP's DNA or collective soul is about independence, self-government and statehood. Social democracy is seen as a way of aiding this. For some in the party it has undoubtedly become the means that matter – and independence the best way of nurturing social democracy in an increasingly hostile climate. But for many others, it is a means to aid the ultimate end: the attainment of statehood.

It isn't accidental that the SNP, like Scottish Labour, have contributed very little to social democratic thinking. Rather they have just drawn from the existing well of ideas and often in a very superficial way. Social democracy to most in the SNP is a given and even self-explanatory set of values and ideas. It isn't too harsh to say that the SNP's version of social justice isn't that different from New Labour's: centred on an inclusive national vision where conflict and division are transcended by a 'one nation Scotland' in the words of Gerry Mooney (invoking Disraeli's 'one nation Toryism' and Ed Miliband's flirtation with 'one nation' Labour).[204] In the SNP's 2016 Scottish Parliament election manifesto, Nicola Sturgeon reduced 'my vision for Scotland' to a nation 'fair, equal and prosperous'[205]: the sort of generalities nearly everyone can sign up to.

This matters because across the developed world social

democracy isn't in the best of health. Moreover, in Western Europe, not one social democratic party is in a good state and on the ideological and political front foot. Neither is this the case in the much vaunted Nordics, or Germany, France, Spain or Italy. Any belief that Scotland has somehow mysteriously bucked this trend with our 'social democratic consensus' and the rise of the SNP is sadly delusional.

Scotland's sense of social democracy links to its centre-left mindset and difference from the rest of the UK. Too much ink has been spent over the years trying to measure, maximalise or minimalise this difference through a literal interpretation, and number crunching, of Scottish Social Attitudes Survey material.

This effort produced a plethora of articles in the run-up to the indyref and afterwards with titles such as 'Scotching a Myth: Scotland is not as left-wing as you think it is'[206] (Alex Massie) and 'The SNP won't admit the truth on most things, Scots and English see eye to eye'[207] (Fraser Nelson). The argument goes that on a number of key indicators of public opinion there are few substantive differences between the Scots and English. Nelson cited that in both Scotland and England 33% suspect that 'most people on the dole are fiddling, in one way or another' and that the two nations weren't that different in their Euroscepticism, with 41% of Scots and 43% of English supporting keeping the UK in the EU but with less powers; that last point didn't exactly turn out well.

Similarly support for a benefits cap in a YouGov 2013 survey was 74% across the UK and 82% in Scotland, while support for removing benefits from those who decline the chance to work was 76% across the UK and 81% in Scotland.[208] A BBC survey in 2015 found that 64% of people in Scotland wanted immigration reduced or stopped completely, while the UK figure was 70%.[209]

However, political cultures are about more than headline figures and more detailed research points to a very different climate in Scotland. A detailed survey by the Migration Observatory at Oxford University into Scottish attitudes found significant differences in answer to the question: 'Would you say that it is generally good or bad for Scotland that people come to live here from outside the UK?' Scots answered this 49:32 good, the English and Welsh 49:35 for bad. Underneath these headlines there was more difference: the most common single response in England was the most extreme bad response with 16%, while the most extreme good had 4%; in Scotland these figures were 9% and 8.5% respectively.[210]

The difference debate has been highlighted in the last few years by the level of UKIP support and Euroscepticism in Scotland compared to England and the rest of the UK. In the 2014 European Parliament elections UKIP finished first across the UK with 26.6% of the vote: this translated into 28.1% and first place in England and a mere 10.5% and fourth place in Scotland – although still enough to give one MEP, David Coburn.[211]

The 2016 European referendum was won by 51.9% to 48.1% for leave. England voted 53.4% to 46.6% to leave – a lead of just under two million votes; while Scotland voted 62.0% to 38.0% to remain. This is an English lead of 6.8% for leave and a Scottish lead of 24.0% for remain: a difference gap of 30.8%.[212] If every single Scottish voter who turned out had voted for remain it would not have been enough to turn the overall result. Similarly, if Scottish turnout had been at indyref levels and split the way it did, it still would not have been enough.

Then there are the diverging patterns of UK general elections which increasingly exist in name alone. The 2015 contest illustrated that not only are homogeneous elections a thing of the past, so are nationwide elections. Instead, there are Scottish, Welsh and Northern Irish contests, along with a variety of sub-English contests – the North, Midlands, South West and London for example.

The Scottish result was as different from the rest of the UK as imaginable. While the SNP vote rose 30% from 19.9% to 49.97%, Labour fell 17.7%, whereas across the UK it rose by 1.5%; the Tories went down 1.8% while across the UK they went up by 0.8%; and UKIP failed to make an impact. The only real UK constant was the universal kicking the Lib Dems got – crashing 11.3% in Scotland and 15.2% across the UK. The Scottish Labour vote of 24.3% was their lowest since 1918 (although worse was still to come); the Tories 14.9% their lowest since 1865 (although they were away to experience a small upswing in the following year's Scottish Parliament elections).[213]

Social Justice Nation?

Scotland has a language of social justice and social democracy, but the real picture of the nation is much more complex than rhetoric would suggest. A Joseph Rowntree Foundation Report *A Scotland without Poverty* declared what should be completely obvious, but isn't: 'Poverty is costly, risky and wasteful for those who experience it – and for the economy and wider society.'[214]

Poverty and inequality are a product of numerous factors – clearly many of which are beyond the current powers of the Scottish Government. In 2014-15 according to official figures relative poverty stood overall at 940,000 (18% of population) after housing costs; in the working-age population 600,000 (19% of working-age population); while relative child poverty was 220,000 (22% of all children) and relative pensioner poverty was 120,000 (12% of pensioners).[215]

Patterns of poverty, deprivation and affluence are heavily shaped by geography mapped by the Scottish Index of Multiple Deprivation published every four years.[216] The most recent figures for 2016 identified the most deprived area as Ferguslie Park, Paisley, for the second time in succession. Near to the area are Phoenix Retail Park and Glasgow Airport – both growing areas of employment. A small spillover employment-wise from these would have a huge impact on Ferguslie Park, but such are the disconnections of poverty aided by poor local transport and employment recruitment that local residents do not necessarily benefit. Just to underline this, the most affluent area in all Scotland is Lower Whitecraigs in East Renfrewshire – a mere eight miles from Ferguslie Park, but existing in separate worlds.

Educational inequality remains a problem and in many respects is getting worse. First, take the example of further and higher education access. A mere 8% of 18-year-old Scots from the poorest areas get to university compared to 14% from Northern Ireland, 15% Wales and 17% England. Sir Peter Lampl, Chair of the Sutton Trust said of these figures that 'Scotland faces a shocking access gap.'[217]

Second, the thorny issue of private education. The proportion of Scottish students at the four ancient universities who were privately educated was 19% in 2004 and rose to 26% in 2014-15. The sum total of 71% of privately educated school entrants gained a place at one of the four ancient universities; the figure for state school entrants was 29%.[218]

Third, a comparison of student debt between Scotland and England shows marked differences. Average debt in England per student five years ago was £16,200, but is now approaching £45,000. This has produced a situation where Scottish students have the lowest debt per student in the Anglophone nations, whereas England have the highest: a stark difference.

Table 7.1. Anglophone nations with average graduate debt per student (2015)[219]
- England – £44,500
- Wales – £19,000
- Northern Ireland – £18,200
- Scotland – £9,400
- United States – US$29,000 (£20,500)
- Canada – CAN$28,500 (£15,000)

- Australia – AUS$39,700 (£20,900)
- New Zealand – NZ$50,000 (£23,300)

This led *The Independent* to comment that 'The Scottish higher education system has long been looked up to with envy from other parts of the UK – and further afield – for its top-class institutions, student funding system, and no tuition fees.'[220] The above figures look like major plus points of the Scottish higher education system and are a deliberate outcome of policy choices. However, from another perspective what they do is entrench middle class advantage. Middle class students in Scotland are likely to leave university with less debt than other comparable groups in the UK; a deliberate consequence of Scottish policy decisions in choosing to target middle class subsidies over other policy goals.

Another arena Scotland has made choices on is universalism. Universal benefits are widely seen as more progressive by buying in the middle classes (as the 'no tuition fees' policy does). There are grounds for this argument: but what often isn't freely admitted is that universal services tend to favour the middle classes and not the poor. In any actual situation rather than just looking at the abstract principle, there are trade-offs and choices about spending. What can be universal is always a form of choice, and therefore, of priority and ultimately, selection.

Jeane Freeman, now a SNP MSP, wrote in *The National* in January 2016: 'Universalism as a means of social provision means that we decide something is a fundamental part of the society we want and therefore we should make sure it is provided for everyone...'[221] This is true of public goods such as free education and health, but the statement that, if 'we abandon the key principles of universalism... we give up on the idea of a fairer, more just and prosperous Scotland' isn't based on any facts, but instead on an article of faith.[222]

The experience of universal services is relevant to this

discussion. Even free health care – a fundamental public good and a gauge of a civilised society – works to the advantage of the middle classes and systematically against poor people and neighbourhoods. This has been underlined by research undertaken by the Deep End GP Group, a network of GPs and health professionals who work in Glasgow's East End, the most deprived part of the city. They cite figures that show, setting a baseline of 100 for the most deprived tenth of the city's population, that there are more than double the number of health consultations (220) in the most affluent tenth of the city population. There is a flatter environment in funding, with the most affluent tenth only slightly higher at 107 but the second most affluent tenth the highest at 134.[223] From this experience they have called for what Professor Michael Marmot described as 'proportionate universalism'.[224] Scottish Government independent poverty adviser Naomi Eisenstadt has endorsed this approach:

...it's about flattening the gradient so that the difference between richest and poorest isn't so great. It's that if you only work with the very poorest you miss a lot of the need... but services for everybody often miss the poorest, and services for the poor often aren't good services.[225]

An unconditional defence of blanket universalism isn't a policy of social justice, but instead hurts the poor and rewards the middle class. We desperately need more nuanced and, on occasion, targeted and intelligent policy and practice that really makes a difference.

The Real Divided Scotland: The Scar of Inequality

Scotland is disfigured by systemic inequality. This is the result of decades and indeed centuries of economic policy, the workings of capitalism, and the ultra-rich engaging in self-preservation and investments. The top 2% of households own 17% of personal wealth; the top 10% own 44% of personal wealth; the least wealthy 30% own 2% of personal wealth. To put the scale of this wealth into perspective the sum total of the wealth of private households in the period studied 2010-12 was £714 billion: at a time when Scottish GDP was £150 billion. The wealthiest 10% own nearly three quarters of all financial wealth in the country; the poorest 30% have no financial wealth at all.[226]

The UK, as widely known, is one of the most unequal countries in the OECD. According to Gini figures, which measure the scale of inequality in a society, the UK comes 29th out of 34 countries, with only five countries more unequal: USA, Turkey, Chile, Mexico and Israel. That means that on these figures the UK is the most unequal European country in the OECD. If Scotland were an independent country it would rank 20th in this table – behind Korea and France, but ahead of Canada and Italy.[227]

Aiding and supporting a political environment which begins to formulate policies and ideas to attempt to address inter-generational, indeed, cross-centurial social injustice and the gathering of privilege by the super-rich and monied elites isn't exactly an easy task. But we hinder ourselves in this if we tell ourselves that Scotland is already a land which champions and acts on social justice. That would be complacent and self-congratulatory anywhere. It just happens in Scotland to be a mixture of denial and disinterest in the reality presented to us and strangely, a continued disinterest in developing a programme that scrutinises and challenges those with power and wealth.

Scotland's big-ticket devolution achievements are often presented as part of the official story of our social democratic polity. Therefore, free tuition fees, free care for the elderly, and the council tax freeze, have been seen by many as proof of our progressive credentials. They are proof of our different choices.

Yet, none of these help poorer families or disadvantaged Scotland. Instead, they skew resources towards the middle classes and above-average income Scotland – all wrapped in the language of social justice and universalism.

Making the case for an explicit Social Justice Agenda from Rich to Poor

In a sense, such totemic policies being constantly cited even acts as a block on social justice because they are seen by many as proof that Scotland is already doing what it can and prioritising the war on social injustice. They thus can provide an obstacle to actual action and to more successful measures on dealing with social justice. A social justice Scotland would address a number of detailed areas[228]:

- The challenge of affordable and available childcare and early education. Scotland has lagged behind England for the devolution era on this, missing out on Sure Start, and is only beginning to prioritise and put funding into this.
- Begin to address in-work poverty. The Living Wage is one part of the answer to in-work poverty and there is a need to develop other approaches from in-work training and support for the lowest paid and least qualified.
- Younger adults who are working and/or renting from a private landlord, are more likely than in the past to be in poverty. This requires policies on transitioning for young adults from education to work, and addressing how the housing market is increasingly failing large parts of society.
- The challenge of educational inequalities. Some of Scotland's most high-profile decisions have entrenched and widened such inequalities, privileged privately educated pupils increasingly know how to work the system, and the poor and disadvantaged are left at the margins.
- The economic and social exclusion of people with

disabilities. They face disadvantage and discrimination in work, welfare and society, underscored by a much higher incidence of poverty.

- The increasingly punitive British welfare system. One huge humanitarian challenge is the widespread use of sanctions. This necessitates greater access to hardship payments, with the Scottish Welfare Fund remaining a source of support. But for how long and to what extent can Scottish welfare decisions mitigate against the harsh climate of UK welfare policy?

- Finally, start articulating a social justice vision of the future which isn't just about the poor and disadvantaged and widening opportunity. We increasingly need to deal with the anti-social behaviour of those at the top of society materially – 'the over-class' – the opposite of the underclass. Measures would include serious land reform, maximum salaries in the public sector and addressing corporate misgovernance.

A combination is needed of two dimensions – policies and action – to create a philosophy of social justice for the 21st century. It is testimony to our conservatism and complacency that nearly two decades into devolution this has not been attempted. There is a propensity in first Labour, and now SNP, to think they don't need to define such a term because Scotland has a consensus and that each party at its peak has somehow captured it.

A suggestion for a meaningful version of social justice – one capable of aligning government, public bodies and business and having public opinion behind it would include the positives of a more equal society, recognising the need to widen opportunities and tackle disadvantages and to aid an inclusive idea of citizenship where every individual has rights and responsibilities, as well as to address the issues of inherited and unearned income and wealth, and its undue power and influence in society.

Secondly, not everything that is wrong and unfair in Scotland can be addressed immediately. A sense of priorities, timescales, and the ultimate destination and character of a socially just nation is essential: in short, we need a road map and an understanding of what the direction and different choices available on the way might be. Strangely social democratic parties across the West have a poor record at acknowledging this strategic terrain – opening them up to endless bouts of short-term pragmatism and being blown off course by crises.

Scotland's Elite World

The Scottish super rich exist in a world apart from most of us. The scale of their wealth is illustrated by the annual 'Sunday Times Rich List'; its 2016 version had 72 Scots in its list of 1,000 individuals.[229] Scotland's super-rich is headed up by the Grant Gordon family – whisky distillers who own the Glenfiddich brand – worth £2.16 billion (49th UK); Mahdi-Al-Tajir who owns Highland Spring and is worth £1.735 billion (60th UK); and Sir Ian Wood of the Wood Group worth £1.4 billion (72nd UK).

Land ownership has become an increasingly high-profile subject and controversy – aided by the pioneering work of Andy Wightman, now MSP, as well as a host of other campaigners and people down the years. After an initial impetus in the 1999-2003 Scottish Parliament, momentum for reform was lost and the SNP have shown for a long time little appetite or feel for the subject. Eventually they came forward with land reform proposals which form the basis of the Land Reform Bill 2015 which have been seen as so tepid they were even defeated at the SNP Annual Conference in October 2015 by 554 to 427 votes.[230]

The organisation Global Justice Now identified seven global capitalists who own large tracts of land in Scotland who are guilty of human rights abuses. These are Anders Povlsen, Rio Tinto, Paul van Vlissingen, the Vestley family, the de Spoelberch family, Majid Jafar and Lovat Investments Ltd. Their activities include unregulated fracking, land grabs, privatisation of national parks in Africa, and large-scale union busting.[231]

Land in Scotland and the UK is just another commodity: another asset to be put on the balance sheet or used as a tax right-off. Land ownership bodies such as Scottish Land and Estates have in recent years become very nervous about the tide of opinion. They and other defenders of unequal land ownership and opponents of reform regularly use over the top, fairly offensive language in a vain attempt to stem the winds of change.

Lord William Astor, David Cameron's father-in-law, owns the Tarbert estate on the Isle of Jura which comprises 18,736 acres, and wrote in *The Spectator* in May 2015 of 'a Mugabe-style land grab' where estates might be 'nationalised' or where land owners 'made to feel so unwelcome that we have to sell up.' He even mused that opposition to land owners like himself might be because of other factors, asking: 'Is it because we don't sound Scottish? We should not all have to speak like Rob Roy.'[232]

Even Scottish Land and Estates said such remarks were 'distinctly unhelpful'[233] – which is a bit rich coming from an organisation which regularly uses inflamed rhetoric over the most mild land reform proposals – talking of, for example, 'raw, anti-landowner sentiment' and 'incessant clamour for radicalism.'[234] Worse, the *Daily Telegraph* and *Daily Mail* regularly run headlines invoking the threat of a 'Zimbabwe land grab' and have even compared proposals to 'social engineering' in Mugabe's country, North Korea and Cuba.[235]

Scotland's Public Sector Elite

The highly paid in Scotland's public sector do not come into the millionaire class, but they live a very different life from the people they are meant to serve and are ultimately accountable to. The burgeoning pay of Scotland's university principals is one example. Top paid is Professor Jim MacDonald, Principal of Strathclyde University – at the time of writing on £343,000 per year.[236] He was recently the beneficiary of the purchase by the university for him of a £1,180,000 five-floored luxury townhouse in Park Circus, Glasgow, and £300,000 – all public monies – to refurbish it. This when the university already had a grace and favour residence in the city which the Principal could use – which the university ultimately sold.[237]

It is a lucrative closed market to get into. Professor Sir Timothy O'Shea, Principal of Edinburgh University is paid £289,000; Professor Pete Downes, Principal of Dundee University £261,000; Professor Petra Wend of Queen Margaret University £228,000; and Professor Louise Richardson of St. Andrews University £294,000. Alastair Sim, Director of Universities Scotland, defended the situation parroting the usual line: 'Decisions on senior pay in universities have strong lines of accountability and oversight by the governing body which includes staff and student members.'[238]

Police Scotland, a creation of the SNP administration, are another example of largesse at the top. The new Chief Constable Philip Gormley is paid £218,280 per year.[239] He has numerous perks including rent-free accommodation for the first six months in post in Tulliallan Castle, Kincardine, which was then agreed at a rate of £599 rent per month, £61.50 utility bills and £129 council tax – coming to £789.50 per month.[240]

Under Police Scotland's first head, Sir Stephen House, a re-organisation designed to save monies and make efficiencies produced four deputy chief constables and seven assistant chief constables. This when the Met in London have, with three million more people under its head, one deputy and four assistant commissioners. Public sector 'modernisation' often seems to lead to more chiefs, and more highly paid chiefs at that, and to fewer frontline staff and services.

Scotland's highest paid public servant outside of universities is Douglas Milligan, Chief Executive of Scottish Water on £245,000[241]. There are 64 individuals in the Scottish Government, quangos and public bodies who earn over £100,000 plus in salary (excluding NHS staff and extra remunerations in bonuses and pension contributions). A further 251 local government staff earn over £100,000 per year, 27 over £150,000, and four over £200,000.[242]

None of these public sector figures compare with excesses at the top of the private sector. A study by the High Pay Centre identified the highest paid boss in Scotland as David Nish, CEO of Standard Life who was paid £5.5 million in 2014; Martin Gilbert, CEO of Aberdeen Asset Management received a £4,757,000 salary and Ross McEwan, CEO of RBS was paid £1,851,000.[243] Just to illustrate what a different world it is at the top, Nish announced in 2015 that he was leaving Standard Life and was rewarded with a £25 million golden handshake after leading the company for six years.[244]

Is there a Distinct Scottish Elite?

Scotland has inequality and a disproportionately rewarded group at the top of the pay tree, both in public and private sectors. But is there actually such a thing as a Scottish elite? A recent David Hume Institute report found that 23% of Scotland's elite went to private schools – including 57% of university Principals and 45% of senior judges – in a country where 5.6% of children of secondary school age get private education.[245]

Scotland's business elite – the CEOs of the top 100 companies – saw 42% attend a school outside the UK and

31% attend a university outside the UK. Those who attended a UK school were 28% privately educated, and of those who attended a UK university, 62% obtained a degree from one of the elite universities. Scotland's media senior positions – top executives and commentators – were 29% privately educated, while about one-third attended an elite university, including half who attended one of Scotland's four ancient universities and 6% Oxbridge. In comparison, UK media elites were 45% Oxbridge educated and 74% attended a Russell Group university. In Scotland's senior civil service positions, nine out of ten went to one of Scotland's ancient universities, Oxbridge or Russell Group universities.

The report concludes by asking if there is a distinct Scottish elite and does not give a clear-cut answer: 'The top of Scottish society is significantly unrepresentative of the Scottish population – though less so than the top of British society.'[246]

A large part of public life, consultation and dialogue is a contentious, self-reinforcing cycle within these groups. A Jimmy Reid Foundation report 'Not By The People' undertook an analysis of 750 people appointed to public bodies and 2000 plus witnesses who gave evidence to Scottish Parliament committees over the past five years.[247] It found that 67% of those giving evidence to committees and 71% of the public appointments came from those earning incomes over £34,000, when this represents 13% of all Scots. In contrast, 11% of public sector appointments and 3% of committee witnesses came from those earning under £24,500, whereas 70% of all Scots are in this group.

Stephen Reicher, report author, said such an elite system led to politics by 'parachuting' into people's lives and that this 'was wrong in practice as well as principle' and 'makes good ideas less likely to succeed.'[248] This is one of the many dynamics of the 'missing Scotland' and reinforces the processes of exclusion and silencing, which removes huge swathes of Scotland from the political processes.

The picture painted in this chapter is of little recent change in post-devolution Scotland in relation to economic and social inequalities, wealth and power. Too many of the same professions, people and elites still run things, make decisions talking to people just like themselves, from the same backgrounds, schools, universities and interests, and face too little scrutiny or formal accountability.

However, we can note too that too much of Scotland's public debate is skewed, and geared towards a mixture of the superficial and the binary. These include a propensity to pose any situation as either triumphant and filled with swagger, or doubting our capacity to bring about change. Thus, our education is either the best or the worst in the world, our public services are either the envy of the UK, or a laggard unable or unwilling to change, or the current SNP Government is beyond reproach, a champion of social justice and competency, or alternatively, keeping Scotland on hold, complacent, and worse, even deceitful.

Missing is the combination of nuance, the Scotland in between these extremes, and also a debate of substance, which goes beyond soundbites and slogans. Similarly, inquiry, curiosity and even the possibility of changing your mind based on debate or fact, are also strangely absent. Instead, too much of political engagement has been about appearance, image, empty rhetoric, not digging below the surface, or where you or your opponent stand in relation to a political party or the constitutional debate.

This situation does not help anyone in Scotland, except those who have power, influence and are insiders: the elites, political classes and those who gain from the maintenance of the domestic status quo. This is, in numerous ways, a continuation of a very long tradition in society, public life and politics – previously reinforced by Westminster control and its one step removed distance from Scotland. The Westminster years of administrative devolution from 1885 to 1999, and in particular, from Tom Johnston's reign as Secretary of State for Scotland from 1941-45 saw the Scottish lobby act as an increasingly effective corporate interest group whose aim was to wrestle monies, resources and rewards out of Westminster.

This contributed to a mindset which aided a politics of dependency and paternalism – looking to get monies out of Westminster with the aim of then spreading that largesse around Scotland. This attitude has been carried forward too much into the formative years of the Scottish Parliament under both Labour and the SNP: an inability to see the answers to our problems in ourselves and a capacity to reach for blaming others about our own shortcomings. Some of this was evident in the indyref and in the immediate period afterwards, around the Smith Commission on greater powers to the Scottish Parliament.

Letting go of such assumptions is scary and threatening. The default position of blaming others and making poses towards Westminster has in past times gained a rich dividend and worked, but at a cost. It has contributed to us not growing up and taking responsibility, infantilising ourselves. Letting go is fraught with all sorts of insecurities and doubts, yet that is the way of the modern world. We have no option but to embrace it, but we need a better set of criteria than just assuming our innate progressive credentials will look after us. We need to have a rigorous set of ideas, values and philosophies to guide us, to help create a Scotland of the future where power and elites are held to account. That future doesn't come about by accident, it requires effort, imagination and boldness: in sum, a radical Scotland of words and action.

Chapter Eight:

Scotland as a Mongrel Nation and Culture

What is the point of culture? Culture functions ultimately to ensure the preservation and continuity of a people… Culture does not make people. People make culture.

Chimamanda Ngozi Adichie, We Should All Be Feminists, 2014

A day or two ago I had a lamb bhuna in Lochranza, Arran and walked past a lot of Dorran bungalows with Gaelic names, several with big black 4 by 4s parked in their driveways, which these days is the mark of having arrived. I don't mention these details to disapprove of them, though the curry was disgusting, but simply to suggest that our culture or ways of being are so heterodox these days – heterodox and also similar – that to define one against another becomes very difficult. Perhaps the main thing about Scottish culture is that it wants to be seen as different to English culture. Which in a hundred little ways it is – a hundred little ways that divide us as against the thousands of bigger ways that connect us.

Ian Jack, personal communication, August 2016

Culture is everywhere about us in the modern world. Therein lies its power and the problem. For if it is universal, that raises the dilemma of defining what it is and what it is not? The same is true of Scottish culture that, in a reductionist sense, could be defined as culture that happens in this country – which is self-explanatory and doesn't get us very far.

Culture is like many other over-used words – confusing, polemical and open to numerous different interpretations. The writer James Clifford observed that it is 'a deeply compromised idea', but one which he 'cannot yet do without.'[249] A useful reference point – Raymond Williams' A-Z of words and isms *Keywords* identifies three different interpretations of culture.[250]

First, there is culture as individual enrichment and growth, as in saying 'someone is cultured' – which is meant as a compliment and term of approval. Second, there is culture as a group's particular way of life and shared attributes – from Scottish and youth culture to multi-culturalism. Third, there is culture as activity, in other words, the act of enjoying or consuming something cultural. To these could be added a fourth – culture as a way of describing and understanding organisations and institutions such as, say, the culture of the British Labour Party, European Union or Tesco. This is something distinct from the formal rules and structures which contribute to how a body operates and feels.

Every time we use the word 'culture' we are drawing upon some or all of the above meanings. This can often happen without the actual meaning being made explicit by the person in question and thus culture's very ubiquity, saturating every corner of modern societies, can lead to problematic conversations and miscommunication.

'Culture' is naturally a term utilised by those who work and inhabit the world of arts and culture. But it is also used by those who see themselves as part of 'the creative class' – that amorphous term which includes arts and culture, but also advertising, marketing, design and fashion and many other activities. It has also been adopted by business gurus and consultants looking to be change agents, and to pitch for lucrative contracts. Politicians increasingly invoke it as well, trying to understand a world beyond managerialism and to work out why 'the levers of government' don't work the way they are meant to. 'Culture' here is often part of the mythical magic silver bullet which will supposedly effect change.

What are Scottish Cultures?

The characteristics of Scottish culture are interwoven with identities, traditions, histories and collective memories. Scottish identity has been endlessly written about and ruminated upon. While it has been taken to be self-evident it has often only been explored in its numerous component parts. Moray MacLaren in his richly rewarding and enjoyable *Understanding the Scots* published in 1956, asked 'Who are the Scots?' meaning in relation to identities and cultures not to DNA, and answered:

One of the many possible answers to that question is that they are about as confusing a collection of opposites as you are likely to meet anywhere in the world. They have more internal differences of characters and opinion than almost any other nation.[251]

This of course draws upon the well-known trope of the 'Caledonian Antisyzygy' of George Gregory Smith, black and white Scotland, and the mantra of 'divided Scotland, which has been articulated throughout most of our history, and still has resonance to this day.' Thus, in the early days of the Scottish Parliament Iain Macwhirter talked of 'the Jekyll and Hyde Parliament' as it struggled to find its feet, and in particular, battled on issues previously unsaid and hidden from the public gaze.[252] Neal Ascherson described the limits of the 'St. Andrew's Fault' – the difference between the dreams and fears of the Parliament and country.[253]

More recently, there has been anger, confusion and dismay from some pro-unionist opinions during the first indyref campaign and its aftermath. From the other side, some pro-independence supporters have equally bemoaned and demonised pro-union sentiment, in what can only be seen as a brutal contest for legitimacy and attempting to delegitimise opponents in a zero-sum game. Politics is a tribal battlefield, filled with sworn enemies for some.

An examination of this manifestation down the years is beyond the scope of this book. Suffice to say, Scottish writers have with great enthusiasm and gusto explored such terrain, but have deliberately held off in recent times from summarising the characteristics of Scottish culture. Part of this is a conscious decision. After years of being stereotyped by a host of clichés, there then followed the embracing of the kailyard, tartan and the sentimental in the late 19th and early 20th centuries, and in the 1970s and 1980s, a critique and distancing from this led by Tom Nairn's description of 'the tartan monster'.[254] Now it seems there is a new sentiment, of trying to understand these phenomena, but not be boxed in. A similar debate has been taking place among writers about the category 'Scottish literature' which many see as limiting and a ghetto. One Scottish writer said about defining culture: 'If such a thing did exist, it would be wrong.'

The Wikipedia definition of 'Culture of Scotland' is 'The culture of Scotland refers to the patterns of human activity, symbolism associated with Scotland and the Scottish people'[255] – a tautology that doesn't really get us very far. Even books which attempt to be guides and compendiums of contemporary Scottish culture choose to not offer any overarching definitions coming after Nairn's 'tartan monster' watershed. This is the case with *A Companion to Scottish Culture*[256] first published in 1981 and completely revised in 1993, and the more staid, *Scotland: A Concise Cultural History*[257] published in 1993.

Faced with this deliberate act of non-defining Scottish culture I asked a range of cultural voices and authorities to summarise their views on Scottish culture, allowing for all the above considerations and complexities. A sizeable majority chose to say that they would prefer not to, putting forth the argument made above. However, a few put their heads above the parapet and some even spoke at considerable length. Extracts from a couple of these reveal something, and identify the inherent problems in such exercises.

First, the writer, activist and campaigner Alastair McIntosh:

What is Scottish culture? For me, Scottish culture derives from a collectively held consciousness of being a community of place. Of being a 'country' in the old sense, a bioregion, out of which grows a social sense of nationhood as community writ large. From there, arises the vexed question: how far does such a nation have political agency? Do we have the outward mechanisms of state sufficient to express this inner cohesion of soul? And the 'we' in all of this? Who is the 'we' of such a culture, if we are never to forget our traditions of hospitality and fostership towards the lost, the victimised and the refugee? Here's a cultural principle. A person belongs inasmuch as they are willing to cherish, and be cherished, by this place and its peoples. That egalitarianism is why, at our best, we refuse to validate such domination systems as social class privilege. Our artists and minstrels, our crafters and grafters, our intellectuals and theologians, our folks who express the raw spiritual verve of a bardic politics – all of these are participants in handing down the ethos that, 'a man's a man for a' that'.[258]

In a very different tone and reflection *the Guardian's* Ian Jack offers the following thoughts:

Our old friend 'Caledonian antisyzygy' must take a good share of the blame. This is really no more than a piece of literary speculation, first put forward by an academic, G. Gregory Smith, in 1919 and later taken up by Hugh MacDiarmid and others who were persuaded – even entranced – by the idea that duality or a tension between opposites was a hallmark of Scottish people/society/culture. The customary literary references will be familiar to you: RLS's Dr. Jekyll and Mr. Hyde, *Hogg's* Confessions of a Justified Sinner. *I'm pretty certain that other literatures contain just as many examples of two-people-in-one:* Dracula, Frankenstein, *etc., but for some reason or other Caledonian Auntie Thingummy developed a real hold among the Scottish or Edinburgh intelligentsia. Protestant v. Catholic, Highlands v. Lowlands, Unionists v. Nationalists. Maybe it began as an explanation of failure – 'this is what's wrong with us'. Latterly, I suspect, it's been worn as a badge of pride, like a patient with an interesting disease.*[259]

Finally, the cultural commentator Joyce McMillan, resisted offering any interpretation, but in so doing offered a contextual landscape:

I think all living cultures are in a constant state of dynamic change, and can – should – never be 'defined', although they can be sketched at any given moment. There is nothing unusual about Scotland in that respect. We simply have to fend off the danger of metropolitan perceptions which would prefer Scottishness to be a non-threatening dead culture, a quaint piece of exotica pickled in nostalgia. Fortunately, Scotland's artists are having none of that.[260]

The three above quotes give very different takes – the first, romantic, even invoking the spiritual and the unknowable; the second, the many multiplicities and divides, and the third, Scotland's uniqueness as part of a universal exploration about art, culture and meaning. The first two are rich in metaphor and mythology. All three deeply share a common rejection of the cultural and political values of Britain over these last forty years, while in different ways wanting to look out from Scotland to the world.

The Culture of Politics and the Politics of Culture

One political definition of culture in Scotland has roots and inspiration in the post-1945 uplift of huge swathes of the people of this country – as well as of people across the United Kingdom. The post-war opening of opportunity, choice and greater living standards came with an implicit cultural set of aspirations – of working class Scots previously held down by poverty, ignorance and exploitation becoming more full citizens and in so doing being enriched and contributing back to the culture of society.

Like many of Scotland's stories, it is one still waiting to be fully written and realised. What has been explored sometimes to near-exhaustion has been the undermining and closing off of that world post-1979. The pain, discomfort and loss which transpired from this, almost amounted to a psychological wound in the collective soul of parts of Scotland. The scale of this has defined much of the last forty years from politics overall to providing a backdrop for the home rule and independence debates, and for much of our cultural considerations – from novels, to plays, films and TV dramas.

The official story of Scotland post-1979 in politics and culture runs something like this: in 1979 politics were blocked due to the first devolution referendum and then the subsequent election of the Thatcher Government. Instead, artists, writers and cultural figures reimagined and reclaimed a different Scotland. This was a place which was more autonomous, self-confident, and increasingly unlike the rest of the UK. Following on from this the newly created, imagined Scotland fed into and shifted our politics, slowly changing how we thought about ourselves and practised our politics.

This for many in the Scotland of the home rule and independence movements has become a compelling story, even in places the conventional wisdom. It is not hard to see why. It offers a route of change which is more interesting than electing Westminster MPs and at a time when Labour were dominant and conservative, and the SNP small and divided. It offered the prospect of a diversion around these forces and an alternative story.

It also happens to be an account with a few problems. First, how politics has understood culture post-1979 has been very superficial. Political parties, elected representatives and leaders of the anti-Tory parties were not exactly well-versed in matters cultural. They took a few hints that there was a change in the weather post-1979 in theatre, novels, music and the visual arts. But beyond say the Proclaimers' music or 7:84 and Wildcat Theatre Company, the radical political content of it at the time would be pretty thin to near non-existent to them.

Second, cultural voices would throughout this period have an equally unrich political knowledge. It would in left cultural circles be based on the idea of Scotland as socialist, collectivist, and even workerist. In some accounts, what would be holding back Scotland from realising its radical potential would be the leadership of Labour here and its dependency on London. There would in the political theatre of the 1980s be too little nuanced understanding of such politics, and more commonly, a thesis of betrayal and letting Scotland down: a new version of a very old story.

The politics of culture as understood by our political class can be illuminated by the very distanced relationship between political and cultural nationalism – with the SNP never quite understanding this wider force and vice versa. There was even a rich cultural nationalist strand, exemplified by Norman and Janey Buchan, ex-Communists who became respectively a Labour MP and MEP who cared passionately about folk music and traditions, but were ferociously anti-political nationalism.[261] There was even a distinct part of Tory unionism that at its peak revelled in cultural nationalism – Walter Scott, Walter Elliot and John Buchan (of *The 39 Steps*) being three examples.[262]

Similarly, to this day the SNP have not exactly been adept on matters cultural, from the creation of Creative Scotland (a Labour idea), to broader cultural policy, media, broadcasting and the BBC, where the main aim has seemed to be at best to create a mini BBC for Scotland, when the world of consumption is fast changing.

In the post-1979 cultural world, Alasdair Gray's *Lanark* (1981), the work of James Kelman and in particular, *A Disaffection* (1989) and Booker Prize winning *How Late It*

Was, How Late (1994) (this award itself a massive contentious UK issue with Simon Jenkins condemning it as 'literary vandalism'[263]), along with Irvine Welsh's *Trainspotting* (1993), Liz Lochhead's *Mary Queen of Scots Got Her Head Chopped Off* (1987), Janice Galloway's *The Trick is to Keep Breathing* (1989) and A.L. Kennedy's *Looking for the Possible Dance* (1993) might all stand a chance of being referenced as the written works of fiction from the period which had cultural and political resonance. The towering force of Edwin Morgan, later to become Scotland's first Makar, who proved such an inspiration might also be mentioned.

From the pre-1979 world, the ripples of John McGrath's *The Cheviot, the Stag and the Black, Black Oil* along with the moral voice and authority of William McIlvanney's *Docherty* (1975) with its 'hard man' of Graithnock, Ayrshire, drawing on his experiences growing up in Kilmarnock and the surrounding areas, followed by *Laidlaw* (1977) credited with starting the 'tartan noir' genre and inspiring Ian Rankin's Rebus. In more recent times, Gregory Burke's play *Black Watch* told a familiar story with a powerful twist – of Scots going off to serve overseas, but this time in the chaotic deception of Blair's Iraq war.

Much of this can be summarised into presenting an account of Scotland which is one of humiliation, exploitation, being expendable whether in the field of industrial capitalism or battlefield, and used by external forces from Empire to Tony Blair. If that is the dominant story of the politics and culture, then the culture of politics has an equally simplistic story. Scotland is presented as radical, rebellious, dissenting and impossible to conquer and to successfully govern – from Romans to Edward II and modern-day Tories.

The salience of the constitutional question is taken as a given about our past. In James Robertson's novel *And the Land Lay Still* 1950s Edinburgh is seen as a place where people talk about the home rule issue without coming over as eccentrics or outsiders.[264] At this time, post-1949 National Covenant and the return of the Tories in 1951, such concerns were an extreme minority pastime in what was that most British of decades. Scottish nationalism, beyond the SNP, was associated in polite society with embarrassing hijinks and student escapades such as the removing of the Stone of Destiny from Westminster Abbey on Christmas Eve 1950 by Ian Hamilton and a group of Glasgow University students.[265]

One example of the cultural-political interface occurred when the writer, poet and academic Robert Crawford confessed, just before the indyref, that while he has increasingly written on politics (or to be accurate, cultural politics) in the last twenty years he has read only one book on Scottish politics – David Torrance's biography of Alex Salmond, *Against the Odds*.[266] Despite his growing moves towards political concerns, Crawford seemed to feel no awkwardness in revealing this.

Scotland post-indyref has seen this cultural-political interweaving of a left-nationalist story become the defining account of much of the Yes community. The two stories mutually reinforce each other, aiding a cultural and political attitude of difference. This is all fine and well, but what should concern us is the flimsy basis of both. The politics has bought into a very complacent view that all is satisfactory in the world of culture, while large acres of cultural Scotland have bought into the idea that we are this radical nation. What are missing from both of these interpretations are inquiry, critique and seeing past surface appearances.[267]

Post-1979 Scotland: 'Thatcher Poll Tax Tony Blair Iraq War'

There is even an issue about using pre- and post-1979 Scotland as the critical hinge of modern times without qualifying it. Sometimes it is unavoidable, but there is way too much simplicity in seeing 1979 as the critical breaking point on its own. In too many perspectives, pre-1979 Scotland is portrayed as this merry, happy, even egalitarian land of communal living and contentment. One where workers had dignity, purpose and built proper physical things like ships, and when crises happened, as in the Upper Clyde Shipbuilders work-in, people rallied round and stood for what was right against might.

This is then counterpoised to the post-1979 world. One which is miserablist, selfish, self-seeking and where we live in a world which has lost its moral compass. This leads to an ultra-one-dimensional account of the last forty years. In some places this was all that was needed to intervene in the indyref, with the writer Alan Bissett claiming:

We voted for New Labour, but they had realigned themselves to appeal to Tory voters. So actually since Thatcher, Scots haven't really been getting any of the governments that they actually really deserved.[268]

If people think this was the passion and excitement of the indyref, many years before that Jimmy Reid said something very similar: 'When New Labour came to power, we got a right-wing Conservative Government.'[269]

This is a rewriting of Scotland's last thirty to forty years. Scotland clearly did not vote Conservative, had a problem with Thatcher and Thatcherism, and experienced a growing democratic deficit in the 1980s. Yet, however appalling Tony Blair ended up being, under his leadership Labour won three convincing elections in the UK and three landslides in Scotland. In the period 1997-99 when Labour was in office, Blair was hugely popular in Scotland, and the experience of the Labour Government of 1997-2010 included many landmark achievements: the Scottish Parliament being the obvious one to cite here. But also worthy of note are the dramatic cutting of child and pensioner poverty, record investment in public services, the national minimum wage, and constitutionally, a Freedom of Information Act and Human Rights Act. And that's without mentioning devolution elsewhere and the Northern Irish peace process. This isn't a defence of Blair in office or New Labour. Clearly there were huge shortcomings and fundamental flaws in how it did politics. But merely to summarise the ebbs and flows of the last three to four decades in seven words as some kind of act of faith: 'Thatcher Poll Tax Tony Blair Iraq War' is a great soundbite but inaccurate history and politics.

This is an unhelpful way of looking at the recent past because it just writes over the last thirty to forty years and does not attempt to understand the nuances and dynamics of changes in society, employment and industry. Many of the most far-reaching shifts would have happened without Thatcherism and New Labour, and indeed many predate them: the decline in manufacturing, the long-term problems of coal, iron and steel, and shipbuilding, the increasing feminisation and fragmentation of the workforce. There is a tendency to see the big economic and social forces of recent times as being synonymous with Thatcherism and New Labour when they actually went with the grain of change. Just as the long-term shift to more individualism isn't reducible to being the same as neo-liberalism and selfishness. There is a British-wide account of this and the Scottish variant tends to often give a blank cheque to the SNP and independence arguments – seeing them as a rejection of the recent past – and even sometimes as a way to rewrite these events in an exercise in radical nostalgia: bring back the industries, nationalisation and council housing, rather than inventing new models appropriate for our age.

All history is of course remembered and digested in short hand: Neville Chamberlain and Munich, Winston Churchill and 'our finest hour' in 1940, Anthony Eden and Suez. In many respects, Tony Blair is forever going to be identified with the deceptions of the Iraq war, as David Cameron will be with Brexit. But the history of a nation state should allow for more complexities and subtexts.

There is a deeper backstory of Scots' long-term alienation from their own history, seen in William McIlvanney's comments that not having been systematically taught our own history at school we have ended up with a 'pop-up picture school of history.'[270] This has lots of disconnected figures and events – Bonnie Prince Charlie, Mary Queen of Scots and more. It is not much of an advance to see our recent history as a continuation of such trends: contributing to disempowerment and alienation from our own collective histories and memories.

Heaven Knows I'm Miserable Now: The Rise of Cultural Miserablism

A powerful connection between this pop-up version of recent Scotland and the emergence of an artistic and cultural take of our country has become known as cultural miserablism. This has become particularly persuasive in the world of film, and has been defined and critiqued by the filmmaker Eleanor Yule in association with the academic David Manderson.[271] This thesis has a number of key characteristics including:

- the male tragic working class hero usually with a fatal flaw – alcohol, drugs, gambling, violence;
- a backdrop of unemployment and economic deprivation;
- a dysfunctional extended family and/or collapsed community;
- secrets, lies and unforgotten misdeeds;
- a lack of redemption and hope;
- reduction of women to secondary roles.

All of this is in a world of bleakness – from weather to setting and language and an overarching worthlessness 'generated by the idea that a "superior" power had the upper hand, be it a gang, an addiction or another nation (inevitably English).' Fundamentally, 'there is no escape and no matter how hard a

Scottish miserablist hero tries he is doomed to failure.'[272]

This set of tropes has been a sort of alternative official story on steroids: a tale of 'it's grim up north' told of Scots supposedly driven to despair and worse by the harsh winds which have blown through communities, turning upside down lives and families, and leaving behind a walking wounded generation of men cut loose from their moorings and anchor points. Strangely, this take on modern life which began as a savaging of complacency and cry of pain has ended up being embraced and repacked by official bodies – including for export. In one of the most unlikely scenarios imaginable the Scotland of young men shooting up, inflicting violence on themselves and others, and adrift from friends and families has become a bizarre 'Scotland the Brand' here and internationally.

Well-known examples of the genre include such films as Peter Mullan's *Orphans* (1998) and *Neds* (2010), Ken Loach's *Sweet Sixteen* (2002), Lynne Ramsay's *Ratcatcher* (1999) and Gillies MacKinnon's *Small Faces* (1996). Beyond this the miserablist script can be seen in theatre, fiction and TV such as *The Scheme*; and the continual objectification and stereotyping of West of Scotland working class life and poverty across the country. There are occasions when this is playful and fun as in the series *Rab C. Nesbitt* about the adventures of Rab C. and Mary Doll in deepest Govan, and *Still Game*. The same case could be made for the film adaption of Irvine Welsh's *Trainspotting* (1996). There are clearly blurrings and boundaries in this, but there is an underlying powerful message in the genre according to Teddy Jamieson writing about the Scottish BAFTAs:

What is their Scotland? It's an urban Scotland, it's usually a Glaswegian Scotland and it's a grey, dreary, defeated, often dangerous Scotland. Yes, there's still humour there but it is a humour riddled with despair. It's a vision of a country that is alcoholic rather than merry, that is ground down rather than fighting back. It's as if someone has turned out the lights and plunged all of us viewers into the dark.[273]

This has had consequences in terms of cultural commissioning, funding and gatekeepers. Scotland has always had a tiny film industry and along with broadcasters it has adopted the miserablist manifesto as one of the key stories of Scotland to represent and play back to us and then send around the world. This story of modern Scotland is of a land gone wrong; with no hope, exits or escapes; a deep set of wounds running through society, and fear and foreboding everywhere. There is no realistic chance of politics or collective action changing things for the better; this is a deeply atomised world which is an extension of Thatcher's 'there is no such thing as society' to the point of dystopia.

This genre was once a breath of fresh air, seen as daring and even a liberation from kitsch, kailyard and tartanry, and all the garish, brightly-coloured confectionery accounts of Scotland, most notably seen in *Brigadoon* (1954). But what it has also lost has been softness, affection, even the importance of whimsy, folklore and the positive of the local. Thus, from Michael Powell and Emeric Pressburger's *I Know Where I Am Going* (1945) which stars the Corryvreckan whirlpool through the Alexander Mackendrick Ealing comedies *Whisky Galore* (1949) and *The Maggie* (1954), up to the more modern Bill Forsyth *Gregory's Girl* (1981) and *Local Hero* (1983). After that there was a cultural desert of bleakness, with the odd isolated oasis popping up through films like *Sunshine on Leith* (2013) based on the Proclaimers' music (and a previous stage version), a joyous exception.

Contrarian Cultural Scotland

There is of course kickback and counter-stories to cultural miserablism. Paradoxically, some of the most siren voices from an even more pessimistic account think Scotland is going in completely the wrong direction and needs an urgent wake-up call. This often but not always comes from those who in many respects were part of the Scottish establishment and now feel alienated and lost from much of contemporary society.

There are numerous platforms and voices articulating this – including the Scottish editions of the *Daily Telegraph* and *Daily Mail*. But arguably outdoing these in his vociferous and strident counterattack has been the classical composer James MacMillan. Over the years he has made numerous high-profile cultural interventions – one of the first of which was his 1999 Edinburgh International Festival lecture on 'Scotland's Shame' which challenged the historic and contemporary anti-Catholicism and legacy of discrimination. His words may have been over the top, but did act as a catalyst to a much needed and long overdue debate.[274]

MacMillan then took up a permanent position of violently shaking up conventional Scottish assumptions, something which can be no bad thing, but doing so in a way which trucked no dissent or possibility for debate: it was us versus them, you were either with him or against him. Despite this the indyref provided him with an ideal opportunity to prick the sensibilities of pro-independent artists and cultural opinion writing: 'Artists can be agents of good in society, but we can see that some of them end up supporting evil, blind to the roots and inevitable ends of their thinking.'[275]

MacMillan recently wrote that 'culture and education are being weaponised by political voices' as if this hasn't always been the case. What he really meant is political forces he disagrees with. Culture has become in his words 'vile, parochial... eschews elitism, but is profoundly motivated by an ideology of resentment and grievance.'[276]

For all MacMillan's megaphone cultural diplomacy there is a debate which needs to be had on culture – and some of the issues which he touches upon in his blunderbuss way. Three years previously, theatre critic Lyn Gardner wrote a *Guardian* piece entitled: 'If Scottish critics love it, it must be good – right?' In it she asked: 'So what is going on? Are Scottish critics protecting their own? Or are other critics just being bone-headed and not getting it?'[277] The motivation for this had been seeing a play called *Claire* which moved many Scottish critics, but left her cold. Such a piece of course could be written about critics the world over: the London theatre and literary critic worlds being renowned for their mutual referencing and backbiting.

There are in vast swathes of cultural production the issue of lack of originality and the rise of recycling culture (not in an environmentally friendly way). This can be seen across the Western world: the gridlock of the babyboomer generation endlessly going on about the 1960s, Beatles and Stones – something former Pulp frontman Jarvis Cocker described as 'children of the echo' – which has produced a law of diminishing returns as people endlessly aped and copied their sixties heroes leading to the worst aspects of 'Britpop' in the 1990s.[278]

Take the cultural bonanza that is the Edinburgh Festival industry which now comprises at least twenty festivals. The Edinburgh Fringe, once a counter-story to the official International Festival has now long been mainstream and mostly safe, very middle class and not very proactive. The right-wing commentator Harry Mount reflecting on the 2016 Fringe asked: 'Where has all the originality gone?' Even more, where is the radical edge and political subversion in plays, comics and performers? No doubt it is true that the current era is a confusing one to be a left-wing comic. Do you for example make fun of Jeremy Corbyn or the confusions of Brexit, and should your savvy comic say anything at all about Scotland or just let it be? There is a whiff of cultural nostalgia which previous generations would have fearlessly undermined, Mount observed: 'Fifty years ago, people weren't doing tribute acts to Noël Coward and Fred Astaire; they were creating new things.'[279] This is after all billed as 'the biggest arts festival in the world' and should be able to showcase leftfield voices and opinions and take risks, otherwise it will be outflanked by others.

There is also the cultural challenge of broadcasting and the media, and how it serves and is ultimately unaccountable to the people of Scotland. Its emergence only came about when the newly appointed Controller Alasdair Milne, new to Scotland, decided to start his job on New Year's Day 1968 and with little to do in an empty office went about changing the signage on the front of the building. Hence 'BBC Scotland' was born.[280] Apocryphal or not it shows the lack of substance to the name, that power has not flown north and there is a continuing absence of accountability.

There has been for quite some time a visible democratic deficit in how BBC Scotland is seen and satisfaction levels compared to the rest of the UK. The BBC's own figures in 2016 found that when asked to rate the BBC out of ten, ten being excellent, Scotland gave a 5.8, England 6.4; a whole host of indicators showed dis-satisfaction: 48% supporting BBC expansion and its current licence fee; 37% saying that the licence fee is good value; 58% viewing the BBC as having too many repeats. Ian Small, BBC Scotland's Head of Public Policy and Corporate Affairs reflected: 'We recognise that there's a deficit in programming in Scotland.'[281]

Another BBC report said: 'Perceptions of the BBC in Scotland have traditionally been less positive than in most other parts of the UK, due to a complex mix of reasons, some cultural.' One of the findings of this report was the minority reach of BBC Scotland's current affairs – reaching a mere 10% of the population in 2015, this up from 6% in 2013, whereas BBC *Reporting Scotland* reached 21% of the population.[282]

All of this is a starting point for proposing substantive reform of broadcasting in Scotland. Yet, much of the debate is nearly twenty years behind in a time lag, still seeing an integrated news service on BBC Scotland, 'the Scottish Six' as the answer. In 1997-98, then Prime Minister Tony Blair, along with BBC Director General John Birt and Peter Mandelson lobbied to make sure this did not happen, aided by the non-leadership of Donald Dewar, Secretary of State for Scotland at the time. Birt feared it would lead to the emergence of an 'English Broadcasting Corporation' and this would spell the eventual end of the UK.[283]

In an emerging age of multimedia devices and platforms, changing patterns of media consumption, and the use of tablets and smartphones, a 'Scottish Six' has the touch of the analogue about it. Fundamentally, it does not address how BBC Scotland adapts to this new environment of choice. BBC Scotland is not accountable to Scottish audiences who can only directly influence it via London (or for a small number, demonstrating outside BBC Scotland at Pacific Quay, Glasgow). This mismatch skews the BBC in all sorts of ways: externally with the public and internally with a host of senior staff all focused in information, paper trails and who they account to answering to London and not Scotland. That creates an intrinsically dysfunctional organisation.

Surprisingly, the Scottish Government has been enormously cautious and timid on broadcasting. This after the welcome initiative and degree of consensus around the Broadcasting Commission which reported in 2008 and recommended a designated BBC digital channel.[284] Since then the main activities of Culture Secretary Fiona Hyslop have been about creating via stakeholder meetings, a community of interest of independent producers who would gain from a BBC Scotland digital channel or greater autonomy. It has been very incremental and inward-looking and what has been missing has been talking about the coming revolution in media or how to make institutions like the BBC thrive and prosper in it, and accountable and responsive to audiences here.

Putting this in the context of the Scottish Government's

continual invoking of 'creative industries' and the absence of any wider cultural policy or perspective beyond numerous anodyne sectoral statements it is clear that the SNP are very conservative on culture, and are content to be basically minding the shop, believing the Scottish landscape is slowly moving their way. In what will shortly be ten years of office, the SNP have very little tangible to show in the realm of culture. Instead, the party rather than trailblazing has been content to follow in the slipstream of the forces of movement and change, to the extent that the old reference points are becoming weaker.

Celebrating Our Counter-Stories: Scotland as a Mongrel Nation

To conclude this chapter, Scotland has throughout its history in the union since 1707 been a counter-story in the UK. It has acted as a counterweight, while being positioned geographically at the periphery and outside the conventional centre, it has had privileged access to the main power elites of the UK, and at key points known how to influence and lobby them – hence the terms, 'the Scottish interest' and 'the Scottish lobby'. However, this position has come at a cost politically and culturally.

Scotland, certainly until the setting up of a devolved Parliament, played a corporate game in the UK – manoeuvring to get maximum benefit and spending from Westminster. This relied upon, as a number of Labour (as well as Tory) Scottish Secretaries of State conceded, over-stating the unity of purpose and opinion in Scotland to maximise influence and leverage goodies out of London: often at the detriment of democracy north and south of the border.

The legacy of this pork barrel, quasi-dependency lingers into the era of the Scottish Parliament. At the same time, for our society and culture to mature and take greater responsibility, we have to in the future let go and abandon this approach. That would be the right approach in a future of greater self-government, even potentially independence, but either way starting to shift our mindset now can only have beneficial effects in the future.

Scotland's embracing of a monoculture at times has hindered the articulation of counter-stories domestically – thus restricting and restraining the public life and vitality of the nation. Scotland is culturally changing beyond formal politics and institutions. One recent tiny example was provided by the small controversy of Celtic FC fans flying the Palestinian flag at Celtic Park at a European Champion's League match with Israeli side Hapoel Be'er Sheva for which Celtic were fined €20,000. This produced lots of comment and controversy, one of the most revealing from lifelong Celtic fan James MacMillan, perhaps looking for a stramash to whip up further, when he wrote: 'At one time the Catholic Church would have been able to intervene among their flock… and knock some sense into their militant tendencies.'[285]

Thankfully, that Scotland is no longer possible and while MacMillan and others rail against the SNP bossiness and nanny state-dom, they should pause and reflect on the long journey Scotland has undertaken. Scotland used to be a dark place for Catholics who faced the twin oppressions of Protestant dominance and discrimination, and Catholic Church authoritarianism – along with silence about this in many parts of public life. It is sad that someone so prominent should feel so disconnected from modern life that they would like to re-invoke the latter. These days are over never to return.

A final observation. Scotland's transition cannot be seen in some tidy, simple, linear, old-leading-to-new journey, as if we leave the shadows and embrace the light. Cue the curtains come down, the show ends and the audience applauds. This is the thinking in MacMillan's earlier piece entitled *Scotland's Art Police* describing modern society thus: 'Old=bad; new=good. English, royalty, bourgeoisie = bad; Scottish, socialist, "down-to-earth"=good.'[286]

In much more sensitive and informed terms, Joyce McMillan's recent collection of theatre reviews, *Theatre in Scotland* has, in its conclusion, theatre director Philip Howard state that her writing is 'about the "doubleness" of Scotland... about the sense of working alongside the opposing half.'[287]

This is one of our oldest stories – one which we encountered at the start of this chapter – of divided, black and white, damned versus saved Scotland. This has been used down the years to pathologise and stigmatise us – even when used as above in the cause of enlightenment and being cultured. There has been a diminishing and internalising of doubt and powerlessness which has gone with such articulations which has fortunately withered and weakened, but not been completely killed off.

Instead, we do not need to search for the beginning of a completely 'new song' for Scotland. We can choose to encourage and more fully embrace some of our other already existing visions of Scotland – the infinite Scotlands of the mind and imagination, and as Willie McIlvanney once put it, champion and see ourselves as the 'mongrel nation' and cultures that we truly are.

McIlvanney's words were cited on a cold Edinburgh December day when the capital hosted a European Union summit and alongside it the biggest ever pro-home rule demonstration. Facing a hostile UK government and anti-Tory political parties more inclined to squabble than co-operate, he made the case for a Scottishness which was not 'some pedigree lineage' but instead 'a mongrel tradition'.[288] Isn't that an intrinsic part of our proud, pluralist and defiant culture: one worth nurturing and nourishing in a world of increasing intolerance and cultural separation? If so isn't it time we started singing that song and standing up for it?

Chapter Nine:

Free Your Mind

In a few hundred years, when the history of our time will be written from a long-term perspective, it is likely that the most important event historians will see is not technology, not the internet, not e-commerce. It is an unprecedented change in the human condition. For the first time – literally – substantial and rapidly growing numbers of people have choices. For the first time, they will have to manage themselves. And society is totally unprepared for it.

Peter Drucker, Managing knowledge means managing oneself, 2000

I thought GalGael was just another programme to keep the DWP off my back while I got on with the business of drinking myself to death, no big deal. But I was wrong. I was shut down, enclosed, bitter, angry and resentful of everything and everybody; then there was GalGael. I'm a changed man, a better man, a man able to properly express his gratitude and appreciation for just about the first time ever, to open up and allow the world to see who I really am.

GalGael user, Govan, Glasgow, 2014

Scotland could be on the verge of fundamental change. Not just regarding the constitution and whether we become an independent nation, but more substantially in terms of the terrain and landscape of society. We have already experienced a series of leaderless revolutions – economic, social and cultural – which we are still coming to terms with and making sense of.

Moreover, it is also true that for most of Scotland's history until very recently there has been a near-complete absence of a persuasive and influential social liberalism. Scotland's main progressive traditions – the Liberal Party in the 19th century, Labour for large parts of the 20th century – did not, despite their championing of radicalism and support for economic and social change, dare to challenge many shibboleths of social conservatism. All of that has changed in recent decades, aided by the establishment of the Scottish Parliament.

This lack of opposition has been due to numerous factors – the Reformation, the long historical influence of the Church of Scotland, and even the reach of a cultural Calvinism into non-religious opinion across society, including into Labour, SNP and Tories. One example of this was the absence of the swinging sixties north of the border and of an equivalent to Harold Wilson's social liberal programme of reforms. This was not the sort of Scotland that Willie Ross was interested in presiding over and aiding into being.

Therefore, while Wilson (and his successor James Callaghan) presided over a substantive range of reforms from legislation of abortion and male homosexuality, divorce reform and the abolition of theatre censorship, there was no matching set of Scottish proposals. In most of these cases Roy Jenkins (as Wilson's Home Secretary) encouraged reform by private members' bills, but whereas abortion was dealt with at a UK level (championed by a young Scottish Liberal MP called David Steel), male homosexual reform only dealt with England and Wales – leaving Scotland and Northern Ireland unreformed. Leo Abse, a Labour MP, was the advocate of this bill and said at the time that there appeared to be 'a curious pattern... in relation to bills which touch[ed] on human relationships as far as Scotland was concerned.'[289]

Some might want to hope or suggest that this was a lingering throwback to darker times that soon disappeared. Events showed the opposite. In a whole host of issues from sex education in schools and society, to family planning, adoption, and the continued debate on lesbian and gay rights, Scotland for the next three decades demonstrated a deep unease, and often organised resistance, with discussing such subjects – let alone doing something constructive and liberalising.

As recently as the first calendar year of the new century, Cardinal Thomas Winning, as then Head of the Catholic Church in Scotland, could call homosexuality 'a perversion' – and survive.[290] Labour MSPs and MPs refused to condemn him. When the abolition of Section 28/Clause 2a was passed the same year he publically commented: 'If this is democracy, then I am no longer a democrat'[291] – a comment which was more revealing than he had perhaps intended.

More recently, the Catholic Church has used similar language in relation to civil partnerships, adoption for same-sex couples and same-sex marriage. Cardinal Keith O'Brien, Winning's successor, referred to gays as 'captives of sexual aberration' in 2004 and later called homosexuality a 'moral degradation'. Same-sex adoption was 'totalitarian', civil partnerships supported relationships 'demonstrably harmful to the medical, emotional and spiritual wellbeing' of people involved, and same-sex marriage was 'madness... which would redefine society.'[292] O'Brien's blatant hypocrisy, as well as overt prejudice, was referred to previously in Chapter Two.

Such over-the-top language more than hinted at desperation of the Catholic Church and other moral conservatives that they were losing influence. It isn't an accident that in the closed order Scotland of the past such outbursts had been few and far between. Such bodies and individuals did not need to assert their power; now they were fighting a losing war and probably knew it. In 2012, Stonewall, the lesbian and gay equality group, awarded O'Brien 'Bigot of the Year'; Alex Salmond demurred by saying that the award did not aid a 'dignified debate on the important issue of equality in Scotland.'[293]

Scotland was belatedly but emphatically changing, aided

by the long-term decline of the Church of Scotland – with membership down from 1.32 million in 1957 to 1,230,000 in 1966 and 504,000 in 2006; Catholic Church membership was steeply down as well with, at the turn of the century, a mere 200,000 Catholics attending mass in Scotland; while support for traditional Catholic positions on abortion, divorce and homosexuality crumbled.[294]

The above changes illustrate the dramatic decline of two of the main pillars of conservative Scotland – the Catholic Church and Kirk – and which also by their character and influence exemplified one dimension of Scottish difference. Add in the collapse of the third pillar – the Scottish Labour Party – and it is clear that this once formidable order no longer has its historical power and force.

It is now possible to see several of the high-profile public controversies at the onset of the Parliament – James MacMillan's 'Scotland's Shame' speech on anti-Catholicism and the Section 28/Clause 2a episode on homosexuality – as representing wider cultural wars of the kind not seen in a long time. In these episodes, previously unexplored public issues broke into open and uncontrolled visible debates. These showed that it was possible to discuss these things, that the moral conservatives could be stood up to, and that change was possible.

By the start of this century, Scotland's conservatives no longer commanded majority public support, but nor did they have the respect and awe of the parliamentary class as had been the case in the 1960s and later. This was a watershed moment and an opening of the floodgates of change. Suddenly, the forces of equality and anti-discrimination were aware that they could win the argument and that once potent forces who had policed the boundaries of debate had been diminished.

It could be argued that in this attitudinal shift, Scotland has become a bit like elsewhere: more cosmopolitan, liberal, and in places, rather like England. But in losing some of the negative differences, many Scots have consciously chosen to accentuate their positive differences. In other respects this has just happened due to the continual rightward drift of English politics. This is something going on all around the world: the balance between the local and global, and it is even called the bifurcation of globalisation.

Scotland's Revolution of the Mind

These changes are dramatic, far-reaching and in all likelihood irreversible, representing the crumbling of once omnipotent authority and the emergence of a more disputatious society. This 'revolution of the mind'[295] has contributed to what I have previously described as 'independence of the Scottish mind'.[296] This manifests itself in ideas; practice, and ways of thinking, communication and identities in what is called the public sphere.

The parameters of what this is and isn't has to be understood. This attitude of independence is a cultural and political mindset – not about formal institutions, politics and practices. Scotland already thinks and talks to itself, and sees itself increasingly as a conscious political agent and community. However, this contains challenges and problems. Sometimes this increased sense of autonomy and difference can have a tendency to become insular and reinforces a sense of Scottish exceptionalism – 'wha's like us' and seen in some of the most over the top hype post-indyref.

Then there is the fragility of the public sphere in Scotland and its limited autonomy, ecology and size. It is affected by all kinds of financial and commercial constraints, economies of scale, foreign and absentee ownership, along with an absence of viable business models both for many alternative platforms and a large part of the mainstream press (affected by declining sales and advertising revenues). All of this is exasperated by the existence of an English/London-dominated public

sphere which influences and intervenes in Scottish debates –
sometimes without any obvious conflicts, and sometimes with
huge insensitivities and the imposition of a very different set of
worldviews.

Two challenges arise for Scotland's independence of the
mind. The first is that this cultural and political mindset and
way of seeing things has to become something that is real,
that impacts policy, practice and ideas – and informs a way of
doing things. Second, this has to be centred upon the notion
of interdependence as an attitude. Insularity, lack of curiosity
in others, or vaguely invoking the Nordics as our future and
not recognising the crises and predicaments they and social
democratic politics everywhere face – does not help us in this
expedition. This cannot be in any sense a separation of the
mind.

Breaking Free from the Dead Hand of Unspace

A number of steps can assist the development of an
independence of the mind. This kind of Scotland has been
increasingly emerging in recent decades. But as with all social
and cultural change, it needs encouragement, support and
even the articulation of a few informal guidelines and accepted
norms.

First, the predominance of unspace which, as previously
explored, has significantly weakened and loosened, with the
establishment of numerous alternative spaces with a very
different feel and ethos – a sort of fuzzy, messy space. No matter
how weakened unspace is it remains in some institutional
settings, places where too much conformity, groupthink and
impenetrable barriers remain to challenge conventions and
conventional wisdom.

Unspace can be found everywhere in the world – the power
and mandate of institutional speak, its footprint and how it
prioritises and rewards certain modes of acting, talking and

exchange, and disavows, marginalises and ignores other forms. It has a narrow range of permissible behaviours, and frowns on spontaneity, frivolity and informality.

What is unusual in Scotland is the broader cultural and historic setting in which our unspace sits. Scotland post-1707 was preserved by an elite autonomy centred around the prestige of the Kirk, law and education. This had far-reaching consequences in that a democratic public culture and set of spaces had little room to emerge. As the Scottish state expanded in the early 20th century and particularly in the post-war era, this public culture became influenced not just by the processes of administrative devolution and the patronage of the Scottish Office, but by official Scottishness being packaged and presented as an administrative set of identities. This version of Scotland was about the people who had permission to do things to us, and the vast majority of us who things were done to.

This was profoundly depowering – making Scots pliant objects and recipients of services, and removing any real possibility of power and voice. Unspace became the cultural practice of the old order, but it still lives in numerous places. It can be found across numerous areas of professional, business and elite Scotland, from the corporate sector to the legal profession, parts of education and health, and is still the dominant characteristic of local government, the Scottish Government and UK Government in Scotland.

It takes time, effort and adaptability to challenge unspace inside the system. There are examples, but it is usually found in semi-autonomous bodies – who have managed to establish a remit which lets them get on with innovative, challenging work. One example in the public sector would be the work of the Violence Reduction Unit. Its activities – because of the multi-disciplinary nature of the work it does along with some of the problems of its main client groups – mean it has to be able to articulate a set of values and practices which are not only human and genuine, but at times, unofficial.

Figure 9.1. Features of Unspace and Fuzzy, Messy Spaces

Unspace	*Fuzzy, messy spaces*
Name Badges	No name badges
Delegates	Individuals
Participants list	No participants list
Corporate or public sector sponsors	No sponsors or trust sponsors
Week day	Often at weekends
Participants attend as part of work	Participants come out of interest
Expensive – often held in costly (and intimidating) venues, participants' organisations pay their attendance	Accessible to people on low or no income. Held in venues that are accessible and welcoming
People talk from institutional roles and mandates	People talk as individuals
Subjects and agendas institutionally-focused	Subjects and agendas values-oriented
Discussions filled with jargons and buzzwords	Discussions mirror everyday conversations
Outcomes either pre-determined or controlled by the power players. Often very low, or no ownership of outcomes or actions	Outcomes demand further engagement of participants and energise towards more collaboration and action

The dynamics and culture of unspace work for some (see Figure 9.1.). It has an obvious structure, logic and people know how it works (or doesn't work). It is safe and people can stay in their comfort zones knowing the role they have to play. It is very mind- and intellect-focused. It draws deeply from an authority based paradigm which is steeped in history, politics and tradition – and has become internalised in many of us even if we resist it. Many of us default to submitting to external authority as it is familiar, and being collaborative and experimental is too scary and unknown.

Fuzzy, messy space demands turning up as a whole human being: connecting head and heart. A shift from a practice of unspace to nurturing different spaces would involve three strands in parallel. First, there is a need to encourage structures that help people in that space know that they can trust their voice and that their views matter. Second, people have to be supported with skills and resources to navigate through the tough, messy territories that entail change. Third, leadership needs to be encouraged and aided which is not about command and control, and permission-based authority. None of this is tidy, linear and controlled, but the old structures and cultures are weakening and no longer work effectively. The alternative future is already there in the margins. The culture of space and place is profoundly about belonging and connectedness,[297] but also offers, via the internet and social media, the potential in the future to dislocate space and place – and create new virtual communities and networks.[298]

It's Good to Talk Dangerously: Jaytalking Scotland

More often, fuzzy, messy space exists at the margins or the edges of the system – where people do not have to act from an imposed, institutional identity, but can speak from a less managed set of identities. In these new spaces, dissent, pluralism and the evolution of counter-stories have to be encouraged.

How do alternative, disruptive voices co-exist and respect each other? How can a culture of 'jaytalking' – the art of dangerous talking (in the spirit of jaywalking) develop – an idea originally floated by the American writer Marshall Berman, inspired by the satirist Jules Feiffer.[299]

Berman wrote that the US lacked critical culture and ability to explore 'how human beings should live and what our life means.' This was written in 2000 and holds even truer now: post-9/11, post-crash, in the world of Trump and even more xenophobic populists. 'Jaytalking' to Berman entails three core ingredients:

- *powerful, provocative ideas;*
- *smart and imaginative people working in various sectors of life, often wholly unaware of each other's existence;*
- *'experimental neighbourhoods', places where people and ideas can bump into each other… and find or imagine new ways to put together, and to act out their new syntheses.*[300]

Scotland saw a glimpse of the shift in the 2014 indyref but by its nature this was temporary. Yet, at the same time, the backstory was of the diminution of traditional power and institutions – with the resultant consequences of opening up spaces, cracks and possibilities. While society cannot and would not want to live in the permanent mobilisation and exchange of the indyref, putting these changes into longer context is helpful. We have to learn from the experiences of this period – and talk about how to experiment, create infrastructure and develop new spaces. Some of this is going to involve tricky issues such as funding, business models, sustainability, the issues of younger people entering the labour market and precarious incomes, and how any ecology of DIY culture nurtures pluralism within it.

All of this has to be seen in the global context of massive changes in technology, science, how we share and understand information and data, and resultant consequences for organisations, societies and the nation state. Some, such as the writer and activist Paul Mason, have argued that the above offers the possibility of shifting from a world of scarcity to one of abundance – one of the first clarion calls of the early socialist movement in the early 19th century – believing it can change the capitalist mode of production and herald in a new age of post-capitalism.[301]

Even if that is utopian or a long way in the distance – the age of imposed identities is in terminal decline. As the quote from Peter Drucker at the outset of this chapter says, a new era of choice is emerging that is more revolutionary than such inventions as the internet.

When many of us grew up class, work, gender and ethnicity effectively defined who you were, and to a large extent your life chances, identity and place and prospects in the world. It is revealing that much of today's left across the West still want to cling to these identities – which we had little control over – as the way to do politics rather than daring to let them go and embracing that liberation. As the novelist Neal Stephenson wrote: 'Our cultures used to be almost hereditary, but now we choose from a menu as various as the food court of a suburban shopping mall.'[302]

This is perhaps too flippant and consumerist, but it makes the point that identity and the self are in flux. There is the option of a wholly marketised, commodified version of the self and a democratic, socially engaged one. Relevant in this is the meaning of some of the most over-used and problematic words of our time: creativity, innovation, complexity, and the notion of genius.

In the modern world nearly everything seems to involve creativity – making it unclear what it actually is. There is, as Michael Bhasker wrote in *Curation*, 'the "creativity myth": the idea that creation and creativity are intrinsic groups.'[303] We conflate two different notions of creativity. One is new, innovative and involves creating things. The other involves making more of things that already exist, or adding existing elements together – an incremental creativity, if even that. The two are very different and most of what is called creativity is the latter, such as adding content or new sites to the internet.

The musician and polymath Brian Eno in a recent BBC *Hard Talk* took this much further to the point of expounding a revolutionary theory of social change, and even of the universe.[304] He questioned the fundamental basis of the idea of complexity and individual genius. Eno stated that all complexity comes from simplicity as is illustrated by evolutionary theory in a post-god world. All of the beauty and intricacy around us began as simplicity with, at its root, the most basic single cell organisms.

This insight, Eno contends, has far-reaching implications for the artistic and creative impulse, pointing against any idea of the artist as a god-like figure and authority. Indeed, he goes much further and poses that the very concept of individual genius is inherently problematic. Talking in the aftermath of David Bowie's death in January 2016, Eno reflected on the 1970s Bowie-Eno Berlin albums that are widely applauded as groundbreaking. Instead of seeing them as the work of a single genius or even two geniuses coming together, Eno views them as the product of what he calls 'scenius' – the intelligence of a whole time and community.

Social Change and Standing on the Shoulders of Giants

Bringing this back to contemporary Scotland there is a widely held view here that because we are different from the rest of the UK, more centre-left, less Tory, and more resistant to the overt undermining of public services, that we are therefore good at, and know how to do, social change.

The version of social change usually implied in this is rather conventional, even old-fashioned and a bit light on detail. It is social change by top-down diktat and the most narrow notion of what politics is. It is also one, as previously described, based on resisting, and in places rolling back, the projects of Thatcherism and New Labour. It is one which in the present lays a lot of responsibility on achievements of past generations, radicals and visionaries, such as building the welfare state, NHS, Hydro-electric schemes in the Highlands, and slum clearances across urban Scotland.

This brings a complacency predicated on the assumption that we know how to do this and have done it successfully before. That we can 'Stand on the shoulders of giants' and repeat the magic recipe. It is profoundly defensive, unimaginative and conservative, seeking our best ideas and politics in the past. Instead, the lesson from past successes is to be of your own time, to be looking outward and towards the future, and to continually evolve, adapt and experiment.

Social change – understanding it, embracing it and making it happen – requires effort. Firstly, change always starts at the edges and margins. Harold Jarche has written about 'moving to the edges' where there is more fluidity and questioning, 'where the answers may not be clear, but they are less obstructed than in the centre.'[305]

Second, such change entails a different kind of relationship with institutional power. The best initiatives don't take the state on in some head-on Bolshevik challenge, coup d'état or complete opposition. Instead, they navigate into a position where they have autonomy and influence on as many of their own terms as is humanly possible. This is the creation of a type of intermediate space and culture: life in the fuzzy, messy spaces and zones.

This was one of the lessons that sprang from the Glasgow 2020 project I created and led. In a two-year initiative which involved every single public body and organisation in the city – people time and time again recognised the value of a space not owned or colonised by the council or a public agency, somewhere they were free from the obligation to shape their interests around that of an authority.

This is simple and absolutely fundamental. In a new context, people acted differently, and more freely and creatively because they didn't feel they had to respond to someone else's agenda. Yet at the same time they wanted to know that all this energy and effort was going somewhere and would be noticed and acted upon by bodies such as the council.[306] On a longer-term basis the work of what was known as London Citizens (and became UK Citizens) springing from faith and community groups, along with trade unions, shows a similar ethos.

Third, this takes us to a different idea of power and politics – one that entails vertical and horizontal networks allowing for a different kind of political party and agency. For all the impressive membership increases in the SNP post-indyref and in Corbyn's Labour Party, they are still in their practices and cultures traditional political parties. More than half of the new members of both parties are inactive. For example, a recent survey of SNP post-indyref members in late 2015 showed that 55% had not attended a single SNP meeting.[307] Similarly, a YouGov survey in June 2016 found that 61% of Labour's new members under Corbyn had never been to a meeting, while 85% of them had never canvassed or campaigned.[308] This is party membership as clicktivism rather than a new age of party activism.

Traditional political authority and parties are struggling with all of this. The new is not yet clear, but there are emerging examples of doing things differently such as Alternativet in Denmark – which describes itself as an 'open source' party, one with 'popular political laboratories' which create a 'network-based politics.'[309]

Fourth, this has consequences for the state, public services and government. For too long on the left and in Scotland there has been a stasis, seeing our highest aspiration as defending the gains of previous generations such as free public health and education services. No one is disputing that these are historic gains – but it is commonplace to slip from defending these as principles of public and common good, to defending the existing delivery model of them – which are very different propositions. What this does is give the credo of change on public services to the right wing and such policies as free schools, foundation hospitals and academies. That puts the left on the side of the forces of conservatism and importantly, conservation: politics as a kind of heritage industry.

Fuzzy, Messy Spaces of Change

There are numerous examples of social change in present-day Scotland which have the characteristics of fuzzy, messy space. One would be the rightly much lauded GalGael project in Govan, Glasgow which teaches long-term unemployed men and women the ancient craft of Viking shipbuilding. In so doing it reintroduced skilled work into areas where it has long been in decline, and brought shipmaking to the Clyde in a socially useful way (rather than BAE Systems' making of warships). It also assists in terms of working with men at the margins in one of Glasgow and Scotland's most deprived areas.

GalGael is an active, living statement of hope and commitment, constituted in 1997, and run by, in its own words, dynamic self-governance with the aim of a flat, non-hierarchical structure. In the front window of the premises its ethos are presented to visitors and the outside world in four circles – We Make, Hope Possible, Life Livable, Work Probable.

Then there is in the most multi-cultural diverse part of Glasgow (and indeed Scotland), Govanhill Baths which were closed by the council in 2001. It was the site of an epic community struggle which saw the council eventually give the premises back to the community in 2008. Now a vibrant, diverse community centre and hub of change, the Baths have secured long-term funding to rehabilitate and reopen the once magnificent swimming baths around a whole cluster of community activities and resources.

Govanhill Baths have also been an unqualified positive in an area undergoing rapid change and many tensions, with slum housing and anti-social landlords, combined with an influx of Roma refugees, from Romania and Slovakia. This has had national media attention because the neighbourhood sits in First Minister Nicola Sturgeon's constituency meaning that some elements of the right-wing press, the *Scottish Daily Mail* and *Scottish Sunday Express*, have felt that gives them permission to describe Govanhill in dismissive and offensive ways. Words like 'ghetto', 'tinderbox' and 'going to blow' have been scattered about – none of which are accurate.[310] Instead, using such terms is part of a bigger political project against immigration, Nicola Sturgeon and 'separatism'.

A final example would be the work of Sistema Scotland in the Raploch estate in Stirling originally inspired by the example of El Sistema in Caracas, Venezuela. A tribute to the power of music and hope, Sistema was established in 2008 setting up the Big Noise Orchestra with local young people. It has become by now a long-term presence for a whole cohort of young children – enriching their and their families' lives by supporting and nurturing them in music, life skills and confidence[311]. A second Big Noise project started in Govanhill in 2013 and moves are currently afoot to set up another project in Douglas, Dundee.[312]

These are just three examples in a nation of over five million people but from the edges and margins. They aren't of the mainstream. Instead they address such big issues as belonging; being firmly rooted in and of the community; emergent, adaptive leadership, and perhaps critically, staying power, which has allowed each to go through several different waves of change. There are lots more examples of organisations and initiatives set up on the edge and challenging old conformities – some not surprisingly considering the state of the mainstream media creating new media spaces. These include the Ferret[313], championing investigative journalism, which has already broken stories on fracking and working conditions in the company Amazon; and CommonSpace[314] which has spun out of the think/do tank Common Weal. We will no doubt see more of their like.

Another important factor in understanding change in Scotland is the issue known as 'Mind the Gap' – namely the closeness of public bodies, institutions and elites and the ease with which they can be engaged with if you speak the right insider language. This has advantages for those who possess the relevant skills and who want access, such as corporates and consultants. But it is a problem for the fermenting of alternative ideas, for it means many feasible proposals have the chance of being considered by government, adopted and colonised. Most of the people with access don't mind this as they want to have influence, but it means numerous initiatives are too quickly adopted by government – and taken from the groups that originally proposed them. There is a positive and negative in this: positive in that unthreatening proposals can be adopted; negative in terms of ownership and the lack of space for genuinely alternative ideas to germinate.

I had direct experience of this in 2010 when I proposed to Alex Salmond as First Minister that the government set up a Commission on Public Service Reform. My reasoning was that money was getting tighter, tough choices had to be made, government needed to be seen to be strategic, and by doing so could reclaim the words 'public sector reform' from the consultant class, while inviting trade unions to be partners. I wrote a paper for Cabinet, it was accepted, and I even suggested that they get a retired trade unionist to chair it, ideally, Campbell Christie, previously head of the STUC.

This came to pass but two significant things happened. First, it was renamed the Commission on the Future Delivery of Public Services[315] – something subtly, but profoundly different, delivery being a very different proposition to reform.

Second, the limits of how government does these things became obvious. Thus, there appears to be a filing cabinet somewhere containing names and contacts of the 'usual suspects' to sit on such bodies. But strangely, despite the Scottish Government having a track record in doing these sort of things there is no central resource in how to do them, and how to engage and experiment in processes. The lesson I took from this is that when you engage with government and succeed, your ideas quickly stop being your ideas and instead become someone else's. That's the world of Minding the Gap.

What do we do with politicians?

The thinker Zygmunt Bauman, in his study of intellectuals, defined their activities in terms of 'legislators' and 'interpreters'[316] – a helpful distinction to use in understanding modern politicians. Legislators believed that change came through the formal act of politics – passing laws, making rules, and engaging in rational discussion. Interpreters embraced the soft, informal and discursive, offering advice, analysis and being more contingent. The first is about hard or institutional power, the second about soft, cultural and subjective power.

In Bauman's analysis, the intellectual world has seen a shift from the first to the second – from a Fabian outlook based on laws, facts and reason, to one which is more fuzzy, argumentative and non-linear. This is often presented today as progress, but critically, the former had a championing of hope and the common good, which is mostly absent or in retreat in the contemporary world.

Politicians still see and present themselves as legislators and interpreters, but both are under increasing pressure and attack. Their role as legislators has become constrained by power in national Parliaments moving upwards to national leaders and executive power, to an extent, downwards, to the emergence of new regional and old national identities in new settings.

This has left them seeing themselves as interpreters, but this too is increasingly challenged. Knowledge and information are blurred by the decline of authority and expertise. What counts as fact is contested, but part of a wider set of arguments that involve alternative facts and figures, as happened in the indyref and Brexit vote. 'Just give us the facts' cry voters, and are then offered a mix of what they see as no facts and an avalanche of rhetoric and confusion.

The gap between public and politicians has shifted. Recently I was watching *BBC Question Time*. It was the usual mixture of unsettling and frustrating, and a telling portrayal of the state of politics: a boorish UKIP woman, poor Labour and Tory politicians, a columnist and a celebrity. A friend observed the following morning that over the years the gap between the audience and panel has been closing, to the point that sometimes it appears non-existent. When the show began in 1979, the panel still had representatives of the great and good, the patrician class, and the generation who fought or remembered the war. Now they mostly represent career politicians, think tank types or commentators, and entertainers or comedians.

This observation is true of politics per se, but it isn't the whole picture, for in other respects, a significant chasm has opened up between public and politicians. This can be seen in the emergence of the term 'political classes' in recent times, which conveys that politicians are 'not like us' and are 'a breed apart'. Increasingly across the Western world politicians have become an insider class, and it has become seen as a profession and vocation, rather than something citizens or people from 'normal' life do for a period with a sense of duty and pride, and of making a contribution. The role and character of a politician is at a crossroads, but we have to ask if it is the most effective means in the long run to form governments and make national decisions. Perhaps more participative forms of direct popular role, referendums and deliberate forums can be considered and experimented with, but it is clear that the traditional model and its modern variant is broken.

The Pull and Limits of Tribes

One way of being human is to be tribal – it can give a sense of belonging, history and tradition – from youth gangs, to football and politics. Sebastian Junger in an extended essay explored the power and problems of the tribe which he describes as 'the people you might feel compelled to share the last of your food with.'[317] The pull of belonging is weakening in modern life, and a modern variant of solidarity is required – one less defined by military conflict, aggression and othering.

Yet, the hold of tribes offers something, as can be seen all across the world and in Scotland. Rather than throw out the notion completely, it can be reframed. In the indyref, the Yes and No camps were in essence 'moral tribes', mutual versions of them and us, which failed to see in their opponent something very similar. Joshua Greene in his book, *Moral Tribes*, identified a number of ways to develop a common dialogue, one of which is to establish 'a common currency of value' and 'a common currency of fact'.[318] How often in our indyref was the latter bemoaned: that we were debating this huge question without an agreed set of facts or an independent adjudicator? But in reality this was about something even deeper – the absence of a shared set of values. That's what is crucial for our future and needs urgent work.

Sue Goss in her reflective book *Open Tribe* notes the allure of the word 'tribe': a term with 'a long and chequered history as an anthropological, cultural and ideological term.'[319] Similarly, 'open' is a term with many meanings – many positive (Open University) and many contested – positive for some, negative for others ('open for business'). Bringing the two words together in 'Open Tribe' gives a notion of 'tribes we can move in and out of' in the words of Robin Murray. As Goss observed: 'we can begin to see the emergence of open tribes rather than a single tribe... We don't have to choose between belonging and openness.'[320]

This is a world that is trying to move beyond binary ideas of them and us, black and white, and the good and bad guys. That is rather apposite to Scotland post-indyref, post-Brexit vote. Too much of our practice and thinking both here and across the West is based on questionable assumptions that 'we' are the good guys, that the world should only work for the good guys, and have them in control. This has the resultant spin-off that many then search in work and politics to try to find the groups with whom we agree on everything to work with. This last assumption is a dangerous and damaging fallacy: it isn't generative or allowing for growth in its search for sameness.

Scotland has too much of that spirit in too many places – from our politics, to our professions, to our elites. A belief that we are the good guys, and that if only our good guys were running everything and/or listened to and treated with the respect they deserve, all would be fine with the world. This has a propensity to spin off in some accounts into the 'Kumbaya Scotland' view: if only we could all be nicer to each other, hold hands, sing songs, and identify that overarching agreement and consensus, somehow contentment – even bliss will happen. It is the wrong way of viewing of Scotland and the world.

Instead, we need to realise the limits of breaking the world into them and us, good and bad, and with it the concomitant attitude of blaming all of our shortcomings on external forces – usually the predictable mantle of villains of Tories, Westminster, the British state, and capitalism. All of these bodies have their own problems to answer for, but this attitude doesn't recognise the power that Scottish elites have and, that some of the mistakes made here have been made in areas where Scotland has been self-governing for decades – and had autonomy – long before the current Scottish Parliament arrived.

The Scotland after the grip of moral conservatism and unspace will be a much less predictable, ordered society. That world is irreversibly on the wane, but we are still clearly in transition from the old to new future. There are several possible Scotlands of the future, both domestically and constitutionally, which will be explored in more detail in the concluding chapters. The opportunities on offer are major: to help shape a Scotland that is vibrant, diverse, pluralist, and has turned its back on monocultures, and instead, is comfortable in its uniqueness and multiplicities. This future Scotland is already here; but it needs nurturing, resources and leadership.

Chapter Ten:

What do we do about Britain?

Never in all my 12 years in Gomorrah [London] on Thames did I find any Englishman who knew anything save those who had come back from the edges of Empire where the effect of the Central decay was showing, where the strain of the big lies and rascalities was beginning to tell.

Ezra Pound, Guide to Kulchur, 1938

Britain is in crisis. That much is agreed by nearly everyone. For some the solution is to dream of a different political union such as a federal UK. But this looks extremely unlikely in the next fifteen to twenty years. Right-wing Brexiteers have a whole different set of political dreams.

A number of consequences flow from the first point. A tidy, ordered, symmetrical or semi-symmetrical, reformed United Kingdom is not going to emerge at this late hour and save the day. However that does not mean that a spectrum of other possibilities abound. Whatever occurs, there will be arrangements and institutions across the isles of the United Kingdom – either in a looser state than present, or involving a set of states. New forms of power sharing, relationships and co-operation are all possible. The question to ask is: what kind of form, and for whom and what purpose? Who would any new order best serve, and whose interests would it aid?

For example, the UK at present is not, nor has it ever been, a unitary state. Instead, it has many of the characteristics of what has been called a union state. James Mitchell in his study of the UK, *Devolution in the UK* made the point that the UK has become 'a state of unions'[321]: a state with a distinct set of unions which have been agreed, remade and revisited and are constantly evolving between the centre and devolved nations. This is a dynamic situation and not a settlement with some more committed to it than others; the English polity having a lingering attachment to the idea of a unitary state.

The UK could potentially be heading beyond this towards a union of states, but if it is, it would, taking Mitchell's argument, be one in which different nations were at different points of enthusiasm about this ever loosening union and set of arrangements. It also raises questions about stability and sustainability in the long term.

Yet, constitutionally re-arranging the furniture and composition of the UK does not deal with the multi-dimensional crises of the UK which we identified in Chapter Five: economic, social, cultural, democratic and geo-political. Instead, it focuses on one aspect alone: the democratic shortcomings of the UK and hopes that by addressing this the other facets will improve. This is an increasingly forlorn hope in the absence of the UK embarking on a serious, systematic democratisation, and even more, considering the lack of a coherent economic and social alternative to the existing order of things.

Mission Impossible? A Different Kind of British State

Talking of such overarching principles as federalism or confederalism or a much looser union requires a fundamentally different kind of state with different characteristics at the centre, and in how it conducts its bilateral relationships with Scotland, Wales and Northern Ireland – let alone what happens with English governance.[322] All of this requires that the state represent and articulate very different economic and social interests from the present.

Sadly, on both of these related counts any serious attempts

at reform have come to very little. On the first – constitutional reform – Labour at its peak in 1945 made peace with what can be called 'the conservative nation' – the Tory account of England/Britain which has assisted them in their dominance via a whole set of institutions sustaining privilege and elite power.[323] Indeed, it could be said that peak Labour became a party more changed by Westminster and all its flaffery and ancient traditions, than one which changed Westminster.

Instead there was an innate belief that capturing hold of the powerful organs of state power and using them for the greater good was not only the right thing, but also something natural. There was in this a missing Labour account of the need for democracy and pluralism, and sadly, a complete buying into of the conservative establishment account of Britain. Even in the 1980s as the Thatcher government remade the UK on a minority vote, Labour could not be won over to Charter 88's programme of far-reaching democratic reform including a written constitution.[324] Such was the party's continual belief in the totems of British statism and myths such as parliamentary sovereignty. This myopia has cost Labour dearly.

The second dimension – often unexplored in these discussions – is just as important. From the early 1960s, Britain's ruling elites became increasingly aware of the UK's relative economic decline in the world and at this point, critically, with regard to its European competitors and the post-war recoveries of Germany, France and Italy. Increasingly, the UK was portrayed by elites as 'the sick man of Europe' due to laggard economic growth, poor corporate management, and archaic industrial relations.

Prime Minister Harold Macmillan became progressively anxious about this in the early 1960s and developed an interest in indicative planning, greater co-operation between business and industry and applied for the UK to join the then EEC which was rebuffed by De Gaulle. Semi-corporate bodies were set up such as the National Economic Development Council (or NEDDY as it became known) that spawned numerous sectoral bodies (known as 'little Neddys') modelled on the French experience; it was cold-shouldered by Thatcher and abolished by John Major in 1992.

Next came Harold Wilson's National Plan and Department of Economic Affairs: the former to aid long-term economic planning, the latter, to try to wrestle economic policy from Treasury short-termism. Both failed, the result of growing weaknesses in the UK economy seen in a Balance of Payments deficit and the need in 1967 to devalue the pound, with Wilson's infamous 'it does not mean that the pound here in Britain, in your pocket or purse or in your bank, has been devalued' TV address of November 1967[325]. Instead what was permanently and irreparably devalued from then was Wilson's reputation.

Ted Heath's Tory Government followed, and after first experimenting with free market reforms and privatisation, he abandoned these in favour of modernisation and an even more assertive corporatism, rigid prices and incomes policies, while trying to engage in one-sided reform of industrial relations challenging the power of trade unions. None of this worked in turbulent global economic times and burgeoning inflationary pressure, but Heath did manage one major achievement: the UK successfully negotiated and entered the EEC (along with Ireland and Denmark), a policy that would last for 43 years.

This was followed by the Wilson and Callaghan Governments of 1974-79 – elected unexpectedly in February 1974 as a minority government, and then October 1974, with a tiny majority on what was then the most radical Labour manifesto in the party's history. It promised statutory planning agreements between the state and private sector, a National Enterprise Board taking shares in profitable private companies, and a social contract between government, unions and business. This was the Bennite Alternative Economic Strategy, but it was quickly diluted once in power, and effectively abandoned as the government faced the reality of huge economic problems from high unemployment by post-war standards and inflation hitting 27%.

It didn't end well, for Wilson resigned in 1976 handing over to the more emollient James Callaghan, but the UK was then bailed out by an IMF loan that year which inflicted crushing public spending cuts. This was seen at the time as a totemic moment, the end of the hopes and securities of the post-war managed capitalism – and shortly after Labour self-destructed in 'the winter of discontent' of industrial strikes over 1978-79 and months later Thatcher was elected.

These four successive attempts – Macmillan, Wilson mark one, Heath, Wilson mark two – all attempted to get the state to become developmental, which meant more long term, strategic, and setting national economic priorities. The aspiration was to use this to change British capitalism and its endemic short-termism, amateurish management, oppositional trade unions, poor investment, Research and Development, and the dominance of financial capital over industrial capital.

It is not an accident that all these previous attempts failed. They did so because they involved taking on powerful vested interests. Until the Thatcher Government came along, it was widely assumed in media and public discussions that trade unions were one of the major roadblocks to reform, and several failed reforms were initiated (Wilson's 'In Place of Strife' proposals in 1969 where he backed down; Heath's Industrial Relations Act 1971). All governments recognised that industry and commerce needed radical change, and that short-termism, lack of investment strategies, the cult of 'gentlemanly capitalism', and finance capital and the City's disconnection from enterprise and even the domestic economy were, if they were talked about, all seen as changeable by voluntary codes and practices. The exception would be the Bennite strategy, but that was quickly jettisoned by Wilson in 1974-75.

This set of failures led to the Thatcher Government: it promised economic renewal by 'setting the people free', dismantling regulations and the post-war managed order, and encouraging entrepreneurship. It became a decade of hyper-triumphalism aided by Labour internecine warfare, but shorn of the rhetoric of 'the great British economic miracle' and 'putting the Great back into Great Britain', the whole decade was kept afloat by the proceeds of North Sea Oil and privatisation: otherwise the UK would have been facing worse constraints and pressures than the 1960s and 1970s.

One of the many tragedies of New Labour was that while it had many noteworthy achievements, it refused to set its face against the Thatcherite consensus, and instead went with the grain of the zeitgeist of elite opinion. This entailed a Faustian pact by Blair and Brown with globalisation and the City not to shake or threaten what they perceived as the British magic money tree as long as they could redistribute some of the proceeds to public spending. The prospect of a more radical approach, mooted in opposition in 1994-95 around 'stakeholder capitalism' and drawing on a critique of British capitalism's shortcomings associated with the likes of Will Hutton and others, was expressly ruled out as being too risky, bold and playing into Tory caricatures of Labour.[326]

There is a cumulative price to be paid for these successive failures – and the conscious decision by the Thatcher Government to go down an alternative route, followed by New Labour deciding on the path of least resistance. It is borne in continued fundamental economic weaknesses, the entrenchment of the Anglo-American version of capitalism, and the failure of the state to reform and set up the kind of collaborative institutions and arrangements commonplace in Western Europe. The ultimate cost has been on the British people – who have suffered in terms of living standards, security, employment and work rights and endemic inequality. The Tory argument post-Brexit is that Britain hasn't had enough of this nasty medicine, while Labour are unfortunately missing from the whole argument.

A reformed United Kingdom would have to entail building a political and intellectual coalition confident and deep enough to address the above. This would mean attempting to shift the entire legacy of the British state and capitalism into becoming a very different kind of state and capitalism. Sadly, that doesn't look like it is going to happen – and the only foreseeable circumstances which might arise to change that would be via an epic and transformational shock to the global economic order of at least 1973 style proportions. Even then success could not be guaranteed, given how dug in the entrenched interests are, and how weak the reformers.

Carry on Britain!

The 'idea' of Britain will continue in numerous respects whatever the future. It will continue as a cultural, historic and geographic term. It will also continue to still have some kind of political meaning as well as geo-political consequences – whatever the form of constitutional and governmental relationships across these isles.

There are many different Britains. There is the island of Britain; there is the creation of 'Great Britain': the three nations of England, Scotland and Wales; and there is a tangible 'idea' of Britain which goes beyond the framework of the United Kingdom. There are many British identities and many different variants and expressions. Britishness is a civic, social and legal term – but our passports, as has long been pointed out, remind us that we are subjects of the 'United Kingdom of Great Britain and Northern Ireland' – as well as for now members of the European Union: to which Bernard Crick remarked: 'I am a citizen of a state with no agreed colloquial name.'[327]

However these isles eventually reconfigure – post-Brexit, Scotland's constitutional status, Northern Ireland and its relationship with the Republic of Ireland – some aspects of

Britishness will remain and rightly so. A cultural Britishness will continue, as will some kind of civic and social dimension. But it is also more than likely that even if Scotland became formally independent, some form of shared institutions would remain across the nations of what is now the UK.

Critically, Scotland will remain in many of its identities and facets 'British' even if independent. Why wouldn't it? We are imprinted with the experience of 300 years in a political union. Modern Scotland is in numerous respects a creation of Britishness – or perhaps more accurately a joint project between the Scottish people and the rest of the UK. How otherwise did some of the great achievements of our society occur, lifting hundreds of thousands of our citizens from the most blighted, deprived lives which continued well into the middle of the 20th century?

At a fundamental level, Scottish nationalism is in part a very British phenomenon, even creation. The antecedents of the Declaration of Arbroath of 1320 – beautiful, intoxicating poetry that it is – weren't directly invoking a nationalist mindset at the time; they were engaged in feudal posturing and positioning, whereas today it cannot but be seen as part of the awakening of nationhood and self-determination. Similarly, in the 19th century and the early 20th century, the absence of a Scottish nationalist movement was widely commented upon. The historian Neil Davidson in his challenging thesis *The Origins of Scottish Nationhood* argues that Scottish nationalism as we now understand it emerged post-1707, and is a creation of recent times.[328] Although he does not use these words, there is a strand of Linda Colley's 'forging a nation' in this:[329] something all nations and nation states do throughout their history, actively selecting what they choose to remember and forget as they make up the folklores of their past and present, and indeed, future.[330]

Scottish independence would leave Scotland in many respects British. To deny or want to whitewash this out of our experience would be to want to deny large parts of our history. Scotland was a partner with England in the United Kingdom, and its people were at points, enthusiastic participants in the expansion and maintenance of the British Empire, and all its resultant activities: conquest, colonisation, exploitation and the slave trade.[331] Large amounts of Scotland's wealth were a direct result of Empire: for example, Glasgow's tobacco lords, Edinburgh's New Town, and Dundee's juteopolis.

Scottish military personnel fought in all Britain's wars post-1707 and were renowned the world over as impressive fighters.[332] There were the two World Wars, the long, bitter process of decolonisation, and the eager role British elites had for the country as an eager supplicant and prop in the American imperial project. Some of this was unfortunate, morally questionable, and occasionally, of dubious legal standing: from the British army's involvement in the Greek civil war from 1944-47, to the brutal massacres in Kenya in the 1950s, and the ill-fated Blair wars of Afghanistan and Iraq this century. But not all of it was of that ilk: Scottish soldiers, sailors and air personnel played their enthusiastic part in the defeat of Nazism and fascism. There are some stories to be proud of.

There is more to it than that. There is a common radical tradition of people coming together to fight against injustice and poverty and for greater democracy: the Chartists, Suffragettes, the first trade unions in the 19th century, and the rising influence of the Trades Union Congress and Scottish counterpart, the STUC; that's before talking about decolonisation, nuclear disarmament and the anti-war movements. These campaigns of what socialist writer G.D.H. Cole called 'the common people'[333] produced many of the civilising, humanising reforms which made Britain a better place for millions: the NHS, welfare state, employment and work rights, and greater equality at work.

Our Friends North, South, West and East

There are relevant examples to us close to home. There is the story of Ireland post-1922 when it became independent after a bitter conflict with the British military, followed by the Irish civil war. Ireland's British dimension had always been more contested and indeed imposed than Scotland's ever was, but despite that a debate about the intersection of Irishness and Britishness began as soon as Ireland became independent.

In recent times, as Ireland has grown more prosperous and self-confident, this debate has evolved. Thus, in 2011, Queen Elizabeth II, the UK's head of state, visited Croke Park, Dublin, the home of the Gaelic Athletic Association, but more importantly, the site of a British massacre of twelve spectators and one player at a Gaelic football match in 1920 in what was the original 'Bloody Sunday'. This was the first ever visit by a sitting British monarch to Ireland since independence and a profound act of Anglo-Irish reconciliation.[334]

As significant was the 100th anniversary of the Easter Rising in April 2016 that was characterised by a recognition in Ireland of memory, commemoration, remembrance and complex and competing histories. Whereas on the 50th anniversary Irish republicans marked the Easter Rising and unionists in the north marked the first day of the bloody battle of the Somme which happened at the same time, by the 100th anniversary, both events were seen as part of the same global conflict. Indeed, the victory of Irish independence can only be understood in the context of World War One and in grotesque, over-extended imperialism – the British Empire included.[335]

There is still one important omission, and loss of memory, about 1916 – and that is the impact on the United Kingdom. Seldom commented upon is that the current boundaries of the UK are less than a century old, dating back to Irish independence in 1922, and therefore originating in the Easter Rising. Ed Vulliamy wrote on the occasion of the 100th anniversary: 'The Easter rebellion was the beginning of the end of empire for Britain...'[336]

Not that distant in history or geography, our Nordic neighbours have gone through a complicated history of realignments, independence movement, and the emergence of new states. Norway became independent from Sweden in 1905 following a referendum in which 184 people voted against it in a free campaign – producing a 99.95% for statehood. Finland emerged from being part of imperial Russia as the Tsarist regime collapsed in 1917 having previously been in union with Sweden. Iceland, after attaining home rule in 1919, held a referendum after twenty-five years of self-government in 1944 which produced an emphatic vote for independence: this time 377 people voting against in a 99.95% vote.

The story has not yet ended. The Faroe Islands voted slenderly for independence in 1946 by a majority of a mere 111 votes (50.7:49.3) and shortly afterwards declared independence – only to settle for a maximal form of home rule from Denmark. To this day, they are one of only two territories to vote for independence and then not progress to it: what is called the ultimate 'buyer's remorse' – the other being Western Australia in 1933.[337] Greenland voted for home rule in 1979 and then with the election of a left-wing government voted to narrowly leave the EEC in a 1982 referendum (53:47), leaving in 1985, and subsequently voting for greater self-government in a 2008 ballot. As things currently stand, both the Faroe Islands and Greenland remain parts of Denmark, but have all sorts of ad hoc arrangements; for example, while Greenland left the EEC, the Faroe Islands never joined. There is in Greenland circles belief that the country is slowly on the way to independence.

What unites the above stories are shared common histories and heritages which have not only endured, but have been enriched and deepened by successive realignments. The Nordic countries are a geographical, cultural and geo-political term for the countries of Northern Europe and the North Atlantic. All of the nations and territories above – as well as Åland Islands (a Swedish autonomous archipelago in the Baltic) and Svalbard (a Norwegian archipelago in the Arctic Ocean) – participate in the Nordic Council which was established in 1952 and has developed on a number of inter-governmental co-operation fronts including foreign affairs and security.[338]

There will therefore more than likely be some kind of Britain, an acknowledgement of British identities, and some kind of arrangement across the nations that are the UK. The salient issue is not whether Scotland is or isn't independent or the continuation of the UK under any circumstances, but what kind of political union and co-operation, and for what purpose?

The UK as it is currently constituted does not, for all its hyperbole, really look after the wellbeing of its people very effectively. That's not very surprising – as the UK was never really designed for that purpose: its basis being, as we have seen, as an unashamed warrior state. The sociologist Colin Crouch has observed that the rise of a radical British right has seen an attempt to shift the UK from a welfare state to a warfare state;[339] in truth, British social democracy made the mistake of trying to build the former on the infrastructure of the latter.

Could a new set of arrangements between the nations of the UK aid a very different political dispensation? One which wasn't about the same problematic central state, advocacy for corporate interests and crony capitalism, and which was not about some of the dubious geo-political and quasi-imperial pretensions which still shape Britain's defence and foreign policies. The question is at least worth asking and the answer isn't automatically in one direction or another.

British Futures after the United Kingdom

There would be numerous challenges to Britain after Scottish independence. That much is obvious. As is for now the unknown nature of Brexit: in terms of membership or not of the European single market, whether there are hard or soft border controls between the UK and EU, and lots more. All of these will have huge implications for Scotland and whatever form independence could take.

First, there is the issue of what happens to England? There is the obvious threat of a reactionary English nationalism and right-wing populism – which rather than going away after the Brexit vote, has felt vindicated and given permission by it. So far such an English voice has always – despite some of the rhetoric of Thatcher and other right-wing Tories – been marginalised by the internal dynamics of the Tory coalition, but that has been weakening as party ties have diluted: hence the rise of UKIP first as a threat to the Tories on their right flank, but in the future, perhaps, more of a challenge to Labour.

What happens to radical, centre-left English politics? There is a proud, heretical, dissenting English tradition, one richer and more challenging of authority than labourism, but in recent times it has been mostly silent and acquiescent in the rightward drift of politics. There is, compounding this, the historic problem of British Labour addressing the English question and its inability to speak with a distinct English voice.

There is also underlying all of this the myth of Conservative England which has increasingly underpinned British Labour and centre-left considerations. There is a historic dimension, but the humbling experience of four election defeats in a row post-1979 and the populist nature of Thatcher's counter-revolution, have left an indelible mark, weakening self-confidence and forcing Labour for years after to question some of its basic assumptions (although maybe in retrospective, not questioning enough). But in recent years this has become a self-fulfilling prophecy, vacating the English landscape to Conservative politics and the conservative imagination.

Beyond the English question, what happens to Wales? In a reconfiguring UK does it put its weight behind attempts to force a federal or quasi-federal solution? That is the strategy of Labour First Minister Carwyn Jones, who has made several high-profile interventions at a UK level in the last few years including in the indyref and post-Brexit vote.[340] However, if as is likely such an approach does not pay dividends, what does Wales strategically do? The nightmare option would be to be left with England, and seen as little more than an appendage by English elites.

There is also the question of Northern Ireland that, like Scotland, voted to remain in the EU. Northern Ireland could be left in a position where, if as is inevitable, the UK comes out of the EU it has to change the internal Irish border from being a very soft border into a hard one. This carries political consequences for the sensitivities if not the ultimate durability of the Northern Irish peace process.

The short-term position for Northern Ireland looks uncertain with very few alternative paths to Brexit for the moment. Independence is not an option, nor is for the immediate, Irish reunification. Irish commentators such as Fintan O'Toole have raised the prospect of a new entity: Scotland Ireland Northern Ireland (SCINI) – which would address Northern Ireland's double identity, while keeping it and Scotland in the EU. It wouldn't be 'an old-fashioned unitary state' and would need to entail 'radical thinking about what it means to be a democracy in the 21st century.'[341] It isn't going to happen as a formal entity, but it is a time for radical thinking.

The challenges of Brexit bring home to roost forty years or more of British geo-political delusions. The UK has paid the price of politics of post-imperial grandeur. That sounds fair, but it isn't the elites who are going to suffer from Brexit, it's the people of the UK. Thus, as the Eurosceptic right indulge their moment in the sun and fantasise about a lean, mean, light touch, newly liberated Britain, freed from Euro sclerosis, it is working people and their living standards and rights who are going to suffer.

Already the Brexiteers are dusting down their long held ambitions of turning the UK into 'the Singapore of Europe' or a Hong Kong sitting off the continent, or being repositioned into the mid-Atlantic and more attuned to North America. None of this is likely to be completely realised, but they indicate the radicalism and ambition unleashed on the right by Brexit and the unfavourable terrain for the centre-left.

All of these dilemmas have been a long time fermenting. Just as Scotland's indyref didn't come out of nowhere, neither did the Brexit debate. It merely brought long brewing issues and controversies to the surface. The domestic and geo-political dilemmas the UK will face post-Brexit are dilemmas and conflicts UK elites have been trying to manage these last forty years.

The UK after decades of prevarication and being an 'awkward partner'[342] in Europe will have to confront these as hard choices which it will no longer be possible to fudge. Will the UK become a recalcitrant 'little Britain' turning its back on its European neighbours? How far will a resurgent right be able to push its fantasyland version of the UK when it hasn't in thirty years addressed any of the fundamental and structural weaknesses of British capitalism? For how long will the centre-left continue in retreat and disarray – an English, Scottish and Welsh story, as well as a British, European and global one? And is it possible that a post-Britain Britishness could emerge post-Brexit and post-Scottish independence that addresses some of the big issues in a more progressive manner?

The nations of the United Kingdom and the UK itself will never be the same again. But compared to that last three or four decades, the near-future could make that experience look positively becalmed – as economic, social and geo-political turbulence beckons. This future poses huge challenges for Scotland, but England's centre-left forces are going to have to recognise that the way they have been doing politics for decades has contributed to their present impotence.

Chapter Eleven:

The Four Dimensions of Scotland International

to seek the truth
is to foment terrorism

to call war state violence
is to foment terrorism

to question the news
is to foment terrorism
to press the mute button
is to foment terrorism

Tom Leonard, Litany: Blair's Britain, in Outside the Narrative, 2009

Once upon a time the world was meant to be about being big, whether military might, economic power, or just sheer prestige and clout. This was true of the age of Empire and also the era of US-led post-war managed capitalism. This was the logic that produced the European Union, with size mattering, to try to match and counter the power of corporations and capitalism.

Those assumptions began to be challenged post-Soviet Union with, after 1989, an unprecedented springtime for nations across the European continent the like of which in scale had never been seen before, surpassing 1848 and 1918. Suddenly small was in; being adaptive, able to act quickly, and set national goals and priorities.[343] Then came the crash of 2008 and suddenly for the newly independent Baltic states, Iceland or Ireland, it didn't look too great being small when a financial tsunami hit. Then again the UK hit the buffers in the same period.

It is too determinist to talk about big or small states being the optimum size, but historically we have seen 'the return of small states'[344] followed by a long economic boom, and then economic and political uncertainty and anxiety. It is hardly surprising then that, in this climate and culture of turmoil and change, Scotland is shifting and repositioning itself geo-politically. This is a continual, never-ending process.

The world historically and contemporaneously is full of such considerations: currently Turkey is shifting how it sees itself in relation to Europe and the Middle East, the US has, at the onset of the 21st century, been rebalancing its interests vis-à-vis Europe and the Far East, and Putin's Russia is in a brutal way attempting to re-stress Russian rights in what it sees as its 'near homeland', and as regional player in the Middle East.

Scotland's geo-political repositioning may seem humdrum compared to the big stakes involved in some of the cases of today, but as this chapter will underline Scotland matters and has impact way beyond these shores, because of history, our membership of the UK and the accident of geography.

Scotland on the Move

Scotland's deliberations have to be seen on a number of dimensions: Scottish, UK, European and globally. It isn't surprising that the British factor should play a part here. There is, as previously examined, Churchill's notion of the three worlds of Britain: Europe, Commonwealth and the English-speaking world, which Andrew Gamble updated to four by talking of the idea of England as a 'world island' in four intersecting circles: union, Commonwealth, Europe and Anglo-America.[345] These notions have been significantly thrown into flux by the Brexit vote, which has contributed to a geo-political crisis for the UK and with major consequences for Scotland.

These four intersecting circles are an appropriate starting point for thinking about the world from Scotland's vantage point and interests, but with very different interpretations. These four strands: the union/post-union; Europe – with a particular emphasis on northern Europe and the Nordics; Anglo-America; and the Commonwealth, will form the basis of a global Scotland's positioning, alliances and networks. To cite the title of a 1970s study of this subject 'power and manoeuvrability' are critical ingredients in the world of interdependence.[346]

Union/Post-union Britain

First, the framework of union/post-union. As Adam Price, former Plaid Cymru MP, said in the indyref when the air was full of talk from the No side of 'divorce', 'separatism' and 'tearing Scotland out of the UK', one way of reframing this from such apocalyptic language is to observe that the union isn't just about England and Scotland. Instead, 'there are four people in this marriage, a domestic arrangement that not even the most liberal Cameroon would sanction' without which such bi-national discussions 'relegates those of us in the rest of the UK to junior partners', or worse render them invisible.[347]

Post-Brexit the UK is hardly a partnership of equals, but one where a very partial version of England has seized control of the vessel and is steering her in the direction of the rocks, without permission of many of its passengers. What happens to England and the remnants of the British state will have a huge impact on Scotland. Will Westminster continue with business as usual in light of Scottish independence? Would a post-UK/ rUK continue to be run by a rump Conservative Party that in 2015 won 41.0% of the English vote, and last won a majority of the vote there in 1955, the same year it won a popular majority in Scotland?

Where there is political will there is always a political way, and all over the world there are numerous fuzzy, messy, hybrid arrangements that offer some pointers. The UK has history here – as it isn't a conventional state – and isn't even a nation (if Scotland has been a stateless nation, the UK is a nationless state – hence its problems with British nation-state building). It has undertaken all sorts of compromises and created numerous ad hoc arrangements that may prove relevant to the situation with Scotland.

First, take Ireland post-independence. It began limited both in sovereignty – with Ireland initially being a Dominion under the Crown and in the Commonwealth – and geography, with Northern Ireland remaining part of the UK. In 1923 the UK and Ireland agreed a Common Travel Area enduring to this day, an open borders area with no border checks. In 1949 the Ireland Act was passed, following Ireland declaring itself a republic and leaving the Commonwealth; this defined Ireland as 'not a foreign country' for all sorts of citizenship rights, such as the right to vote in all UK elections.

Relevant here has been the Northern Irish peace process with the UK government prepared to see its sovereignty over the province compromised and in part shared with the Republic. Significant measures include the 1985 Anglo-Irish Agreement signed by Thatcher and Irish Taoiseach Garett FitzGerald which for the first time formalised Irish Government influence over Northern Ireland much to unionist chagrin in the north.[348] Then, when the first tentative steps in the Northern Irish peace process were being explored, the then Secretary of State for Northern Ireland Peter Brooke declared in November 1990 that Britain has no 'selfish strategic or economic interest' in Northern Ireland and would accept unification if based on the popular will; this intervention had a huge impact on Irish republican thinking and gave impetus to the peace process.[349]

Subsequently, the Downing Street Declaration of December 1993 between UK Prime Minister and Irish Taoiseach Arnold Reynolds accepted the principle of self-determination based on consent for all the people of Ireland. It included recognition of the right to a united Ireland, should the people of north and south want it, while the Irish Government accepted that this had to include the right of unionists in the north to object to unification.

All of this culminated in the 1998 Good Friday Agreement (GFA) between the UK and Irish Governments and most of the main parties in Northern Ireland (the exception being Ian Paisley's Democratic Unionists and Sinn Féin offering qualified support in the referendum). The GFA set out provisions for Northern Ireland devolution, North-South and West-East co-operation, and eventually saw Provisional IRA decommission its weapons arsenal and declare the formal end of the conflict.[350]

The agreement was backed by simultaneous referendums in May 1998 held in the province with a 71.1:28.9 endorsement and in the Republic with a 94.4:5.6 margin of victory.[351] This paved the way for the establishment of the Northern Irish Assembly with the first elections in July 1998 and the beginning of power sharing between the unionist and nationalist traditions. The Northern Irish peace process, nearly two decades since the Good Friday Agreement, can be judged a qualified success with the absence of armed conflict, established institutions and agreed political processes. But there remains profound and entrenched mistrust between the two communities in Northern Ireland, and little scope for a politics which transcends that in the near future.

There are other less dramatic examples of British ad hoc arrangements. A pertinent one is the case of the Isle of Man and the Channel Islands of Jersey and Guernsey. None of these are in the United Kingdom, but nor are they in the EU. Yet at the same time they sit inside the Common Travel Area of the UK and Republic of Ireland established in 1923 and they are in law 'British subjects'.

The Isle of Man and Channel Islands are known as Crown

Dependencies – rather than being part of the British Overseas Territories – which are the random remnants of the British Empire scattered around the world that include Bermuda, the British Virgin Islands, the Cayman Islands, the Falkland Islands and Gibraltar. These two external sets of territories provide the world's biggest tax havens – with the acquiescence of the UK Government – and also in many respects offer a vision of a 'little Britain', worlds where what it means to be British is stuck in some sepia-like manifestation of the past.

The Isle of Man is not in the Commonwealth, but chooses to take part in the Commonwealth Games entering its own team. Jersey and Guernsey are in the Commonwealth; and the Isle of Man and the Channel Islands are members of the British-Irish Council. The UK Parliament can legislate for them and has responsibility for defence and foreign affairs. Even though they are not part of the UK they can be seen as part of the 'idea' of Britain. They are part of the archipelago of 'the British Isles' – the Isle of Man by geography and geo-politically, the Channel Islands, geo-politically, while geographically they sit twelve miles off the coast of France.

One observation on the above relevant to Scotland is the balance between when the UK has chosen to be flexible and loose in its arrangements, and when it has chosen to act in the opposite manner. For example, with regard to Ireland post-independence, the UK has shown enormous pragmatism – particularly in the initiation and development of the Northern Ireland peace process; it has also made many mistakes – from its tolerance of the unionist one-party state of Stormont of 1922-72 to some of the worst repressive acts by the British military in Northern Ireland over the course of the troubles.

Yet, the British record in Ireland pre-1922 is not only a deplorable and shaming one, it illustrates the worst aspects of British statecraft: a capacity at points to be stubborn, believe in military might, and perhaps, worst of all, to believe your own myths: namely the idea of Britain as this benign, civilised, enlightened force and of course, the abstract totem of parliamentary sovereignty.

A British framework of co-operation will matter greatly to Scotland. This will have an inter-governmental dimension, a body such as a council of ministers, and could go further, having some kind of democratic input and oversight on shared areas of interest, which could range from strategic defence and security concerns to maritime rights and the civic and social union of the countries. Moreover, the nature of these institutions is dependent on the nature of Brexit and the future direction of the UK/rUK and in it, the character and ethos of the British state. How possible is it to conceive of the British central state – a pre-democratic entity in the age of post-democracy – finally catching up and embracing the 21st century? The omens do not look good for the moment.

The European Dimension

Post-Brexit vote we face the prospect of the UK leaving the EU and either negotiating to remain a member of the European single market, or sitting outside it and having to pay duties on exports. While any details of what Brexit will be remains for now shrouded in ambiguity, the vote to leave the EU seems to have indicated a public desire for a return of control over migration, monies, and laws.

A Scotland that attempts to retain its current EU membership raises all sort of questions. Is such a settlement possible without Scottish independence? Would the EU be open to such a compromise, and what about the UK/rUK government? First Minister Nicola Sturgeon has spent considerable time and effort post-Brexit attempting to create a political space to allow this to be explored: namely, Scotland not being dragged out of the EU against its popular will, while attempting to build cross-party co-operation and a wider mandate, and keep party members on board with regard to the prospects of independence and a future second indyref. This is a sensitive balancing act which entails speaking in different languages and giving messages to differing audiences; it has so far mostly worked, but will entail big challenges further down the line as details of Brexit become clear and the SNP have to decide on the content of any future independence offer.

There are also, with independence in the context of Brexit, a whole host of sticky issues. For example, if the UK/rUK was not a member of the European single market what would be the nature of the Scottish-English border? Is it possible to imagine a 'hard' border with border controls and checks – the spectre of separatism – or is that always going to remain a nightmare for use in anti-independence campaign propaganda?

Then there is the big issue of the future of Europe. The Franco-German-dominated version of Europe that has driven the EU since its inception, overseen deeper integration, and seen it through many crises and reverses, is no longer the force it once was. The Germans are the undisputed hegemon of Europe while France faces numerous crises: economic, demographic, and in relation to Islamic communities and the French republican idea of integration. The EU hasn't exactly shown the principles of European solidarity in relation to Greece's debt crisis, running roughshod over the left-wing Syriza government and ignoring the wishes of the 2015 anti-austerity referendum in what can be seen as a brutal fiscal authoritarianism, jointly administered by Berlin and Brussels.[352]

Accentuating all of this is the crisis of the Euro: the single currency of the European project launched to great fanfare on 1 January 1999. It was always a political project of the union, more than a monetary and economic creation but despite this was floated without the commensurate mechanisms to make it work. It has been a failure on nearly every level: economic, social, and democratic. The only measurement on which it is a success is that despite everything it still exists. This failure is one of the entire European project. Aditya Chakrabortty commented that 'the noble European project is turning into: a grim march to the bottom... brought in by agreeable-looking Wise Folk often claiming to be social democratic.'[353]

This is the European project that Scotland aspires to be a member of – and while this is an understandable aspiration a reality check is much needed. The Scottish Government wants to show its European credentials: that it doesn't buy into Euroscepticsm and 'little Englanderism' and that it will not allow Scotland to be taken out of the EU against the democratic will of the people of the country.

Scotland's pro-Europeans do not face these stormy waters alone. It has lots of friends, well-wishers and supporters across the continent and in positions of power in the EU and European Governments. Some of this is on the democratic argument of a nation being taken out of the EU against their will, another about supporting pro-European opinion, while a powerful driver is sheer weariness at decades of British arrogance, semi-detachment and being difficult in EU summits.

One significant ally of Scotland will be the Irish Government. In the story of the UK's two recent referendums – the Scottish and EU votes – it was always the prospect of the latter which concerned the Irish more, with threats to the Northern Irish peace process, nature of the border, and also, critically, Irish influence in EU corridors of power which traditionally involved working with the British on many issues. Compared to that and their own experience of independence, the prospect of Scottish independence was viewed in a more sanguine light.[354]

Scotland will have to start thinking about the membership terms on which we want to be a member of the EU. Do we really want to agree to sign up to the Euro with all the resultant problems, which would pose two currencies on the island of Britain? Or do we consider the realpolitik approach of signing up to a long-term commitment to the Euro – like the Swedes –

without having any intention of joining it? Finally, we have to ask if the EU is the only show in town in which to display our European credentials? More than likely the answer is yes; but we should not rule out completely consideration of the EEA. The more options Scotland can explore the better. Europe is, as Eurosceptics point out, more than the EU.

Anglo-America

The Anglo-American relationship has been one of the key pillars, if not the key pillar, of the UK in post-war times.[355] It has been an asymmetrical relationship with one dominant and one junior partner, and the imbalance of it has at times proven troublesome – from Britain attempting to develop its own nuclear deterrent, Suez, Wilson keeping the UK out of Vietnam despite pressures from the Americans, the Falklands, the US invasion of Commonwealth country Grenada in 1983 without informing the British, or the US bombing Libya in 1986 from UK bases – but it has endured because the two nations have bigger strategic interests in common.

The UK and US have, apart from defence and foreign affairs interests, established close collaboration between their security and intelligence forces which sit within the wider Five Eyes intelligence alliance, and also includes Canada, Australia and New Zealand, which was established in 1941.[356]

Anglo-American capitalism also has a propensity to see the world in a similar light – based on a view of the free market economy that encourages free trade, market liberalisation, privatisation, and restricting state subsidies. This account has become pronounced since the Reagan-Thatcher 'special relationship' of the 1980s based on their shared right-wing ideological outlook, but it has long outlived them and survived through successive Tory and Labour administrations.

Scotland matters in this geo-political alliance way beyond its size and population. First, there is the small matter of the

Trident nuclear deterrent situated in the Firth of Clyde on Scottish land and sailing from Scottish waters. Second, there is the issue of NATO membership and planning, and Scotland's position in north-west Europe being of importance.

Both of these are well known, but what is less known is the geo-political issue of the waters beyond Scotland's north-west coast and why this makes Scotland matter so much. Our country is a crucial part of what is known in military and security circles as 'the GIUK Gap', which stands for the Greenland Ireland United Kingdom Gap.[357]

The GIUK Gap represents the sea channels between Greenland and Iceland and Ireland and the north-west coast of Scotland: 'a choke point in the world's sea lanes'. It had huge importance in the Second World War, the Cold War and now again in the rising tensions of the post-Cold War. It offered the most realistic access for the Nazi Kriegsmarine, Soviet naval forces and now Putin's Russian navy from their main bases into the North Atlantic; the only other alternative being the narrow and well-defended English Channel.

It was critical in the battles of the North Atlantic in the Second World War – and was one reason for the British military occupation of Iceland and American occupation of Greenland – the result of the German invasion of Denmark. This is yet another reason why Scotland's independence referendum outcome mattered across the West and in the US White House. Tim Marshall wrote:

The GIUK is one of the main reasons why London flew into a panic in 2014 when, briefly, the vote on Scottish independence looked as if it might result in a Yes. The loss of power in the North Sea and North Atlantic would have been a strategic blow and a massive dent to the prestige of whatever was left of the UK.[358]

This means that who controls and runs Scotland matters well beyond our shores, and is of supreme concern to the West and any US administration.

Scotland's Commonwealth Connections

Finally, Scotland's soft power extends across the world, one of the significant institutions of which is the Commonwealth that emerged out of the shadows of the British Empire and was formally established in 1926 as 'the British Commonwealth of Nations'. It dropped British from its title in 1949 and now contains 53 nations and 2.2 billion people, representing nearly three in ten of all the people in the world (all of which were previously part of the Empire plus Mozambique and Rwanda).[359]

At significant points, such as the campaign against South African apartheid, the Commonwealth played a role in the sanctions debate and the isolation of the regime and also contributed to the isolation of the Thatcher Government's opposition to sanctions. At other times, such as the human rights abuses of Mugabe's Zimbabwean regime or rising concerns about the genocide of the Sri Lanka authorities in the Tamil part of the island, the Commonwealth has compromised its principles and not taken a clear, ethical stance. Suspensions of membership have been few and far between.

An independent Scotland would be able to take part in the Commonwealth and to advocate for a more pronounced and ethical position on human rights abuses, authoritarian and dictatorial regimes, and other ethical and moral considerations. In particular, it would be able to work closely with countries with significant Scottish diasporas such as Canada, Australia and New Zealand as well as elsewhere.

Scotland would also be a member of international forums, either as part of the European Union or independently as in the case of the United Nations. This raises the issue of the basis of what an independent Scotland's defence and foreign affairs would look like. Inevitably as a small nation these would be different from the current policies of the UK, entailing less defence spending, an absence of post-imperial delusions, and a foreign policy which was more based on negotiation and collaboration, as we see with the Nordics and other similar small-sized states.

Possible Scotland International

Scotland has been invisible as a modern nation on the international stage – as we explored in Chapter Four – until first the Abdelbaset al-Megrahi controversy and then more substantially the experience of the indyref. As previously explored the Scottish Government has for the foreseeable future a foreign affairs and diplomacy deficit and gap in resources. This will have consequences as we navigate the choppy climate of the UK post-Brexit and in any post-independence Scotland.

Other nations such as Estonia, Latvia and Lithuania found themselves in a similar under-resourced diplomatic position at the end of the Soviet Union. The solution their pro-independence governments proposed was to set up cultural organisations that acted as Shadow Foreign ministries. The Catalan government has a track record of building an impressive network of overseas representatives in a flexible structure and often in partnership with others. This is, according to Michael Keating, 'not merely the projection of Catalan interests, but the internationalisation of Catalonia.'[360] Scotland already has representation in a host of British embassies as well as in Brussels, but the Scottish Government should urgently review the environment and look legally at how far it can support and aid the creation of such a nascent diplomatic service.

Much of the above falls into the category of what is known as paradiplomacy[361] – the art of international policy pursued by governments and territories not yet formally independent such as Scotland, Catalonia and Flanders. We also have to have a discussion about the uses and reach of soft power diplomacy and cultural diplomacy.[362] Scotland is already blessed with numerous advantages: the English language, being a member of the Anglo-sphere of English-speaking democracies, and an ability to make numerous global connections and conversations. We also have such international gatherings as the Edinburgh Festivals every year, along with the draw of Celtic Connections and other events that could become more vibrant and mix the local, national and international in an independent country. What would a Scottish equivalent of the British Council look like? What public faces, values and interests of the country would we present to the world? What is the modern Scotland that we want the world to know? We need to start discussing these issues now in preparation for future challenges.

Scotland as a Pioneering Nation

As Scotland enters uncharted waters on the international stage there are numerous recent examples and case studies to draw from. First, as already explored in the previous chapter, the lessons of Ireland are germane – in negotiating a form of independence which was not separation, but maintained co-operation, shared sovereignty and a virtual union in travel and work arrangements.

Second, is the example of Iceland, a nation with a mere 320,000 population who have post-crash dared to jail bankers and embark on an economic recovery which has learnt from the unsustainable previous bubblenomic version. It has also put democracy and integrity central to its public life and institutions.

Third, the collapse of the Soviet bloc did produce a golden era for the creation of new nation states, with two dozen independent countries emerging onto the international stage. Not one of those countries, whether it is the Baltics, the Czech or Slovak republics, or Slovenia, started with the advantages, skills and international reach that Scotland has. All of the states cited have ended up as economic successes and become viable and prosperous.

What all these experiences illustrate is the limits of independence in an age of globalisation and interdependence or, as the economist John Kay put it discussing the Scottish example: 'the gain in sovereignty would be limited by the realities of globalisation.'[363] Scottish independence to some seems a very 19th-century solution to 21st-century problems, posing the parameters of the nation state as the most appropriate vehicle for solving problems and advancing statecraft. To answer that charge independence has to be about inter-independence – recognising that this is about degrees of autonomy – whether in or out of the political union that is the UK.

There are real constraints in the modern-day world, compared to the simplicities of crying 'freedom' and 'sovereignty' and assuming that such concepts cleanse us overnight from the grubby deals and illegal wars that come with membership of the UK. Independence allows Scotland to make certain choices, priorities and trade-offs as a society and have an international profile, but none of this is about absolutes.

An independent Scotland is going to have to find allies, friends and alliances, and to live and thrive as a network nation on the wit of its values, reputation and diplomacy and international alliances. This will involve Scotland setting out on new global adventures but that, like many other aspects of our future, is a very new story which is also part of an older, familiar one: the re-emergence of Scotland as explorers, adventurers and discoverers in this time of ideas and soft power rather than Empire and conquest. It could indeed offer a new age of Scottish pioneers and pioneering: this time a little more humble but filled with curiosity and energy for new challenges and new opportunities.

Chapter Twelve:

A Republic of the Mind

The republic of outsiders shows us that we are more than our money and that we cannot be entirely rendered into a sellable cliché – that creating obstinate, unusual identities for ourselves is more than possible. Their tools are now in all of our hands.

Alissa Quart, Republic of Outsiders, 2013

We are like a house that hasn't been lived in for a long time you know. You go in, and you can see familiar things, but nothing really works, and you know the water needs [to be] sorted out and switched on again, and there is a lot of dust around. There is a lot of great things from the past. There is a wonderful treasure trove of historical memories.

Andy Wightman, interview with author, 2011

These are dramatic times to be alive in Scotland. Exciting and exhilarating for some but deeply frustrating – and even filled with foreboding – for others. In discussing Scotland's recent experience and trying to put it in a more historical and comparative context we can see that while so much has changed, there is also a high degree of continuity. There are often repeated patterns and characteristics in how Scotland is governed and in some of our public debate. As Peter Geoghegan observed: 'Everything has changed and everything has stayed the same.'[364]

The indyref was historic in defining a nation that in many respects will never be the same again. The Scotland of pre-indyref cannot be returned to. Yet it is also true that there are multiple truths and stories about that experience, and no one perspective can be privileged above others.[365]

Learning from Our Near Past: Putting the Indyref in Context

First, we have to recognise that for all the democratic impulse and spirit many people found the whole thing disturbing and disquieting – even something that made them a stranger in their own home. This should make all of us pause and reflect. It is a modern-day tragedy that anyone should feel so alienated, unwelcome and their opinions unvalued – and of course in some circumstances, much worse. We can never tolerate or acquiesce in the politics of intolerance.

Second, the limits of Yes and No as offers, and the parameters of debate put forward should also cause us to reflect. Both of the official campaigns were fatally flawed, offering visions of the future which weren't completely honest, didn't treat voters as adults and refused to be open and truthful about the hard choices in front of us, either independent or in the union. Both campaigns presented apple pie and motherhood visions of respective futures: of a union of social justice and partnership, or an independence that was a land of milk and honey. Both Yes and No offered the prospect of certainty and stability in their offers, a world where risk, doubt and ambiguity were banished completely. It was a problematic way to conduct a referendum and for all the 'festival of democracy' rhetoric during the campaign and afterwards, it left a lot of people feeling uneasy. They were in effect faced with the prospect of two offers, both of which had an element of faith-based, evangelical political sentiment in them.

Post-indyref reflections have tended to concentrate on Yes Scotland's journey from being miles behind to winning 45% overall and 37% of Labour's vote. However this isn't a vindication of Yes Scotland but is due to a host of other factors including Better Together's weakness and the decline in trust in the British state. This, combined with the longer story of Scottish distinctiveness and difference, meant that Yes tapped into some of the key trends of society, but not by enough to produce a winning coalition.

The reasons for this rewind are that any future indyref will be very different from the first time. Any next time will see a short indyref campaign of two to three months, rather than two-and-a-half to three years. There will also only be another referendum with Yes significantly ahead and clear favourites to win. The idea of independence in its SNP colour will, in all likelihood, become the continuity and normalcy offer, particularly in the context of Brexit. All of this will require a very different independence offer, one that moves away from the catch-all 'Big Tentism' of 2014.

The Seven Stories of any Future Independence Vision

The 2014 independence offer of the Scottish Government and SNP was fatally flawed: economically, fiscally, in its lack of acknowledgement of difficult choices and much more. Some of this was avoidable, but a large element was the product of the circumstances of the genesis of the SNP offer: the surprise victory of 2011 with a mandate for an independence referendum and the need to fill in the detail of such an offer in record quick time. The process and methodology of this left a lot to be desired and the end result was the White Paper, *Scotland's Future*.[366] Any future independence offer cannot have the same shortcomings and has to address seven key areas and seven basic stories.[367]

The Economic Case

The UK does not work for the vast majority of the people who live here. It is a political and economic system that appears in many respects to be broken, but that actually works perfectly well for a small self-aggrandising elite. This matters to the case for independence, as Scotland needs a robust economic case for independence based on this country being affluent, wealthy, developed, and more than capable of running its own affairs.

This means developing an economic case which just doesn't go along with neo-liberal assumptions and the managerialist mantra that Scotland can grow itself out of difficult choices via growth, and that this can be achieved by getting hold of the economic levers. Similarly, the Salmondnomics independence offer based on oil at $113 a barrel was never very viable or attractive; it would have posed a Scottish economy where oil and gas took 15% of GDP versus 2% in the UK, giving the oil companies huge influence, and which wasn't exactly eco-friendly or sustainable.

Whatever one thinks of the Government Expenditure and Revenue Scotland (GERS) figures they point to Scotland in the short to medium term having difficult fiscal choices. This is true of most developed countries that become independent – the cost of establishing new services, pulling out of bigger systems, and establishing a record for credibility with markets. The 2014 offer just tried to pretend all this didn't exist and that from the first days of statehood the social democratic land of our dreams could be established. A prevailing mood in Yes was that current Tory austerity was as bad as it could get and things could only get better post-independence. This after all was the basis for mobilising those in Scotland's most disadvantaged communities, many of whom were desperate to escape the parsimonious, punitive nature of the British welfare state.

Any future independence offer has to start from the honest position that the first five to ten years of self-government will involve bumpy times and hard choices, but by the end Scotland would be in a better place. That entails talking about what we prioritise, how we decide winners and losers, and how we identify strategic long-term investment priorities. It is also true that Scotland holds an ace in any future discussions with the rUK Government: the placing of Trident in Scottish waters and the geo-political position Scotland sits in, which we will return to.

The Social Justice Case

Scotland is scarred by inequality, poverty and exclusion: a human tragedy and disgrace in one of the richest countries in the world. Perhaps worse than the material hardship, people suffer from a profound feeling of powerlessness and have given up believing anything can be done to rectify this.

Many of the drivers of social justice are already in Scottish hands, such as education and health with some welfare powers devolved to the Scottish Parliament from September 2016.[368] But independence will need a more convincing offer than the slogan that 'Britain is for the rich', from the Radical Independence Campaign (RIC) leaflet which worked so well on some of Scotland's council estates. There will need to be a serious offer at the heart of any future proposals that isn't just based on the negative. Stopping policies such as the bedroom tax and sanctions is not enough. One measure worth consideration is a citizen's income and perhaps even using this as a right to ask from each Scottish citizen that they have responsibilities to others in a new social contract.

The Cultural Case

Scotland is already, in how it sees itself culturally, partially independent, but there is an assumption in the SNP version of self-government that it has to do as little as imaginatively possible here and that the cultural ecology, individuals and institutions, along with the infrastructure, will just fall into its lap.

In recent years there have been enormous cultural stramashes about the establishment of Creative Scotland, its remit and funding decisions,[369] along with the role of broadcasting and in particular, the BBC. These and many other episodes point to continued tensions about how Scotland represents and reflects itself back to itself and the wider world.

Yet, there is a much bigger cultural dimension than just talking about what happens in the world of arts and culture, or dubious notions such as 'the creative class' or 'creative industries'. That is exploring and advancing the notion of cultural change. The SNP version of independence in modern times has consistently been about 'the full powers of the Parliament' to the exclusion of wider societal transformation. One SNP senior minister even told me post-2011 that all independence entailed was 'extending the Scotland Act 1998 into every aspect of public life until one day we find that we are independent.' Apart from the fact that such a version of independence is never going to happen, what they were envisaging was a restrictive, institutional version of change: one both very British and Scottish in the elite myths it bought into.

Such top-down, tidy, managerialist politics are not only the continuation of the 1950s 'Labour Scotland' vision of society in its new Nationalist colours, but exclude the potential of independence to be about society changing. Scotland needs transformation in large parts of public life and that does not come solely from politicians, the Parliament and a permission-based version of change. It comes from power shifting in society, attitudinal change and encouraging cultural change. For all the undoubted energies and engagement of 2014 such an approach was missing from the official SNP independence proposals, as it has been consistently from their portrayal of statehood. In the second decade of the 21st century such a limited idea of independence as 'all power to the Parliament' is both debilitating and anachronistic to the spirit of the times we live in.

The Democratic Case

There are several irrefutable democratic arguments for independence. One has been provided by Brexit. The other is the experience of the UK Parliaments elected 1970-2020 which have produced 32 years (64%) of Tory or Tory-dominated governments, none of which Scotland voted for. However, this is not an adequate or substantive enough measurement of democracy. It is an indicator of the failings of British politics, not our own credentials. There needs to be a homegrown democratic argument, one that is about more than power being concentrated in the Scottish Government and Parliament and around Edinburgh.

Scotland is already one of the most centralised countries in Western Europe.[370] We have a mere 32 local councils with a population of 5.3 million, when Finland has 313 districts with a 5.5 million population. To make matters worse local government is barely worthy of the name, considering financially and legally it is heavily controlled and constrained by the Scottish Government.

Scotland needs a new democratic framework that matches the public engagement, hopes and spirits evident in the indyref. This should include consideration of democratising public services, institutions, and even, changing the governance of the voluntary sector and business. Why shouldn't Scotland begin to dare to imagine and map out what a social and economic democracy would entail? Clearly, democratisation and decentralisation should not stop with the devolution of powers from London to Edinburgh. A new compact is needed which recognises both that the old paternalism and its new incantation are fundamentally not fit for purpose, when people live in an age of choice, diversity and pluralism in so many aspects of their lives.

The Philosophical Case

The official philosophical basis of the 2014 offer tried to be all things to everyone. The White Paper declared that its future vision of independence was 'to create a more democratic Scotland; to build a more prosperous country; [and] to become a fairer society.' The prospectus which brought all three strands together was the belief that 'it is time for the people of Scotland to take responsibility for our own future...'[371]

Underlying this was the assumption that Scotland is a social democratic country, an assumption, as we have seen in Chapter Six, never explained in any great detail. Nor has there been a particular Scottish take on social justice forthcoming from the SNP, or from Scottish Labour when they were in office. Instead, all of this has been continually viewed as self-evident with good intentions taken as read. Thus, we had in the indyref from the SNP and Yes lots of virtue signalling, subliminal messaging and the less than subtle leaflets like '*To End Tory Rule Forever*', which equated Scotland's centre-left credentials and majority with the democratic characteristics of self-government.

Any future independence offer is going to need as a backstory a much more rigorous philosophical grounding. This at the time social democracy is on the wane in its appeal, reputation and results across the globe. Scotland cannot be expected to buck the global trend, power of markets and single-handedly rebuild social democracy in one country, even though that was the implicit in the hopes of 2014.

We learn from the success of political opponents such as Thatcherism and Reaganism that the path to success is to go with the flow of economic and social change. They did not create the culture of individualism. Instead, they championed it, encouraged it and made it something that became identified with their political projects. In a similar vein, Scottish independence should recognise the greater desire for individual autonomy, self-determination and interdependence, and articulate it in a philosophy of self-determination which isn't just about the nation state, but power, choice and voice within society.

The Psychological Case

The psychological dimension was probably one of the biggest – along with being one of the least understood – weaknesses of the 2014 offer. The Yes side offered a confident, upbeat, panglossian tale of optimism, security and certainty. In its lack of acknowledging doubt and uncertainty it left very few ways in which No voters could connect with it. For all its borrowing from positive psychology, it had a very limited, almost one-dimensional awareness of the psychological dimensions of the debate. This isn't entirely surprising as the Martin Seligman school of positive psychology[372] that they tapped into is, as Seligman himself conceded in Scotland, not about collective change at the level of a culture or a nation, but about individuals.[373]

Yes were asking people to give up something with which they were familiar, even in many respects comfortable – the UK – and take, in the words of Better Together, 'a leap in the dark'. Something was potentially being removed from people that many regarded as important and even precious, and this came over as an existential threat.

There will always be an element of this in a binary Yes/No vote on statehood, but an approach which acknowledges doubts and fears and places at its centre a very human, emotionally intelligent offer would mitigate some of this. It would recognise the importance of psychological reasoning in how people decide to vote and interpret the world. That would entail an independence offer that did not just pretend that everything would be all right on the other side of statehood, and instead would acknowledge risks, uncertainty and the unknown. It isn't convincing politics in a world characterised by huge uncertainty to counter it with certainty. That is a sort of faith-based politics and will work even less effectively second time around.

The Geo-Political Case

The final dimension of the seven tests any independence plan has to pass is the geo-political one explored in Chapter Eleven. The last independence offer did not succeed in this. It attempted to neutralise the NATO issue, tried to blunderbuss on the EU, and did not really want to openly talk about Trident. The implicit message was that the UK had successively eroded its moral authority to breaking point, and that Scottish independence allowed the chance for us to recover it – domestically and internationally – in what can be described as a very old-fashioned Scottish sentiment.

An independent Scotland has to address geo-political concerns using soft power, cultural diplomacy and an effective paradiplomacy and has to take on the big questions. These include where Scotland sits as a nation in the north-west corner of Europe and why it is of much wider importance. This strays into sensitive areas which Scottish politicians including even SNP ones are wary of such as the US-UK military-industrial-intelligence complex. But on the plus side, these factors give Scotland a strong hand to play in any independence negotiations.

Brexit raises a number of thorny issues. It makes the democratic argument for independence much more compelling but weakens the economic basis – considering most of Scotland's exports go to rUK, not the EU. There are unintended consequences from the kind of Brexit deal that the UK Government will finally negotiate with Brussels. If the

UK ends up with a hard Brexit outwith the single market, it makes it more likely that Scottish independence could see a hard border between Scotland and England. This is the sort of UK that Scottish independence supporters want to run a mile from, but it threatens the economic and civic wellbeing of these isles, and raises the spectre of bitter division. A soft Brexit landing whereby the UK remains in the single market would be better for Scotland and throw up less dilemmas, but leaves the pragmatic case for the union stronger. At the moment, a hard Brexit looks the more likely scenario – and with it a bumpy ride for all concerned – Scotland included.

An independence package that can convincingly succeed and win the popular and intellectual argument needs answers in all seven areas. The 2014 offer in this respect fell spectacularly short. At most it emphatically had the better of two of the seven areas: the democratic and cultural terrain, despite its shortcomings in both. At the same time it had a foothold in the social justice case. It failed on the economic, philosophical, psychological and geo-political. Overall it is a measure of the weaknesses of the Better Together argument that independence got to 45% of the vote.

Underlying these seven strands any offer has also to be seen as practical, addressing real concerns and problems with solutions that are realistic, plausible and believable. It also has to be, to an extent, idealistic – in that it aims and aspires for the higher ground while not being naïve. The 2014 independence prospectus could only pass muster in the last of these three, while still leaving something to be desired.

The Power of Stories

An important facet of any future independence vision and other competing versions of the future will be how they present and articulate themselves via stories. They have to create stories that are plausible and personally connect, inhabited with real people and characters we can identify with. The best example in the indyref was probably Nicola Sturgeon's Strathclyde University lecture in December 2012 when she talked of the life chances of an imaginary child called Kirsty.[374] Subsequently post-indyref Kirsty became 'adopted' by *Holyrood* magazine to popularise the different factors and pressures facing a baby born in a disadvantaged community in today's Scotland.[375]

The language of politics matters and reveals much. Too often politics is described by politicians, and those who live and breathe it, in abstract and depersonalised terms that lack emotional connectedness. This is the story of too much of the left in Scotland, Britain and the West. Then there was the discombobulated experience of how New Labour did its politics: which produced a generation of politicians who forced their centre-left values into a managerialist straightjacket lacking passion and authenticity.[376] This has cost Labour dear subsequently as its elected politicians have struggled to reclaim a convincing language and is one small factor in the rise of Jeremy Corbyn: someone who emerged unscathed from the New Labour era because he was never a participant.[377] This was evident in Scotland post-indyref where SNP politicians somehow inhabited a political language and passion connected to having a big vision which came over as much more genuine and less mangled. Some of the outstanding examples of oratory such as the maiden speeches of Mhairi Black and Tommy Sheppard in the 2015 SNP intake had discernible echoes of the 'Red Clydeside' tradition.

Pivotal in this is the power of talking in an obviously human way and conveying a reflective and empathising manner. This is a threshold that many politicians and much of public life consistently fail. Much of the debate and reporting in the indyref would not succeed on this criterion. One stark exception in the Scotland of permanent campaigning over the period 2011-14, little to do with politics, was the journalist Peter Ross's collection of essays *Daunderlust* which honoured personal, unique and individual stories.[378] They were also a recognition that not all public life can or should be about politics.

Shifting from the abstract to the personal dramatically alters so much. It offers a better chance to connect, personalise and popularise, and a deeper way of reframing and presenting arguments and concepts. For example, much of the UK political debate on the economy uses terms that many people struggle to understand such as 'austerity', 'deficit' and 'debt'. Compounding this further is an insider class way of talking and describing politics, very different from how people generally think about their own lives and those of their families.

This carries big implications for how we think about, describe and organise public services and spending, and even the role of the state. Institutional language, and with it the resultant view of the world, is very different from the language individuals use to talk about their life and the things that concern them.

What are Scotland's Political Counter-Stories?

Critical to the power of stories is accepting the need for political counter-stories. Just as Labour Scotland never represented a majority of the popular vote (49.91% its highest vote in 1966) and hence non-Labour Scotland was always a popular majority, the same is true of Nationalist Scotland. It too at peak popularity in the form of the SNP's electoral prospects just failed by a whisker in the 2015 UK elections to achieve a popular majority (49.97%), with the resultant consequences that non-Nationalist Scotland has throughout this period of SNP dominance remained in the majority.

If Nationalist Scotland is now the official story of present-day Scotland this carries with it the seeds of its own overreach and eventual decline. Always in political traditions at their peak popularity and ascendancy, a diminishing of the political antenna begins to occur which eventually leads to mistakes that slowly add up and take their toll. The SNP have over nearly a decade in office proved enormously resilient in popularity, but nothing in politics in terms of opinion poll ratings lasts forever. Eventually the party leadership will begin to see the world from inside their elite position as the default view. This outlook will overwhelm the need to see things first and foremost from outside their political bubble.

It is possible the SNP can have a couple more years at peak or near-peak popularity, but all of this carries implications for a second referendum. For just as Labour had to come to terms with the basic math that it could not win the 1997 devolution referendum, and to win convincingly needed not just Lib Dem, but SNP voters, the same is true of the SNP today. The SNP need non-SNP voters to win the referendum and to win convincingly they need Greens, Lib Dems and Labour voters. That requires keeping your political antenna attuned to non-Nationalist Scotland on a range of subjects other than independence.

This brings us to the counter-stories. There are a number in circulation. For decades until recently the main rival to Nationalist Scotland was Labour Scotland. It was the dominant story for fifty years until a decade ago and since then its decline has been dramatic and steep and may not yet have reached the bottom. It is also one of the most sharp declines of a centre-left party anywhere in the world – falling from 49.9% in 1966 to 19.1% in 2016 – a fall of 30.8% and loss of 61.7% of their peak vote. Probably only the decline of PASOK in Greece from being the country's leading political force in 1981 is of comparable proportions. In short, Labour Scotland looks like it will have its work cut out stopping the decline and rot, let alone providing the main opposition to the SNP.

This has left the terrain open for a different challenger to emerge to the Nationalists and that is centre-right moderate Scottish Toryism. Under the leadership of Ruth Davidson the party has enjoyed a small but very significant recovery going from 14.9% of the vote in the 2015 Westminster election in Scotland – the party's lowest share since 1865 – to 22.9% in the 2016 Scottish elections and second place in votes and seats – their highest since 1992 – with the party winning more No supporters than Labour (33% to 32%[379]).

Scotland post-indyref has provided fertile terrain not just for the SNP but also for the Tories, for reasons that aren't difficult to fathom. As with the SNP people know where they stand on the constitutional question with the Tories and feel they have a clear, unapologetic position – unlike Labour. Factor in the strong positive that is Ruth Davidson's moderate and modern Conservatism which avoids the dog-whistle and xenophobic tones of south of the border, and the re-emergence of the Scottish Tories makes sense. The Tories, given the state of Scottish Labour, look in prime position to form the main opposition and challenger to the SNP, a scenario that would have been unimaginable pre-indyref.

There are other minority interest and niche counter-stories. There is the Green Party account of a very different independent Scotland, economics and society to that proposed by the SNP. The Greens had a good indyref, gaining much publicity and showcasing that independence wasn't all about the SNP, but since then they have shown their limitations. Even though they won six seats in 2016 in the Scottish Parliament they fought a campaign seemingly bereft of any strategic considerations, and in effect put a popular ceiling on their appeal.

Other forces include the independent supporting left force of RISE that originated in the Radical Independence Campaign (RIC) and includes the remnants of the Scottish Socialist Party. While the RIC phenomenon displayed energy and vigour in the indyref, its shoehorning into a political party narrowed it to a tiny base which polled a miniscule vote in 2016. Finally, there is a contrarian and miserablist account of modern Scotland, usually but not exclusively associated with older pro-union voices, which really thinks that everything has gone wrong and we are slowly going to the dogs under the influence of separatism and political correctness. That tendency is one found throughout the developed world.

A Warning from a Future Scotland: The Dystopia of Right-Wing Fantasies

There is however another influential account of Scotland, one which poses a warning from the future and which comes from right-wing commentators including a disproportionate number of London Scots. Already they have a damning caricature and critique of Scotland and via their media status gain easy access to platforms from which they tell a right-wing audience what it wants to hear. In talking about Scotland they are discussing two things. The first is a defence of the neo-liberal orthodoxies that they advocate, and the second is to get people to accept that in the famous words of Thatcher, 'There is no alternative'. 'Look at Scotland,' they can say, 'well-meaning, trying to show its care and compassion, best intentions and all that, but a disaster and nation in decline.'

This is the view of Scotland from *The Economist* of 'Skintland'[380], the continual drip of condescension from the likes of Andrew Neil, Fraser Nelson and Iain Martin amongst others. *The Economist* sees itself as a global, cosmopolitan force for economic and social liberalism but pre- and post-indyref it chose the most pejorative language to describe Scottish independence. In addition to separatist, we were secessionist, and even partition – the last completely inaccurate given there is a recognised and agreed legal border. I pointed this out to the editor Zanny Minton Beddoes and Jeremy Cliffe who writes the 'Bagehot' column – the latter defending such usage – but subsequently the magazine seems for now at least to have dropped partition.[381]

This version of Scotland will continue if we become independent. We will be used as a convenient test case to show the folly of our ways, and of any attempt to break out of the economic, social and ideological straightjackets of our time. Therefore we need to understand and challenge that critique now to be able to challenge and displace it more effectively in the event of independence. The shape of the Scotland after Britain they will launch at us will have familiar lines, as it will be a souped up version of their current critique.

First, they would describe Scotland as a land of bitterness, division invoking the spectre of partition, finding the most embittered voices of anti-independence to portray the country as a virtual collective gulag of the mind.

Second, the intolerance and anti-democratic nature of Scottish nationalism would be wheeled out. They would say these people are zealots and fanatics who don't understand opposing views and the need for pluralism. Instead, they will say they crush dissent in their totalising view of Scotland. They will argue that Scottish studies, history and culture will brainwash every child and turn them into future nationalists.

Third, is the othering of England, London and Westminster. This is portrayed as xenophobic, bordering on racist, and linked to any incidents of anti-English prejudice found in Scotland. Usually the SNP are given a mostly clean bill of health on this, but the charge is that they have released passions they cannot control that are ugly and frightening.

Fourth, they will say that while all that is happening in Scotland might have good intentions, it isn't based in the real world. North of the border has been captured by public spending, crowding out private investment in an attitude close to totalitarian. Andrew Neil once even cited that Scottish public spending is among the highest in the world: 'This is the land of the big state… more important than in any country in the world, bar Cuba, North Korea or Iraq.'[382]

Finally, economic and business policy will be remorselessly picked over. If Scotland tries a race for the bottom on corporation tax it will be approved as vindication that this is how the world operates. But any attempt at higher taxation, or asking those at the top to pay a bit more, will be portrayed as unrealistic and the start of a Scots 'brain drain'. Any post-independence difficulties such as spending cuts or painful adjustments in relation to international markets will be jumped on with glee as proof of our collective folly.

Scottish opinion now has to start preparing for a politics of transition and turbulence. This will be a world where numerous opponents with influence and access to the media and other opinion formers will say a self-governing Scotland is a failure – even before we get started. This could in the future boil over into anti-Scottish prejudice and Scotophobia.[383] The Irish experience offers some warning here, with anti-Irish sentiment and bigotry unleashed post-1922. Scotland wasn't immune from this with two Protestant parties winning significant support in Glasgow and Edinburgh – in the former winning one quarter of the vote in 1933 while in the latter, the party's leader, John Cormack remained a councillor until 1962.[384] The Church of Scotland issued a racist, xenophobic tirade against the Irish in their 1923 Church and Nation Committee report, 'Menace of the Irish Race to Our Scottish Nationality' which it took until 2002 to apologise for.[385] Clearly, sentiment will not reach the low of these offensive opinions, but when an establishment is rattled they do have a tendency to lash out.

The Republic of the Mind

The Scotland of the last few years has seen pre-2011 independence shift from something on the margins, something which institutional Scotland and large parts of authority and expert opinion consistently did not take seriously or think was ever going to happen. All that changed in the Scotland post-2011 when the debate on independence normalised it as an idea. Irrespective of the clear limits in the SNP's version, the very idea of independence coming centre stage, being taking seriously and being debated, changed everything. Firstly, the idea clearly won the referendum debate – which is very different from the SNP's offer. Second, this gap between the real and the idealistic allowed a whole host of serious and radical ideas to be debated, from the currency and EU membership in the former, to imaginative ideas in the latter.

Now in the aftermath of the indyref and the Brexit vote it is clear that independence has the prospect of becoming the new normal. Nicola Sturgeon in July 2016 posed independence as offering 'the greatest certainty, stability and the maximum control over our destiny.'[386] This was always likely to be the terrain the SNP and respectable society would come together on: independence as the politics of security, stability and continuity. This is the story of Scotland throughout most of its history: the institutional and elite autonomy that has characterised the country's distinctiveness and public life.

It was not then surprising that post-Brexit the SNP's positioning of independence as the new normal brought cries of disappointment from some of the more radical currents who had been galvanised by the indyref.[387] This was always going to be so. But while independence's search for the right reassuring message is understandable it is trying to do this in a world moving in the opposite direction. First, Scotland in recent years and decades has experienced, as we have explored, a revolution whereby the old institutions, authority and order are reduced and in retreat. That will not be reversed. Second, the world itself has increasingly become not one of stability and certainty, but disruption and uncertainty.

Part of Scotland's self-government and independence vision has been the yearning for a return to a 'little Britain' of the post-war era, where solidarity and compassion were seen as the driving forces of government. Apart from the sepia nostalgia for the past, that world cannot be returned to because it doesn't exist. The managed international capitalist order of 1945-75 has gone forever, and this new world of change and movement is what we have to get used to. Instead, we have to use flow, fluidity and uncertainty not to aid and reward featherbedded elites, but to make new coalitions of solidarity and inter-connectedness.

Independence also has to be about more than nationalism. Scottish nationalism contributed hugely to Scotland getting where it is today: the constitutional debate of the last fifty years, the establishment of the Parliament, and most recently, the independence debate. But consideration of what kind of Scotland we want to achieve and live in requires more than nationalism that has little constructive to offer post-independence.

The most common answer on this predicament is to cite Scotland's social democracy and the fusing of class and nation seen in the indyref, but as we have explored, the SNP isn't first and foremost, a social democratic party. Scottish social democracy is threadbare in its ideas and uber-pragmatic, and tellingly, is in a poor state of health across the developed world. Thus, it isn't clear that social democracy offers us a compelling and convincing road map to the future. We need to think afresh with radicals the world over about a centre-left politics beyond social democracy or the retro-politics of the Corbynistas in British Labour. That is a set of conversations we will not be alone in but is taking place all over the world as people recognise the wreckage of the false promises of crony capitalism and the collusion of the near-left era of Blair, Brown and the Clintons.

Our future has to be, and will be, about more than the competing claims of two nationalisms, so why don't we start creating that future now? The indyref saw many positives. Democratic debate and engagement reached into many corners and communities that politicians and authorities had previously written off: 'the missing Scotland' whose views could just be run roughshod over and our complacent progressivism claim to speak for.

Yet, there was too much discussion that involved lack of substance. It is good to dream, and it is good to engage in 'Caledonian Dreaming': it is part and parcel of the human condition, but there has to be a link between words and deeds, otherwise it is all just hot air and platitudes. Such an attitude has been too prevalent on the left over the years, and the Scottish left and nationalist traditions have too often talked the great talk, the abstract, the utopian, the perfect society, but not addressed the practicalities of our endemic poverty or lack of opportunities for working class children.

This lack of interest in substance could be seen in the emergence of a politics of symbolism in the indyref and Yes and No supporters flying the flags of Scotland and the United Kingdom. The study of flags is called vexillology and is an intricate craft and tradition, but in the indyref, we witnessed on both sides the rise of what can only be called 'Vex Nats' – those foot soldiers of their respective moral tribes.[388] In the last few weeks, Downing Street took to flying the saltire and urging local authorities and public bodies up and down the land to do the same, while in numerous rallies of Yes supporters the saltire came more and more to prominence. This is politics as ritual, something even primordial, and does little to contribute to our future. In actual fact, beyond the true believers and the noise of the crowd, on both sides, but on Yes more, it scares lots of uncommitted voters with its passion and zealotry. There is a place for flags but they shouldn't be a lodestar of our politics and define who we are and who we are not.[389]

Finally, what is the most desirable path for us as a nation to navigate to the Scotland of the future? How does it engage with the independence question – which some see as the only show in town, and others see as a diversion or worse? First, we will have another independence debate – indeed, it hasn't really stopped since the 2014 debate. Second, that debate has to have, for the huge part of the population who are not card carrying members of independence or the union, the question 'independence for what purpose?' upfront, rather than just pose the trappings of statehood, flags and symbols which excite the 'Vex Nats'.

There are a lot of boundaries and obstacles on this path: tribalism, past histories, bruised and hurt emotions from last time, but part of Scotland's debate will be between two very different approaches and mindsets. One is an unconditional blank cheque towards independence. It says Britain is over, let's get on with building a new nation and fresh start: 'Scotland Year Zero' and all that. The appeal of that is understandable for many, but it isn't enough. The other is a conditional and qualified support for independence that looks for content and detail as well as reassurance and recognition of doubt. The first is very much a nationalist mindset, irrespective of whether people call themselves nationalists; the second is far removed from nationalism.

The unconditional supporters have given their faith and loyalty to the SNP, at the very least to the day after independence. Any influence or leverage they have as a result has been significantly reduced. Post-Brexit, warning signs are evident. As the SNP leadership reassured business and corporate interests, there is an assumption that left-wing independence supporters outside the SNP have burnt their bridges with the union and are assumed as banked in the Yes column.

A conditional support for independence clustered around some of the elements of 'the third Scotland' and DIY activist nation which emerged in the indyref, but addressing and reaching out to swing voters and don't knows, has the prospect of having more influence and being better politics.

A conditional support would clearly state the minimum standards and conditions it wanted from independence. It would pose not just a 'Not in My Name' outlook towards the UK about the wars, elites and crony capitalism, but also a 'Not in My Name' approach to Scotland: to say we have some difficult home truths to face up to as a nation. These would include a new economic model that isn't the broken financial capital vision of the City of London or Salmondnomics, but instead which practises what it preaches on social justice. One that reaches out and attempts to heal the bitter divides of poverty and hardship scarring our society; and that is more thoroughly democratic and aims for higher than just rejecting Westminster rule and traditions. Maybe above all it would demand a different tone, a little humbleness, the ability to listen, and preparedness to admit that there will be difficult times and choices ahead, as well as an upside.

Some have already turned their backs on Britain and the future is now Scottish. Yet, that is not where a huge number, maybe even a majority of Scots, situate themselves. Scotland, despite appearances, does not comprise two armed camps made up of 45% and 55%. Underneath the noise there is much more fluidity, churn and movement. If you want an independent nation, first, you need to listen to the waverers and not try and win them over by hectoring and self-righteousness, and second, concentrating on such groups and specific detail gives a higher chance of a better debate and more convincing majority emerging.

We stand on the precipice of seismic change. We should not be scared or wary because we have already come a long way in our journey. There is no turning back that change. We are a society less deferential; where authority is more conditional there have been massive shifts in the economy, employment and work, and we are a society more feminised and more diverse. But it is still true that we face multiple futures and possible Scotlands, and we need to reach out to those anxious and concerned about the pace and direction of change and the very prospect of independence.

We have to find in this a new sense of national pride, one not based on false traditions, sentimentality or invented pasts of communal living. It has to be based on the age-old and timeless sense of people coming together and the collective power we can have in a shared mission and purpose: one that creates an appropriate kind of confidence. That confidence would not be based upon a hollow rhetoric or overblown grandiose delusions, but a humble awareness that we can change this nation for the better.

This has to be a Scotland which knows its stories, folklores and myths – but knows them as such – and has the wisdom and insight to know the difference between the myths we act on and live out and those we don't. If we want to be the warm, welcoming land of egalitarianism then we are going to have to make some tough calls about the present-day state of Scotland. Those at the top and our elites may have to make some sacrifices, while we will have to think anew about poverty, and how we organise public services and spending.

We need a sense of balance and an acute ear to sensitivity in this. The writer Iain Crichton Smith raged against 'the cult of the individual' and posed as the answer, 'the cult of the community' – but both can be equally suffocating and problematic.[390] We know that tradition and practice from our own past experience. Fintan O'Toole surveying Ireland after the crash wrote:

There has to be a new kind of individualism – not the rugged cowboy ethic of doing whatever you can get away with, but the idea of taking personal responsibility for the public realm. There has to be a new kind of collectivism – not the tribal and parochial loyalties that have shaped the political culture, but a wider sense of mutual obligation.[391]

O'Toole concluded:

There has to be a new idea of the republic, not as an end which will be achieved at some mythical point in the future, but as a beginning, a set of conditions in which people are given the chance to live with dignity.[392]

Scotland, of course, isn't yet a republic, but we can become a republic of the mind: a society where each of its citizens is treated equally, with respect, and has a stake in the future of the nation. A republic of the mind where arbitrary power, influence and wealth is held in check and accountable to the common good, and where we create a modern 21st-century public ethic which isn't about flunkery, outdated traditions and insider credentials.

Then, once we have done that, we can even if we so choose, decide whether we want to become a formal republic. By then we will have learned by experience the important difference between a politics of symbolism and substance. We will know the qualities in us that have the capacity and commitment to change our nation and the lives of all its citizens for the better. We will have learnt what really matters and what values and ideals we should cherish and choose to live by. That Scotland – a republic of the mind – is tantalisingly close and within our reach.

Appendix One: Some of the Detailed Contributions to the Manifesto

This section outlines policies, practices and ideas for an alternative Scotland. It is not intended as a final word or finished manifesto. Instead, the notion is to act as a prompt, provocation and invitation to radical thinking and do-ing.

A request was sent out inviting respondents to imagine a future Scotland that is a democracy and a society where people felt that their voice and interests were respected. They were asked what one policy, practice or idea – irrespective of independence – would make a tangible stake to the country? It was indicated that this could be a single big-ticket policy, or something smaller, that illustrated a wider sense that the country was on the right track.

The responses were enthusiastic and filled with ideas, energy and impatience. A total of eighty people gave their time and views, an interesting cross-section covering professionals, academics, NGOs, business, media practitioners, campaigners, activists and even a few who defy any neat and easy categorisation.

A number of common threads emerged from the responses. The first was support for greater localism, more local democracy, and for that to extend beyond the structures of councils. Second, was a citizen's income or basic income. Third, land reform which deals with injustice and the inequity of ownership. But perhaps one of the most significant trends was a general one: an overwhelming desire for Scotland and the Scottish Government to be bolder, to focus on more substance, and also to be more internationalist in its thinking and action here in terms of where it draws from, as well as in our emerging global profile.

There was also a distinct feeling of quiet but definite disappointment towards the Scottish Government and the SNP. There was felt across the political spectrum, from some of the radical voices of the indyref, to more conservative Yes supporters, No backers, and people across public life, a growing discontent at the safety-first, cautious approach which is nervous at embarking on much of substance or 'scaring the horses'. Yet, at the same time there is a trend to gather powers, to assume the centre and elites know best, and enforce a sort of modernist, top-down, very conventional view of politics and change. Now as any student of late 20th and early 21st-century politics will know such an approach never now works in a developed country. Scotland won't be an exception.

A caveat to the list below: as said above this is not meant to be a final manifesto but to prompt debate and encourage further suggestions. One problem inherent in Scotland – and particularly found on the left – is in believing that policy is easy. It asserts that it can be done either by acclamation and platitudes ('we are against austerity'), or through leadership and good intentions.

Second, policy is not everything. The world seen through policy levers – evident in New Labour, SNP and managerialist outlooks – is a limited one. Instead, as this book has argued, policy, practice and ideas have to be seen in the context of wider cultural and social change, reflecting the lived lives and experiences of people. Life happens not in neat policy categories, but in the cracks between people, policies and institutions, and public interventions and thinking have to address this.

Therefore, this book and the resultant suggestions are filled with hope and enthusiasm, but there is also a note of caution in them as well: in that the future Scotland that is coming and the future Scotland many of us want to live in cannot and will not be just a pale version of today. As this book has argued the changes of recent decades aren't going to be put into reverse or even stasis, so we had all better get prepared for some difficult times, turbulence and heated discussions. Scotland has changed and is changing: that is a process, rightly, without end.

When we are 64: A Menu of Possible Actions

1. A written constitution – not written by the Scottish Government.

2. A Bill of Rights which includes basic economic rights as well as social, civil and political rights.

3. A Citizen's Chamber as a second advisory chamber to the Scottish Parliament. It would be made up of a random selection of 50-100 people with the same social weighting as a citizen's jury.

4. A right to recall to allow voters to challenge elected national politicians with a minimum ten percent threshold required in any constituency required to trigger a ballot.

5. A new fiscal agreement between the Scottish Government and local government based on local government becoming entrenched in Scotland's first ever evolving constitutional settlement.

6. Let cities choose if they want to have elected majors and provosts with real executive responsibility for running local affairs.

7. A Central Bank of Scotland set up under democratic oversight with as its main aims: sustainable growth and prosperity, the primacy of the public good, and strengthening social justice.

8. A National Investment Bank set up to prioritise and lead public investment with responsibility for the Scottish Government's capital investment budget.

9. The creation of a People's Banking Network of local banks which offer cheap loans to individuals and small businesses.

10. A definition of economic prosperity and wellbeing which is not defined by growth and chasing GDP. Faster GDP growth in a resource-scarce world is a limited and often damaging measurement.

11. Increased investment in SME-driven transition away from a carbon-based economy towards an innovation-based, jobs-rich, higher wage/tax Green New Deal.

12. A fully empowered national audit office to cover the entire public sector, with similar powers to the Government Accountability Office in the US to demand documents, which is legally required to publish whole government accounts for Scotland.

13. A moratorium for five years on national commissions and inquiries made up solely of professionals and experts.

14. A statutory register of all public affairs and lobbying companies with full disclosure of all clients and all contracts which involve public monies.

15. Significant land reform with full openness and transparency about who owns land.

16. A land value tax.

17. Participatory budgeting at a local level.

18. Reconnecting the link between local businesses and local democracy – which needs fundamental overhauling.

19. A citizen's income or basic income: a signal to everyone who lives in Scotland that they are equal and matter.

20. A working committee in Holyrood representing local communities, peopled by representatives of those communities – not involving councilors or public bodies, but members of the public.

21. A pay structure for councillors which reflects the recognition that decisions taken locally are as (or nearly as) important than those taken nationally.

22. A public register of beneficial ownership covering companies and land – and addressing shell companies.

23. Publish everyone's, individual and corporate, tax returns online – as in Norway.

24. Full child and adult literacy.

25. Free universal childcare from 0-14.

26. A universal education voucher of £250.00 (paid from not reducing air travel duty) for each Scottish citizen aged over 18 to be spent on an approved full/part-time or evening class course that is accredited by a Scottish educational institution.

27. Every secondary school pupil has access to a therapist if they require one. All pupils would receive a mental health assessment.

28. Every Police Officer, School Teacher and Social Worker must spend 100 hours in a youth club in an area of multiple deprivation before professionally qualifying.

29. Follow the Finnish example of starting school at seven, reduce testing, invest in further education, continue to provide free education at the point of access and invest in adult education.

30. Don't just narrowly focus on closing the attainment gap in education, the new mantra, which is all about exam performance on leaving school. Consider other characteristics and attributes we need for life and for work: perseverance, getting on with people, problem solving, being reliable, ability to talk and listen.

31. Introduce into schools a more formal and structured study of democracy and what being a citizen means from primary years upwards.

32. Educate and encourage young people to be more entrepreneurial – whether economic, social, civic or cultural.

33. Incorporation of Scotland's network of elite private schools into the public sector so we have one integrated system of school education.

34. Within the public sector experimentation and choice of models including self-governing schools.

35. Invest in getting our country truly multilingual so we can be global citizens at home and abroad.

36. Student funding for further and higher education which

isn't skewed towards the middle class and affluent. Set up a funding system which allows the poorest to enter further and higher education without being straddled in debts.

37. Continue to invest in and raise the status and importance of health visitors.

38. A national strategy to combat loneliness and isolation – particularly amongst older people – with a priority on reducing physical barriers and aiding social connectedness.

39. A comprehensive approach to homelessness prevention that matches the commitment to dealing with homelessness once it arises in the spirit of the groundbreaking 2003 legislation.

40. The contribution of care and caring – for children, family members, relatives and friends – to be recognised as a contribution to the Scottish economy and made visible in the national accounts.

41. A national approach to personal assistance for disabled people offered in a person centred, flexible way to allow disabled people to make informed choices.

42. A root and branch review of the Scottish legal profession, since ensuring that the system of law is fit for purpose is an essential requirement of any democracy. This should include reform of the archaic and elitist Scottish court system and the modernisation and simplification of language.

43. Public sector reform not to be just driven by professionals, experts and 'stakeholder' groups, but to involve practitioners and people who work and use services.

44. Democratise 'City Deals' so they are not cliques of

politicians and businesses.

45. Orkney, Shetland and Western Isles to be given special status recognising and protecting their unique character and cultures.

46. The establishment of Scottish Energy – a publically owned utility – with the remit to regulate the energy market, support public ownership and develop renewables.

47. Scottish Energy guarantees a mixed source of 100% renewable supply to houses on a non-commercial subsidised rate.

48. Subsidies for Community Wind Turbines and Solar Panel Schemes which would generate profits back to communities.

49. An Energy Innovation Strategy to develop across the public sector, academia and business – the framework to make Scotland an internationally recognised centre of innovation in energy systems, storage and renewables.

50. New Place Standards are applied to Scotland as a country.

51. Make it compulsory for every company with a board to have a designer at that level – it would radically improve product and service design.

52. Full control of immigration, allowing asylum seekers the chance to work and live as equal citizens and removing the fear of deportation.

53. An international programme encouraging young people from Scotland to contribute to anti-poverty, welfare and empowerment initiatives around the world.

54. The development of an embryonic network of Scottish global ambassadors drawing on the Catalan example.

55. Scotland remains a member of the European Union.

56. Scotland becomes a full member of UNESCO.

57. A New Digital Deal to prioritise ending the digital divide with a specific priority for connecting rural and disadvantaged communities.

58. A tailored citizen's income or basic income for artists and members of the artistic and cultural community.

59. The creation of a Scottish Broadcasting Corporation from assets and resources of BBC Scotland.

60. A new Scottish Film Agency is set up to fund, promote and market film alongside a designated Scottish film studio.

61. A designated public fund to support independent media run at arm's length without political involvement and would provide a small pot of money to support and encourage independent media and a diversity of voices.

62. An annual National Festival of Stories and Storytelling.

63. A Defence Diversification Strategy to safeguard and develop for socially useful ends the skilled jobs and resources in the defence sector in Scotland.

64. Call time on Trident.

Appendix Two: Some of the Detailed Contributions to the Manifesto

Here are some of the direct comments and suggestions from people when they were invited to offer a minimum of one policy, practice or idea. They range far and wide – and include from the thoughtful and detailed, to the more philosophical and even satirical.

★

A root and branch review of the Scottish legal profession, since ensuring that the system of law is fit for purpose is an essential requirement of any democracy. The review would cover the following:

- the recruitment, training and regulation of lawyers
- the operation of the Crown office
- the functioning of the courts
- the judicial appointments' process
- the conduct and reporting of fatal accident enquiries
- the representation of lay people on tribunals
- the frequency with which interdicts are granted to prevent media reporting of events
- the appeals' process (particularly as there would be no recourse to the Supreme Court if Scotland becomes fully independent)

Such a review would involve looking critically at one of the main institutional bulwarks of Scottish civil society.

On the question of land reform, it would shine a brighter light on who owns Scotland, what they contribute to the common good via taxation, what they withhold in tax avoidance, what their justification for such avoidance is. It would challenge the ludicrous idea that land ownership is a solely private matter for anyone also wishing to claim the rights and privileges of citizenship (and the public services which go along with that). It would hopefully also be another step towards the mental de-feudalisation of Scotland, which is still overly deferential to people who have only their own interests and self-protection at heart. It might remind us that our cities and urban areas are also built on actual land!

*

Advocate the idea that we're all in this together, all responsible – in our different ways – for making Scotland prosperous in ways that are sustainable, in terms of supply chains, markets, the environment and so on; it is this that will enable us to deliver on our assumptions about our commitment to social justice and equality.

*

Genuine participatory cooperative local government. Powers and budgets devolved to regional, local and community councils, co-operatives and community owned companies.

*

Prevention and early intervention with young people around mental health – a meaningful policy and real resources into educating young people about mental health and how to keep themselves mentally healthy. And early intervention for those young people encountering mental health difficulties (as opposed to mental illness).

★

A pay structure for councillors which reflects the recognition that decisions taken locally are as (or nearly as) important than those taken nationally. Higher pay would also hopefully make it more viable for ordinary folk to play a greater role in local politics, rather than the same old cadre of business people, doctors and architects.

★

How about a country that does not use the word 'nationalism' in its rhetoric?

★

A policy that sums up a free Scotland is one that puts storytelling at the heart of the conversation about our identity and future. There is no one Scotland, but many Scotlands. Five million Scotlands.

★

An annual National Festival of Stories held in Dundee. The aim would be to improve literacy, visual literacy and give some experience working with other media. This would be delivered though a partnership of government, education (Schools, Universities), third sector, business partners. The ultimate goal would be to foster creativity, entrepreneurship and engagement in political life by encouraging the population to embrace the power of story, and to each become involved in shaping a story about the future of our society.

★

Scotland seeks to become the first country that seeks to fulfill the promise of the Welfare State – that people live longer, happier, healthier, purposeful and productive lives.

★

Full adult literacy to a high degree (e.g. between a quarter and a half of people in prisons are functionally illiterate; they can read and write but struggle with anything complex).

★

The removal of Trident nuclear weapons from Scottish waters - as a result of an act of the Scottish Parliament or after a campaign of mass civil disobedience – would be the most dramatic rejection of Scottish provincialism I can think of, giving concrete expression to the radical ideals so many people in this country subscribe to but so few do anything about.

★

Fully abolishing Scotland's network of elite private schools – which exists for one overriding reason: to reinforce the class privileges of Scotland's richest families - would signal a radical turning point in our national politics.

★

The integration of health and social care is a mess because it has been layered on top of old-fashioned ways of delivering health services (12 regional health boards) and jigsawed together with a mismatching 32 local authorities. If I only got to choose one policy that would give us all a tangible stake it would be to have a new way of looking at how local people get to say how their local services run in a fair and equitable way. I would make sure that within this policy there was co-terminus health and social care services.

★

The radical reimagining of the current welfare system (where this was sufficiently devolved) to establish a citizen's income. To my mind, this would radicalise how we use and value our time, how we define work and enable us to achieve a society in which all citizens had time for not only productive labours but also for reproductive labours which Guy Standing defines as activity of 'bringing ourselves and others into being – creating the space for altruism in contrast to paternalism.'

★

I would introduce in schools a more formal and structured learning about democracy and what being a citizen means. Not just in Modern Studies but in primary school too. A curriculum that includes making clear the importance of relationships and personal responsibility, the need and benefits of being involved in your own community. Not teaching what view to have but providing a clearer understanding of how to seek out information and use it to gain a stake in our society. And the importance of being involved and interested. A better informed and engaged electorate might also make politicians raise their game and it might curtail that tangible sense of entitlement firmly held by many local politicians in our poorest areas. Some of them have an influence and power that far exceeds their capabilities and mandate. In the land of the blind the one-eyed man is king.

*

I would like a government to implement and deliver sustainable and inclusive economic growth. As it happens, this has been the stated purpose of the SNP government since 2007. What has been missing is a concerted effort to deliver the policy. Delivering inclusive growth requires efforts in education, support for families and young people.

*

That local communities are both allowed to properly constitute themselves and empower themselves through taking local control of services and assets on a contracted basis of management and that the presumption of the state is that this should happen. The effect of this would be the gradual rebuilding of local capacity on a bottom-up basis to govern themselves as they see fit. There would be a 'golden share' in community enterprises to prevent full privatisation but that would not mean barring private sector involvement.

*

Where the state is running a loss making asset then the local community should have the capacity to run the asset for a payment at the same level as the current subsidy. It should have the power to borrow using this guarantee (for instance the last recorded loss figures for the Rhubodach ferry to Bute showed a loss of £900k pa. If Bute and the local community chose to build a bridge they should be guaranteed that subsidy to cover capital cost). What we then have is a drive to efficiency where the local communities are rewarded for efficiencies they can introduce.

Shorter working week (30 hours), or long weekend (Friday-Sunday), or shorter working day (6 hours), without wage reductions. It would imply that we had a Scottish government/democracy that was willing to set humane rules and collective goals for capitalism, than just accept its demands for efficiency and flexibility. (Of course, it could easily improve productivity and performance, qualitatively, in the long term). And it would begin to open up free time and space for Scots to care, play/create, self-develop/educate, organise, be citizens, even just contemplate the universe.

★

A series of codes and structures at Holyrood to prevent the ruling party from controlling the committees system; empowering MSPs who chair committees to feel their role is to represent the public interest and not the party's, to act as watchdogs, not puppies.

★

A smart global asylum policy that reverses forever Scotland's declining population and brings new generations of innovation into the nation. This would be aligned to a greater commitment to social housing.

★

Free universal childcare from 0-14. The impact of this would be huge. Childcare is central to both society and economy – such a policy would help alleviate poverty, with huge percentages of some families' income being spent on childcare and, in many cases, the prohibitive cost of childcare actively preventing parents from returning to or taking up work. It would address gender imbalances, with more women being able to take up or return to work (for it is often, though obviously not always, to women whom the weight of responsibility of childcare falls), and in turn address elements of the gender pay gap and wage discrimination. Essentially it's about power and choice – a word I hesitate to use as I usually associate 'choice' with Tory plans – but this would enable people to make the best choices for themselves and their families, and have more control of their lives.

★

Scotland is a democracy already. Most people aren't very democratically active – which is fine – but not choosing to be active (e.g. not voting) isn't a conspiracy against you: it's your choice. We have endless platforms for voices.

★

Ghent is vegetarian every Thursday!!

★

Planning permission for local renewable energy proposals (and possibly other categories of development) to be mediated not only through existing planning law, but through the primary filter of local community consent (possibly, down to community councils, thereby giving them real influence). This calibrated so that communities either gain substantial benefit from land owner developments, or, by rendering the development value of land greater when it is held by community trusts, create a driver for the transfer of land from private to community hands, and in so doing, open up future potential revenue streams by which to cover the purchase price of the land as assessed under the existing land reform legislation.

*

Education is crafted round the 50% who go on to study for a degree. From day one at primary you can see that a whole bunch of children are left behind at the races. Attainment – closing the attainment gap, the new mantra, is all about exam performance on leaving school. What about all the other characteristics and attributes we need for life and for work – perseverance, getting on with people, problem solving, looking people in the eye, being reliable, ability to talk and listen? Our big measure is doing well in leaving exams. Those that do well then get a free university place and a grant for the next 3 or 4 years. Those not 'lucky' enough to be in the top 50% get what? A small number get a job or college place (less than before – colleges suffer more from cuts than unis), a smaller number an apprenticeship – costs largely met by employers. The big group are left dangling – and the state intervention, if any, is for a tiny amount of support for a 26-week period.

*

Watching this government is like watching previous governments, centralising and pulling the levers of power. The municipalism and paternalism of Glasgow City is now reproduced in Holyrood. Just like the Czar who sent the people he did not like to Siberia, the Soviets did the same only in larger numbers. Agency – giving a feeling that self-help matters and pluralism is cherished – and that all these are equally important. A society that I like and want to live in has a sense of the state supporting people, enabling.

*

We create a House of Food in Glasgow based on the Copenhagen model to train and inspire public food workers, caterers and staff for councils, schools, hospitals, nurseries and old folks' homes. This should aim at creating a joyous innovative and delicious food culture, healthy eating and reconnection with land and place.

★

My suggestion is that the NHS needs to be reimagined, not as a shrine for worship, nor as a political football managerial project way of paying doctors or indulgence for the worried well, but as a continuing test of whether we live up to the original challenge that illness is a misfortune whose costs should be borne and shared by the entire community. We're good at doing this in emergencies, but not in helping people to live long and well in the community with multiple conditions – a predicament that will face most of us in due course. The NHS should not be something we only receive when ill, but a project we are engaged in all the time as citizens.

★

I would like Scotland to be a Good Country. For me, this would mean that we wouldn't host weapons of mass destruction, we wouldn't invade other countries, we wouldn't allow absentee land ownership or tax evasion, nor would we tolerate child poverty, domestic violence or intolerance and discrimination in any shape or form. We'd exemplify non-confrontational politics that recognise that what unites us is more important than what divides us, we'd acknowledge that injustice anywhere is injustice everywhere and we'd pursue foreign policy based on an understanding of our inter-dependence with other countries.

Two big changes would be radical transformation of local government so there are far more councils raising more of their own cash. If power devolved from London just stays centrally in Edinburgh then the top-down pattern of Britishness is still with us. Likewise, serious and fearless land reform would mean Scots had finally put fear of the Establishment behind them and would demonstrate to citizens that the needs of the many finally really mattered more than the inheritance of the few.

Making the views and experiences of the individuals affected more fundamental to local and national decisions. We rely too much on 'stakeholder engagement' through third sector bodies. Most people directly affected by policy changes (or budget cuts) are voiceless, their views at best filtered through organisations which may have their own agendas. There's too much of a culture of negotiation behind closed doors, secret gardens, professionals know best, too much playing down the competing interests between different groups in Scottish society, too great a readiness to play down concerns which don't fit whatever grand story is being shared between those at the top table. We need more honesty about how choices often create losers as well as winners.

The reform of an archaic and elitist Scottish court system. This should involve the modernisation and simplification of language, procedure, dress and communication – including pre-trial protocols in civil procedure seeking to shift the balance from an overly adversarial culture towards the use of more inquisitorial and mediation-based approaches. The overall aim here would be to improve access to, and engagement with, key parts of the justice system by ordinary people.

*

We want a fairer social security system that puts the rights and needs of claimants first, against the logic of profit, exploitation, and bullying that underpins the current one: we want the end of sanctions, workfare, and compulsory employability schemes; we want no involvement for private companies in disability assessment processes and that evidence from health professionals is fully taken into account; and we want the right to be accompanied at all disability assessments and job centre appointments to be guaranteed.

*

I take the view that, at one level, all professions are conspiracies against the laity but there are important differences between law on the one hand and education and health on the other. Much of my own writing on education has been concerned with exposing the way its 'leadership class' operates. By that I mean senior figures in the major institutions (Education Scotland, SQA, GTCS) and the 'policy community' controlled by government. 'Safe' people who never question the rules are appointed to key posts. The government patronage system – the way public appointments are made – is a key component of this. At senior levels, Scotland is actually a deeply conformist society (despite our self-image as frank and forthright). Upwardly-mobile working class recruits are socialised into following the conventions. And I think the SNP, notwithstanding its boasts about a new kind of democracy, has become part of this process: it has drifted in a progressively more centralist and authoritarian direction.

★

The SNP's record in government has been aligned to a strategy of 'don't scare the horses'. Demonstrate competence. Incremental improvement. Some radical change, but this was centralising Police and Fire. This demonstrated their agenda. Centralise power and control. This was disconcerting to many democrats, recognising change was important, yet unhappy at the loss of local democratic input to these key bodies, particularly Police Scotland.

★

Just imagine we were creating our own system for public services from scratch. What would we create? Hopefully not just an IT system to administer welfare payments! We need vision and imagination applied to these problems. And, once the ideas are distilled, we need strong leadership to balance what's pragmatically possible with the courageous action needed to implement needed change. I'd like to see a much wider discourse on power in Scotland. Where is power? Who holds it? How are they held to account? How can we widen participation?

★

I think the solution is in part to open the windows/closed doors/garden gates on how decisions are made. I suspect the population is ahead of the professional castes here in having absorbed the individualistic implications of consumer culture.

★

Though I agree with the philosophy behind the curriculum for excellence, the fact that the curricular content is not exam driven and the curriculum can be broad as well as deep allowing pupils to explore different subject areas in as much depth as they want. We are still caught in the need to know exactly how each pupil is performing at any one time. Is this about pressures on the profession from business, educational institutions, government, public? We haven't allowed ourselves to really take a leap, a chance, and a risk maybe into practising the philosophy. So to be involved in educational change at any level one would have to have a background in education and preferably at the 'chalk face' as it were.

★

Establish an 'Institute for the Social Imagination' – this would be charged with looking out into the world and providing Scotland with a meta-narrative – an ability (regardless of how 'good' things were) to debate other ways of doing things.

★

Scottish football has had a golden era in recent years relatively speaking. Rangers in the lower leagues has spread TV, media interest and monies and been a boon for the profile for smaller clubs. Why not institutionalise the breaking of 'the Old Firm' by permanently splitting them? Rangers' four-year journey through the lower leagues could be mirrored with them returning to the Premiership, Celtic being put down to the lowest league. This should be repeated ad nauseam until Scottish football becomes more competitive. Sound crazy? Anybody got any better ideas to make our game more competitive?

★

No one policy will achieve this but in terms of putting down a marker of the kind of society I would like to see, I would go for the nationalisation of the landed estates in Scotland: these would fall under common ownership and their resources, output and products used for the benefits of all Scottish society. This could also be used to fund anti-poverty programmes. The other policy for me is the complete removal of all anti-trade union legislation, and the right of free assembly with the ending of the criminalisation of football fans.

*

I think Scotland is unique because the community deliberately gave up political independence to maintain itself. The Enlightenment invention of 'society' as an object to represent itself was so successful that we forget how odd and original it was. Scottish writers rewrite everyone else's history as a version of Scotland's story. So the tension/contradiction between union and independence is played out at psychological, social and political levels.

Notes

[1] Statista, Unemployment Youth Rate in Europe, May 2016.

[2] United Nations High Commissioner for Refugees, 20 June 2016.

[3] Giada Zampano, Liam Moloney and Jovi Juan, 'Migrant Crisis: A History of Displacement', *Wall Street Journal*, 22 September 2015.

[4] Gerry Hassan, *Caledonian Dreaming: The Quest for a Different Scotland*, Luath Press 2014.

[5] Tom Devine, *The Scottish Nation 1707-2000*, Allen Lane 1999, p. 609.

[6] Daniel Goldman, *Emotional Intelligence: Why It Can Matter More than IQ*, Bloomsbury 1996.

[7] Stuart Cosgrove, 'Crushed by the Wheels of Industry: Scottish Football and the New Economy', *Nutmeg*, No. 1, September 2016.

[8] Lesley Riddoch, 'Look north, Scotland', *The Guardian*, 5 December 2011; *Blossom: What Scotland needs to Flourish*, Luath Press 2013.

[9] Gerry Hassan, 'The third Scotland: self-determining, self-organising, suspicious of the SNP', *The Guardian*, 24 April 2014.

[10] Iain Macwhirter, *Disunited Kingdom: How Westminster won a Referendum but lost Scotland*, Cargo Books 2014.

[11] Iain Macwhirter, 'After Doomsday: The Convention and Scotland's Constitutional Crisis', in Alice Brown and Richard Parry (eds), *The Scottish Government Yearbook 1990*, Unit for the Study of Government in Scotland 1990, p. 21.

[12] Tom Devine, in Carol Craig and Tom Devine, 'Scotland's "Velvet Revolution"', in Gerry Hassan, Eddie Gibb and Lydia Howland (eds), *Scotland 2020: Hopeful Stories for a Northern*

Nation, Demos 2005.

[13] Christopher McCorkindale, 'An Accidental Referendum', *Scottish Constitutional Futures Forum*, 16 August 2013.

[14] Ian Fraser, *Shredded: Inside RBS: The Bank that Broke Britain*, Birlinn 2014.

[15] Phil Mac Giolla Bhain, *Downfall: How Rangers FC Self-Destructed*, Frontline Noir 2012.

[16] For an alternative take on the Catholic Church and more: Tom Gallagher, *Divided Scotland: Ethnic Friction and Christian Crisis*, Argyll Publishing 2013.

[17] Catherine Deveney, 'UK's top cardinal accused of "inappropriate acts" by priests', *The Observer*, 23 February 2013.

[18] Gerry Hassan and Eric Shaw, *The Strange Death of Labour Scotland*, Edinburgh University Press 2012.

[19] G.A. Ponsonby, *London Calling: How the BBC Stole the Referendum*, NN Media Ltd 2014.

[20] Gerry Hassan, *Independence of the Scottish Mind: Elite Narratives, Public Spaces and the Making of a Modern Nation*, Palgrave Macmillan 2014, p. 71.

[21] *BBC Annual Report 2015-16*; *The Observer*, 17 July 2016.

[22] *BBC News*, 15 August 2012.

[23] *The Guardian*, 27 April 2014.

[24] Fintan O'Toole, *Enough is Enough: How to Make a New Republic*, Faber and Faber 2010, p. 20.

[25] Jeffrey Meek, *Queer Voices in Post-War Scotland: Male Homosexuality, Religion and Society*, Palgrave Macmillan 2015.

[26] Electoral Reform Society Scotland, *One Party to Rule Them All: Does Scotland have a Predominant-Party Problem?*, Electoral Reform Society 2016.

[27] David Morley, *Gorgeous George: The life and adventures of George Galloway*, Politico's Publishing 2007, pp. 22-24.

[28] John Grindrod, *Concretopia: A Journey around the Rebuilding of Postwar Britain*, Old Street Publishing 2013, p. 378.

[29] 'The Politics Show', *BBC One*, 3 April 2011.

[30] Fraser Nelson, 'Scotland Files for Divorce', *GQ*, 13 February 2012.

[31] *Daily Telegraph*, 4 April 2015. See also: Fraser Nelson, 'Leaked memo shows Nicola Sturgeon admitting that the SNP prefers Cameron to Miliband', *Spectator Coffee House*, 3 April 2015.

[32] Nicola Sturgeon, *Twitter*, 3 April 2015.

[33] *The Herald*, 6 July 2015.

[34] *Daily Telegraph*, 17 July 2016; *Daily Mail*, 17 July 2016.

[35] Chris Deerin, 'Scotland has gone mad', *CapX*, 7 April 2015.

[36] *Spectator Coffee House*, comment, 18 April 2015.

[37] Alex Massie, 'The SNP has replaced the Church of Scotland', *Spectator Coffee House*, 18 April 2015.

[38] Eric Hobsbawm, *Nations and Nationalism since 1780: Programme, Myth, Reality*, Cambridge University Press 1990.

[39] Gerry Hassan, 'Scotland and the clash of two nationalisms', *New Statesman*, 7 April 2015.

[40] Fintan O'Toole, 'It is not that Scotland might become a new state but that it might become a new kind of state', *Sunday Herald*, 9 September 2014.

[41] William W. Knox, *Industrial Nation: Work, Culture and Society in Scotland, 1800-Present*, Edinburgh University Press 1999.

[42] Ian Johnston, *Ships for all Nations: John Brown and Company Clydebank 1847-1971*, Seaforth Publishing 2015.

[43] *The Herald*, 19 July 2016.

[44] *The Strange Death of Labour Scotland*, op. cit., p. 6.

[45] *The Scotsman*, 10 March 2011.

[46] *The Independent*, 30 August 1993.

[47] *The Strange Death of Labour Scotland*, op. cit., p. 7.

[48] W.G. Beaton, *Glasgow: Our City: Yesterday, Today and Tomorrow*, Corporation of Glasgow Education Department revised edn. 1957.

[49] Elizabeth Lebas, 'Glasgow's Progress: The Films of Glasgow Corporation 1938-78,' *Film Studies*, Summer 2007, pp. 33-52.

[50] *The Strange Death of Labour Scotland*, op. cit., Chapter One.

[51] John Curtice, *2012 Scottish Local Government Elections: Report and Analysis*, Electoral Reform Society 2012.

[52] Allan McConnell, *Scottish Local Government*, Edinburgh University Press 2004.

[53] Andy Wightman, *Renewing Local Democracy in Scotland*, Scottish Green Party 2013.

[54] Michael Shermer, 'How the Survivor Bias Distorts Reality', *Scientific American*, 1 September 2014.

[55] Rafaer Behr, 'Labour's answers lie in its losses, not its victories', *The Guardian*, 25 May 2016.

[56] Gerry Hassan, 'The missing voices of public life and how we create a different Scotland', *The Scotsman*, 9 November 2013.

[57] *BBC News*, 19 September 2014.

[58] Hassan, *Caledonian Dreaming*, op. cit., p. 82.

[59] Willie Sullivan, *The Missing Scotland: Why over a million Scots choose not to vote and what it means for our democracy*, Luath Press 2014.

[60] Gaby Hinsliff, 'Left see itself as good guys', *The Guardian*, 29 April 2016.

[61] Nick Cohen, *What's Left? How the Left Lost its Way*, Fourth Estate 2007.

[62] *The Guardian*, 28 April 2016.

[63] Edward S. Herman and Noam Chomsky, *Manufacturing Consent: The Political Economy of Mass Media*, Pantheon Books 1988.

[64] *The Guardian*, 20 June 1983.

[65] Lord Ashcroft, 'How Scotland Voted, and Why', 19 September 2014.

[66] Rob Shorthouse, 'Key Takeaways from Scotland's Better Together Campaign', *Campaigning Summit, Vienna*, March 2015.

[67] See the superb account of Better Together in: Joe Pike, *Project Fear: How an Unlikely Alliance Left a Kingdom United but a Country Divided*, Biteback Publishing 2015.

[68] Kenneth O. Morgan, 'The High and Low Politics of Labour: Keir Hardie to Michael Foot', in Michael Bentley and John Stevenson (eds), *High and Low Politics in Modern Britain*, Clarendon Press 1983.

[69] *Royal Commission on the Constitution: Minutes of Evidence: Volume Four: Scotland*, HMSO 1971, pp. 32-33.

[70] Colin Rallings and Michael Thrasher, *British Electoral Facts 1832-2012*, Biteback Publishing 2012.

[71] Ibid.

[72] *BBC News*, 8 May 2015.

[73] *Daily Telegraph*, 5 September 2014.

[74] Tom Holland, 'How we drew up our love letter to Scotland', *Daily Telegraph*, 8 August 2014.

[75] 'Please, stay with us: The Best of the Spectator readers' letters to Scottish voters', *The Spectator*, 13 September 2014.

[76] *Huffington Post*, 26 April 2015.

[77] *The Guardian*, 21 April 2015.

[78] *PoliticsHome.com*, 26 April 2015.

[79] *The Herald*, 8 June 2016.

[80] *Daily Telegraph*, 9 June 2016.

[81] *The Independent*, 15 July 2016.

[82] *BBC News*, 19 September 2014.

[83] *The Scotsman*, 25 April 2016.

[84] Hugo Rifkind, 'Why no one's telling the truth about Scotland', *The Spectator*, 21 March 2015.

[85] Vernon Bogdanor, *Devolution*, Oxford University Press 1979; James Mitchell, *Devolution in the UK*, Manchester University Press 2009.

[86] *Report of the Royal Commission on the Constitution*, Cmnd. 5460, HMSO 1973, Para. 232, p. 76.

[87] *Scottish Social Attitudes 2015: Attitudes to Government, the National Health Service, the Economy and Standard of Living*, Scottish Government 2015.

[88] Rob Johns and James Mitchell, *Takeover: Explaining the Extraordinary Rise of the SNP*, Biteback Publishing 2016, p. 76.

[89] *Scottish Social Attitudes 2015*, op. cit.

[90] *Through Our Eyes 2: How the World sees the United Kingdom*, British Council 2002.

[91] *Washington Post*, 21 August 2009.

[92] *Sunday Times*, 1 August 2010.

[93] Ibid.

[94] Neil Blain, David Hutchison and Gerry Hassan (eds), *Scotland's Referendum and the Media: National and International Perspectives*, Edinburgh University Press 2016.

[95] *Time*, 18 November 2011.

[96] Consultative Steering Group, *Shaping Scotland's Parliament: Report of the Consultative Steering Group on the Scottish Parliament*, Scottish Office 1998.

[97] Scottish Government, *Scotland's Future: Your Guide to an Independent Scotland*, Scottish Government 2013, p. 355.

[98] Andrew Tickell, 'Challenging Scotland's law acts as a safeguard', *The Times*, 4 August 2016.

[99] Ibid.

[100] Andy Wightman, *The Poor Had No Lawyers: Who Owns Scotland (and How They Got It)*, Birlinn 2010.

[101] Duncan Sim (ed.), *Housing and Public Policy in Post-Devolution Scotland*, Chartered Institute of Housing 2004.

[102] Irene Maver, *Glasgow*, Edinburgh University Press 2000.

[103] S.G. Checkland, *The Upas Tree: Glasgow 1875-1975*, University of Glasgow Press 1975.

[104] Christopher A. Whatley, *The Scots and the Union*, Edinburgh University Press 2006, pp. 34-35.

[105] Tom Devine, *Independence or Union: Scotland's Past and Scotland's Present*, Allen Lane 2016, pp. 20-21.

[106] James Mitchell and Gerry Hassan, 'Leadership of the SNP' in James Mitchell and Gerry Hassan (eds), *Scottish National Party Leaders*, Biteback Publishing 2016.

[107] Alan Finlayson, 'Making Labour safe: Globalisation and the aftermath of the social democratic retreat', in Gerry Hassan (ed.), *After Blair: Politics after the New Labour Decade*,

Lawrence and Wishart 2006, pp. 41-42.

[108] Colin Crouch, *Coping with Post-Democracy*, Fabian Society 2000.

[109] From a right-wing perspective but influenced by Crouch's concept of post-democracy: Peter Oborne, *The Triumph of the Political Class*, Simon and Schuster 2007.

[110] Bagehot, 'The Osborne Doctrine', *The Economist*, 26 September 2015.

[111] Fraser Nelson, 'The British jobs miracle, in six graphs', *The Spectator*, 13 June 2014; 'A jobs miracle is happening in Britain, thanks to tax cuts. Why don't the Tories say so?', *The Spectator*, 21 March 2015.

[112] *The Guardian*, 15 February 2016.

[113] Resolution Foundation, 'The housing headwind: the impact of rising housing costs on UK living standards', *Resolution Foundation*, 28 June 2016.

[114] *The Guardian*, 7 March 2016.

[115] *City AM*, 9 November 2015.

[116] *The Economist*, 14 March 2015.

[117] *The Guardian*, 18 February 2016.

[118] *The Guardian*, 19 January 2012.

[119] Hay Book Festival 2016, quoted in *The Economist*, 13 August 2016.

[120] *BBC News*, 18 June 2016.

[121] *The Independent*, 21 September 2015.

[122] Sophia Parker 'Introduction', in Sophie Parker, (ed.), *The Squeezed Middle: The Pressure on Ordinary Workers in America and Britain*, Policy Press 2013.

[123] William Beveridge, *Social Insurance and Allied Services*, Cmnd. 6404, HMSO 1942.

[124] T.H. Marshall, *Citizenship and Social Class: And Other Essays*, Cambridge University Press 1950.

[125] See Andrew Neil, 'The Rise of the British Underclass: The Great British Class Survey', *BBC Two*, 25 January 2011.

[126] Neal Ascherson, 'Scottish independence: Why I'm voting

Yes', *Prospect*, August 2014.

[127] *The Guardian*, 24 February 2006.

[128] Johnny Gailey, 'Serco in Scotland', *Bella Caledonia*, 15 May 2012.

[129] *BBC News*, 26 July 2016.

[130] Richard Florida, *The Rise of the Creative Class: And How it is Transforming Work, Leisure, Community and Everyday Life*, Basic Books 2003.

[131] Simon Reynolds, *Retromania: Pop Culture's Addiction to its own Past*, Faber and Faber 2012.

[132] Jonathan Freeland, 'British stereotypes: Do mention the war, please!', *The Guardian*, 26 January 2012.

[133] Ibid.

[134] Dominic Sandbrook, *The Great British Dream Factory: The Strange History of Our National Imagination*, Allen Lane 2015; 'Let Us Entertain You: The New British Empire', *BBC Two*, 4 November 2015.

[135] *The Great British Dream Factory*, pp. 407-25 on John Lennon and pp. 140-42 on Keith Richards.

[136] *BBC News*, 15 February 2005.

[137] House of Commons Library, *Parliamentary approval for military action*, House of Commons Library, 13 May 2015.

[138] House of Lords website, accessed 4 August 2016.

[139] *Daily Mail*, 19 September 2015.

[140] *Daily Telegraph*, 18 July 2009.

[141] *The Guardian*, 11 October 2014.

[142] *BBC News*, 8 March 2016.

[143] Andrew Gamble, *Between Europe and America: The Future of British Politics*, Palgrave Macmillan 2003.

[144] Daniel Hannan, *How We Invented Freedom and Why It Matters*, Head of Zeus 2013.

[145] Christopher Hitchens, *Blood, Class and Empire: The Enduring Anglo-American Relationship*, Atlantic Books 2006, p. 23.

[146] Peter Riddell, *Hug Them Close: Blair, Clinton, Bush and the 'Special Relationship'*, Politico's Publishing 2003.

[147] Stockholm International Peace Research Institute, *Trends in World Military Expenditure 2015*.

[148] Global Firepower Index, *2016 World Military Strength Rankings*.

[149] *World Economic Forum*, 20 August 2016.

[150] Stuart Laycock, *All the Countries We've Ever Invaded: And the Few We Never Got Around To*, History Press 2012.

[151] Ian Cobain, *The History Thieves: Secrets, Lies and the Shaping of a Modern Nation*, Portobello Books 2016, p. 67.

[152] *The Guardian*, 6 June 2016.

[153] Brian Cathcart, *The Test of Greatness: Britain's Struggle for the Atomic Bomb*, John Murray 1994, p. 21.

[154] John Baylis and Kristan Stoddart, *The British Nuclear Experience: The Role of Beliefs, Culture and Identity*, Oxford University Press 2015.

[155] *The Economist*, 4 April 2015.

[156] David Faber, *Munich, 1938: Appeasement and World War II*, Simon and Schuster 2008.

[157] Keith Kyle, *Suez*, Weidenfeld and Nicolson 1991.

[158] Martin Woollacott, *After Suez: Adrift in the American Century*, I.B. Tauris 2006.

[159] Richard J. Aldrich and Rory Cormac, *The Black Door: Spies, Secret Intelligence and British Prime Ministers*, William Collins 2016.

[160] *The Economist*, 4 April 2015.

[161] *The Economist*, 6 August 2016.

[162] Boris Johnson, 'Scottish independence: Decapitate Britain, and we kill off the greatest political union ever', *Daily Telegraph*, 8 September 2014.

[163] Ed Balls, 'The union is the most successful multinational state in the world', *Sunday Times*, 22 June 2014.

[164] *BBC Scotland*, 26 June 2016.

[165] Bernard Crick, 'On Devolution, Decentralism and the Constitution', reprinted in *Political Thoughts and Polemics*, Edinburgh University Press 1990, p. 113.

[166] 'Brexit: The Battle for Britain', *BBC Two*, 8 August 2016.

[167] Roger Davidson and Gayle Davis, *The Sexual State: Sexuality and Scottish Governance*, Edinburgh University Press 2012.

[168] David T. Evans, 'Keep the Clause: Section 28 and the Politics of Sexuality in Scotland and the UK', *Soundings*, No. 18, 2001.

[169] Alison Park, 'Scotland's Morals', in John Curtice, David McCrone, Alison Park and Lindsay Paterson (eds), *New Scotland, New Society?*, Edinburgh University Press 2002; Rachel Ormston, John Curtice, Susan McConville and Susan Reid, *Scottish Social Attitudes Survey 2010: Attitudes to Discrimination and Positive Action*, Scottish Centre for Social Research 2010.

[170] Gerry Hassan, *Independence of the Scottish Mind*, op. cit.

[171] SNP Annual Conference, *BBC Two*, 15 November 2014.

[172] Lord Ashcroft, 'How Scotland Voted, and Why', Lord Ashcroft Polls, 19 September 2014.

[173] Rob Johns, 'It wasn't "The Vow" that won it: the Scottish independence referendum', in Philip Cowley and Robert Ford (eds), *More Sex, Lies and the Ballot Box: Another 50 Things You Need to Know About Elections*, Biteback Publishing 2006, p. 187.

[174] Gerry Hassan, *State of Independence: The Scottish Political Commentariat, Public Spaces and the Making of Modern Scotland*, University of the West of Scotland, PhD Thesis, 2013.

[175] Alastair Hetherington, *News in the Regions: Plymouth Sound to Moray Firth*, Palgrave Macmillan 1989.

[176] Gerry Hassan, 'Minority Interest Nation: The Changing Contours of Reporting Scotland on BBC and STV', *Political Quarterly*, 2017.

[177] Bob Crampsey, *The Scottish Football League: The First 100 Years*, The Scottish Football League 1992.

[178] Gerry Hassan, 'A Question of Empathy', *Nutmeg*, No. 1, September 2016.

[179] Mike Russell, 'Leadership in Perspective', in James Mitchell and Gerry Hassan (eds), *Scottish National Party Leaders*, op.

cit., p. 24.

[180] Sidney Hook, *The Hero in History: A Study in Limitation and Possibility*, John Day Company 1943, Chapter Nine.

[181] Joris Luyendijk, *Swimming with Sharks: My Journey into the World of Bankers*, Guardian Books 2015, p. 194.

[182] Robert Z Aliber and Zoega Gylfi (eds), *Preludes to the Icelandic Financial Crisis*, Palgrave Macmillan 2014; *Huffington Post*, 5 January 2016.

[183] Lucy Lee and Penny Young, 'A disengaged Britain? Political interest and participation', in Alison Park, Caroline Bryson, Elizabeth Clery, John Curtice and Miranda Philips (eds), *British Social Attitudes 30: 2013 Report*, NatCen Social Research 2013.

[184] *Financial Times*, 3 June 2016.

[185] *The Independent*, 18 January 2016.

[186] Ibid.

[187] *The Scotsman*, 17 February 2003.

[188] *STV News*, 20 March 2016.

[189] Anna Marcinkiewicz, Ian Montagu, Jennifer Waterton and Susan Reid, *Scottish Social Attitudes 2015: Attitudes to Government, the National Health Service, the Economy and Standard of Living*, ScotCen Social Research, March 2016.

[190] *The Herald*, 10 August 2016.

[191] *The Scotsman*, 21 July 2016.

[192] *The Herald*, 23 July 2016.

[193] Thomas Carlyle, *On Heroes, Hero-Worship and the Heroic in History*, Chapman and Hall 3rd edn. 1846, p. 1.

[194] Jimmy Reid, *Reflections of a Clyde-Built Man*, Souvenir Press 1976, pp. 99-105.

[195] *The Independent*, 12 April 2010.

[196] Paul Routledge, *Gordon Brown: The Biography*, Simon and Schuster 1998, pp. 45-46, 54-57.

[197] Peter Hennessy, *The Prime Minister: The Office and its Holders*, Penguin 2001, p. 397.

[198] Jonathan Powell, *The New Machiavelli: How to Wield Power*

in the Modern World, Bodley Head 2010, p. 78.

[199] Uffe Elbæk, 'Lessons from abroad: There is always an alternative', in Lisa Nandy, Caroline Lucas and Chris Bowers (eds), *The Alternative: Towards a New Progressive Politics*, Biteback Publishing 2016, p. 249.

[200] Bernard Crick, 'Equality', in Ben Pimlott (ed.), *Fabian Essays in Socialist Thought*, Heinemann 1984, p. 158.

[201] Robin Cook, 'A manifesto like this would actually mobilise our voters', *The Guardian*, 4 February 2005.

[202] Stephen Maxwell, 'Can Scotland's Political Myths Be Broken?', reprinted in *The Case for Left-Wing Nationalism*, Luath Press 2013, p. 17.

[203] SNP website, www.snp.org, accessed 12 July 2016.

[204] Gerry Mooney, 'Scotland and independence: questions of social welfare, nationalism and class', *Soundings*, No. 63, 2016, p. 71.

[205] SNP, *Re-elect: SNP Manifesto 2016*, SNP 2016.

[206] *Spectator Coffee House*, 21 May 2014.

[207] *Daily Telegraph*, 26 June 2015.

[208] Peter Kellner, 'Welfare reform: who, whom?', *YouGov*, 7 January 2013; Alex Massie, 'Welfare reform is this government's most difficult, but popular policy', *Spectator Coffee House*, 4 April 2013.

[209] *BBC News*, 10 March 2015.

[210] Migration Observatory, *Immigration and Independence: Public Opinion on Immigration in Scotland in the Context of the Referendum Debate*, Migration Observatory 2014.

[211] Oliver Hawkins and Vaughne Miller, *European Parliament Election Results: Research Paper 14/32*, House of Commons Library 2014.

[212] *BBC News*, 24 June 2016.

[213] Philip Cowley and Dennis Kavanagh, *The British General Election of 2015*, Palgrave Macmillan 2015.

[214] Joseph Rowntree Foundation, *A Scotland without poverty: Manifesto for a prosperous and poverty-free Scotland*, Joseph

Rowntree Foundation 2016.

[215] Scottish Government, *Poverty and Inequality in Scotland 2014-15: Communities Analysis,* July 2016.

[216] Scottish Government, *Scottish Index of Multiple Deprivation,* 2016.

[217] Sutton Trust, 27 May 2016.

[218] Lucy Hunter Blackburn, Gitit Kadar Satat, Sheila Riddell and Elizabet Weedon, *Access in Scotland: Access to higher education for people from less advantaged backgrounds in Scotland,* Sutton Trust 2016.

[219] Philip Kirby, *Degrees of Debt,* Sutton Trust 2016.

[220] Aftab Ali, "Significant challenges" ahead for Scottish higher education as graduate debt set to almost double', *The Independent,* 8 July 2016.

[221] Jeane Freeman, 'Targeting Benefits and Support? It's simply missing the real point', *The National,* 29 January 2016.

[222] Ibid.

[223] Deep End GP Group, Twitter, 26 July 2016.

[224] *Fair Society, Health Lives: The Marmot Review: Strategic Review of Health Inequalities in England post-2010,* Marmot Review 2010.

[225] *Holyrood Magazine,* 21 December 2015.

[226] *The Times,* 25 March 2015.

[227] *The Herald,* 8 June 2015.

[228] Some of these principles are drawn from Peter Kenway, Sabrine Bushe, Adam Tinson and Theo Barry Born, *Monitoring Poverty and Social Exclusion in Scotland 2015,* Joseph Rowntree Foundation in association with New Policy Institute 2015.

[229] 'Sunday Times Rich List', *Sunday Times,* 24 April 2016.

[230] *CommonSpace,* 16 October 2015.

[231] *Third Force News,* 18 August 2016.

[232] William Astor, 'Should we fear a Mugabe-style land grab in rural Scotland?', *The Spectator,* 23 May 2015.

[233] *The Spectator,* 18 August 2016.

[234] *Daily Telegraph,* 16 March 2016.

[235] *Daily Telegraph,* 20 March 2016.

[236] *The Herald,* 10 February 2016.

[237] Sunday Herald, 2 February 2014.

[238] *The Herald,* 10 February 2016.

[239] *STV News,* 2 December 2015.

[240] *Scottish Sun,* 9 August 2016.

[241] *The Scotsman,* 29 December 2015.

[242] *BBC News,* 6 April 2016.

[243] *High Pay Centre,* 12 October 2015.

[244] *Financial Times,* 19 June 2015.

[245] Social Mobility and Child Poverty Commission, *Elitist Scotland,* David Hume Institute 2015.

[246] Ibid.

[247] Stephen Reicher, *Not By the People: The Launch of the Commission on Fair Access to Political Influence,* Jimmy Reid Foundation 2013.

[248] *The Herald,* 3 February 2013.

[249] James Clifford, *The Predicament of Culture: Twentieth-Century Ethnography, Literature and Art,* Harvard University Press 1988, p. 10.

[250] Raymond Williams, *Keywords: A Vocabulary of Culture and Society,* Flamingo 2nd edn. 1983, pp. 87-93.

[251] Moray McLaren, *Understanding the Scots: A Guide to South Britons and other Foreigners,* Frederick Muller 1956, p. 8.

[252] Iain Macwhirter, 'Scotland Year Zero', in Gerry Hassan and Chris Warhurst (eds), *The New Scottish Politics: The First Year of the Scottish Parliament and Beyond,* Stationery Office 2000, p. 17.

[253] Neal Ascherson, *Stone Voices: The Search for Scotland,* Granta Books 2002, p. 298.

[254] Tom Nairn, *The Break-up of Britain: Crisis and Neo-Nationalism,* New Left Books 1977, Chapter Two.

[255] 'Culture of Scotland', Wikipedia entry.

[256] David Daiches (ed.), *A Companion to Scottish Culture,* Edward Arnold 1981; *The New Companion to Scottish Culture,*

Polygon 1993.

[257] Paul H. Scott (ed.), *Scotland: A Concise Cultural History*, Mainstream 1993.

[258] Alastair McIntosh, personal communication, 23 August 2016.

[259] Ian Jack, personal communication, 30 August 2016.

[260] Joyce McMillan, personal communication, 5 September 2016.

[261] Norman Buchan, *101 Scottish Songs*, Collins 1962; Norman Buchan and Peter Hall, *The Scottish Folksinger*, Collins 1973. There is also the Janey Buchan Political Song Archive at Glasgow University in memory of her cultural activism.

[262] James Mitchell, *Conservatives and the Union: A Study of Conservative Party Attitudes to Scotland*, Edinburgh University Press 1990, Chapter One.

[263] *New York Times*, 29 November 1994.

[264] James Robertson, *And the Land Lay Still*, Hamish Hamilton 2010.

[265] Ian Hamilton, *The Taking of the Stone of Destiny*, Lochar Publishing 1991.

[266] In Scotland, Stirling Centre for Scottish Studies, Stirling University, 23-24 August 2014.

[267] There are of course notable exceptions to this. See for example: Christopher Silver, *Demanding Democracy: The Case for a Scottish Media*, Word Power Books 2015.

[268] *Scotland Yet: A Film about Independence*, Rough Justice Films 2014.

[269] Quoted in *Daily Telegraph*, 11 August 2010.

[270] William McIlvanney, 'Freeing Ourselves from Inner Exile', *The Herald*, 6 March 1999.

[271] Eleanor Yule and David Manderson, *The Glass Half Full: Moving Beyond Scottish Miserablism*, Luath Press 2014.

[272] Ibid., pp. 22-24.

[273] Teddy Jamieson, 'Drawn to the Dark Side', *The Herald*, 12 November 2011.

[274] James MacMillan, 'Scotland's Shame', in Tom Devine (ed.), *Scotland's Shame? Bigotry and Sectarianism in Modern Scotland*, Edinburgh University Press 2000.

[275] James MacMillan, 'Arts and the Referendum', *The Scotsman*, 30 April 2014.

[276] James MacMillan, 'Tartan-ing up the Arts', *Spectator*, 13 August 2016.

[277] Lyn Gardner, 'If Scottish critics love it, it must be good – right?', *The Guardian*, 6 August 2013.

[278] Jarvis Cocker, 'The John Lennon Letters, edited by Hunter Davies', *The Guardian*, 10 October 2012.

[279] Harry Mount, 'Can anything stop the curse of the sequel?', *Spectator Coffee House*, 13 August 2016.

[280] Alasdair Milne, *DG: The Memoirs of a British Broadcaster*, Hodder and Stoughton 1988, p. 49.

[281] *The Guardian*, 20 May 2016.

[282] BBC Trust Service Review, *BBC Nations' news and radio services: Summary Report*, BBC Trust 2016, pp. 7-8.

[283] John Birt, *The Harder Path: The Autobiography*, Time Warner 2002, pp. 483-84.

[284] Scottish Broadcasting Commission, *Platform for Success: Final Report of the Scottish Broadcasting Commission*, Scottish Government 2008.

[285] James McMillan, 'The SNP has played Scotland's Catholic Church for a fool', *Spectator Coffee House*, 24 August 2016.

[286] 'Tartan-ing Up the Arts', op. cit.

[287] Philip Howard, in Joyce McMillan, *Theatre in Scotland: A Field of Dreams*, Nick Hern Books 2016, p. 406.

[288] William McIlvanney, Democracy Demonstration, Edinburgh, 12 December 1992.

[289] *The Sun*, 18 February 1967. Quoted in Davidson and Davis, *The Sexual State*, op. cit., p. 138.

[290] Stephen McGinty, *The Life of Cardinal Winning: This Turbulent Priest*, Harper Collins 2003, p. 402.

[291] Ibid., p. 419.

[292] *Daily Telegraph*, 29 April 2012; *Sunday Times*, 24 July 2008.

[293] *BBC News*, 2 November 2012.

[294] Tom Gallagher, *Divided Scotland: Ethnic Friction and Christian Crisis*, Argyll Publishing 2013, pp. 235, 238.

[295] Drawing from the phrase 'revolution in the head' from Ian McDonald, *Revolution in the Head: The Beatles' Records and the Sixties*, Fourth Estate 2nd edn. 1997.

[296] Hassan, *Independence of the Scottish Mind*, op. cit.

[297] Doreen Massey *For Space*, Sage 2005.

[298] Manuel Castells, *Networks of Outrage and Hope*, Polity Press 2012.

[299] Marshall Berman, 'Blue Jay Way: Where Will Critical Culture Come From?', *Dissent*, Winter 2000.

[300] Ibid., pp. 31-32.

[301] Paul Mason, *Post-Capitalism: A Guide to Our Future*, Allen Lane 2015.

[302] Neal Stephenson, *Some Remarks: Essays and Other Writing*, Atlantic Books 2013, p. 265.

[303] Michael Bhasker, *Curation: The Power of Selection in a World of Excess*, Piatkus 2016, p. 55.

[304] Brian Eno, BBC 'Hard Talk', 11 May 2016.

[305] Harold Jarche, 'Moving to the Edges', 21 January 2014, blog.

[306] Gerry Hassan, Melissa Mean and Charlie Tims, *The Dreaming City: Glasgow 2020 and the Power of Mass Imagination*, Demos 2007.

[307] Rob Johns and James Mitchell, *Takeover: Explaining the Extraordinary Rise of the SNP*, op. cit., p. 249.

[308] Tim Bale, 'Corbyn's Labour: Survey of post-2015 Labour members and supporters', Queen Mary University of London, 28 June 2016.

[309] Michel Bauwen, 'Alternativet: The New Danish Open Source Party', P2P: Foundation, 13 December 2013; Uffe Elbæk and Neal Lawson, *The Bridge: How the Politics of the Future will link the Vertical to the Horizontal*, Compass/Alternativet 2014, p. 7.

[310] *Scottish Daily Mail,* 4 May 2016; S*cottish Sunday Express,* 3 April 2016.

[311] Glasgow Centre for Population Health, *Evaluating Sistema Scotland: initial findings report,* Glasgow Centre for Population Health 2015.

[312] *BBC News,* 25 June 2013; *The Courier,* 2 July 2016.

[313] The Ferret, https://theferret.scot/, accessed 4 June 2016.

[314] CommonSpace, https://www.commonspace.scot/, accessed 27 June 2016.

[315] Campbell Christie, *Commission on the Future Delivery of Public Services,* Scottish Government 2011.

[316] Zygmunt Bauman, *Legislators and Interpreters: On Modernity, Post-Modernity and Intellectuals,* Polity 1989.

[317] Sebastian Junger, *Tribe: On Homecoming and Belonging,* Fourth Estate 2016, p. xi.

[318] Joshua Greene, *Moral Tribes: Emotion, Reason, and the Gap between Us and Them,* Atlantic Books 2013, p. 352.

[319] Sue Goss, *Open Tribe,* Lawrence and Wishart/Compass 2014, p. 17.

[320] Ibid., pp. 32-33.

[321] James Mitchell, *Devolution in the UK,* op. cit., p. 6; *The Scottish Question,* Oxford University Press 2014.

[322] David Torrance, *Britain Re-Booted: Scotland in a Federal Union,* Luath Press 2014.

[323] Andrew Gamble, *The Conservative Nation,* Routledge, Kegan and Paul 1974.

[324] Peter Facey, Bethan Rigby and Alexandra Runswick (eds), *Unlocking Democracy: 20 Years of Charter 88,* Politico's Publishing 2008.

[325] Dominic Sandbrook, *White Heat: A History of Britain in the Swinging Sixties,* Little Brown 2006, p. 407.

[326] Will Hutton, *The State We're In,* Jonathan Cape 1995; Gavin Kelly, Dominic Kelly and Andrew Gamble (ed.), Stakeholder Capitalism, Palgrave Macmillan 1997.

[327] Bernard Crick, 'An Englishman considers his Passport,' in

Political Thoughts and Polemics, op. cit., p. 94.

[328] Neil Davidson, *The Origins of Scottish Nationhood*, Pluto Press 1999.

[329] Linda Colley, *Britons: Forging the Nation 1707-1837*, Yale University Press 1992.

[330] Ernst Renan, 'What is a Nation?', reprinted in Homi K. Bhabha (ed.), *Nation and Narration*, Routledge 1990.

[331] Michael Fry, *The Scottish Empire*, Tuckwell Press 2001; Tom Devine, *Scotland's Empire 1600-1815*, Allen Lane 2003.

[332] Edward M. Spiers, Jeremy A. Crang and Matthew J. Strickland (eds), *A Military History of Scotland*, Edinburgh University Press 2012.

[333] G.D.H. Cole and Raymond Postgate, *The Common People 1746-1946*, Victor Gollancz 2nd edn. 1949.

[334] *Daily Telegraph*, 18 May 2011.

[335] Richard S. Grayson and Fearghal McGarry (eds), *Remembering 1916: The Easter Rising, the Somme and the Politics of Memory in Ireland*, Cambridge University Press 2016; Kirsty Lusk and Willy Maley (eds), *Scotland and the Easter Rising: Fresh Perspectives on 1916*, Luath Press 2016.

[336] Ed Vulliamy, '100 years on, the Irish lay to rest the ghosts of the Easter Rising', *The Guardian*, 24 March 2016.

[337] Matt Qvortrup, *Referendums and Ethnic Conflict*, Pennsylvania Press 2014; 'New Development: The comparative study of seccession referendums', *Public Money and Management*, January 2014.

[338] Nordic Council, www.norden.org, accessed 11 August 2016.

[339] Colin Crouch, 'The State and Innovations in Economic Governance', *Political Quarterly*, 2004.

[340] *BBC News*, 30 June 2016.

[341] Fintan O'Toole, 'Three-state union may be solution to Brexit', *Irish Times*, 26 June 2016.

[342] Stephen George, *An Awkward Partner: Britain in the European Community*, Oxford University Press 2nd edn. 1994.

[343] Alberto Alesina and Enrico Spolaore, *The Size of Nations*,

MIT Press 2003.

[344] Michael Keating and Malcolm Harvey, *Small Nations in a Big World: What Scotland Can Learn,* Luath Press 2014, p. 29.

[345] Andrew Gamble, *Between Europe and America*, op. cit.

[346] Tony Carty and Alexander McCall Smith (eds), *Power and Manoeuvrability: The implications of an independent Scotland,* Q Press 1978.

[347] Adam Price, 'The national identity question is for the whole UK, not just the Scots', *The Guardian,* 23 October 2013.

[348] Arthur Aughey and Cathy Gormley-Heenan, 'The Anglo-Irish Agreement: 25 Years On', *Political Quarterly,* July-September 2011.

[349] Quoted in *The Guardian,* 28 November 1993.

[350] Paul Bew, *The Making and Remaking of the Good Friday Agreement*, Liffey Press 2007.

[351] *BBC News,* 23 May 1998.

[352] Larry Elliott and Dan Atkinson, *Europe isn't Working,* Yale University Press 2016.

[353] Aditya Chakrabortty, 'Greece is a sideshow. The Eurozone has failed, and Germans are its victims too', *The Guardian,* 22 June 2015.

[354] Alex Massie, 'No, the Irish are not afraid of Scottish independence', *Spectator Coffee House,* 13 December 2013; *Irish Times,* 2 July 2016.

[355] William Roger Louis and Hedley Bull (eds), *The Special Relationship: Anglo-American Relations since 1945,* Oxford University Press 2nd edn. 1997.

[356] Carly Nyst and Anna Crowe, 'Unmasking the Five Eyes' Global Surveillance Practices', *Global Information Society Watch 2014.*

[357] Tim Marshall, *Prisoners of Geography: Ten Maps That Tell You Everything You Need to Know About Global Politics*, Elliott and Thompson 2015, p. 92.

[358] Ibid., p. 92.

[359] The Commonwealth, www.commonwealth.org, accessed

17 May 2016.

[360] Michael Keating, *The Independence of Scotland: Self-government and the Shifting Policies of Union*, Oxford University Press 2009, p. 160.

[361] Francisco Aldecoa and Michael Keating (eds), *Paradiplomacy in Action: The Foreign Relations of Subnational Governments*, Routledge 1999.

[362] Ien Ang, Yudhishthir Raj Isar and Philip Mar (eds), *Cultural Diplomacy: Beyond the National Interest?*, Routledge 2016.

[363] John Kay, 'To the brink, but no further', *Prospect*, June 2011.

[364] Peter Geoghegan, *The People's Referendum: Why Scotland will never be the same again*, Luath Press 2014, p. 162.

[365] Arianna Introna, 'Nationalist and institutional horizons in (post-)referendum Scottish politics', *Renewal: a journal of social democracy*, Vol. 23 No. 1-2, 2015.

[366] Robin McAlpine, *Determination: how Scotland can become independent by 2021*, Common Print 2016.

[367] Christopher Booker, *The Seven Basic Plots: Why We Tell Stories*, Continuum 2004.

[368] *BBC News*, 14 July 2016.

[369] Joyce McMillan, 'Three Deadly Sins of Creative Scotland's Bad Funding Review', *The Scotsman*, 25 May 2012.

[370] Lesley Riddoch, *Blossom: What Scotland needs to Flourish*, op. cit., Chapter Seven.

[371] *Scotland's Future*, op. cit., pp. 40-44.

[372] Martin Seligman, *Authentic Happiness: Using the New Positive Psychology to Realise Your Potential for Lasting Fulfilment*, Nicholas Brealey Publishing 2003.

[373] Martin Seligman, 'Towards a Confident Scotland' conference, Glasgow, 24 November 2003. See: Iain Ferguson, 'An Attitude Problem? Confidence and Well-Being in Scotland', in Neil Davidson, Patricia McCafferty and David Miller (eds), *Neoliberal Scotland: Class and Society in a Stateless Nation*, Cambridge Scholars Publishing 2010.

[374] Nicola Sturgeon, 'Bringing the powers back home to a better

nation', Strathclyde University speech, Glasgow, 3 December 2012.

[375] Tom Freeman, 'Her chances, your chances – introducing Kirsty, the Holyrood Baby', *Holyrood Magazine*, 23 May 2016.

[376] Alan Finlayson, *Making Sense of New Labour*, Lawrence and Wishart 2003.

[377] Richard Seymour, *Corbyn: The Strange Rebirth of Radical Politics*, Verso 2016.

[378] Peter Ross, *Daunderlust: Dispatches from Unreported Scotland*, Sandstone Press 2014.

[379] *The Times*, 12 April 2016.

[380] 'Skintland', *The Economist*, 13 April 2012.

[381] Gerry Hassan, 'An Exchange with "the Economist" on Scottish Independence', blog, 12 and 24 March 2015.

[382] 'The Politics Show', *BBC One*, 3 April 2011.

[383] David Stenhouse, *On the Make: How the Scots Took Over London*, Mainstream 2004, Chapter Nine.

[384] Tom Gallagher, *Glasgow: The Uneasy Peace*, Manchester University Press 1987; *Edinburgh Divided: John Cormack and No Popery in the 1930s*, Polygon 1987.

[385] Harry Reid, *Outside Verdict: An Old Kirk in a New Scotland*, St. Andrew Press 2002.

[386] *The Scotsman*, 25 July 2016; Julia Rampen, '10 times Nicola Sturgeon nailed what it's like to be a Remain voter post-Brexit', *New Statesman*, 25 July 2016.

[387] Jamie Maxwell, *Twitter*, 30 June 2016.

[388] Gerry Hassan, 'We are One Scotland: Anatomy of a Referendum', *Scottish Review*, 24 September 2014.

[389] Tim Marshall, *Worth Dying For: The Power and Politics of Flags*, Elliott and Thompson 2016.

[390] Iain Crichton Smith, 'Me and the Little White Rose', reprint of Hugh MacDiarmid Annual Memorial Lecture, 30 November 1989, *Cencrastus*, Spring 1990.

[391] Fintan O'Toole, *Enough is Enough*, op. cit., p. 236.

[392] Ibid., p. 237.